COMMON PRAISE

COMMON PRAISE

Large Print Edition

A new edition of Hymns Ancient and Modern

CANTERBURY
PRESS
Norwich

Common Praise is published on behalf of
Hymns Ancient & Modern Ltd
by Canterbury Press Norwich.

Canterbury Press Norwich, St Mary's Works,
St Mary's Plain, Norwich NR3 3BH,
a division of SCM-Canterbury Press Ltd, a subsidiary of
Hymns Ancient & Modern Ltd, a registered charity.

Common Praise Large Print Edition. First published January 2002
Second impression January 2005

A catalogue record of these editions are available from the British Library.

ISBN 1-85311-467-7 *Cased edition*

Typesetting:
Andrew Parker, Ferndown, Dorset BH22 8BB, United Kingdom
Printing and binding:
William Clowes Ltd, Beccles, Suffolk NR34 7TL, United Kingdom

CONTENTS

COPYRIGHT

For permission to print copyright hymns, whether in permanent or temporary form, by whatever means, application must be made to the respective owners.

GRANTS

Liberal grants of copies of *Common Praise* from the Council of Hymns Ancient & Modern Ltd are arranged through the Publishers to help parishes and others in the introduction of the book, or in the renewal of existing supplies. An application form for a grant can be obtained from the Canterbury Press Norwich, St Mary's Works, St Mary's Plain, Norwich, Norfolk NR3 3BH.

EXPLANATORY NOTES

Refrains are usually printed in *italic.*

An asterisk by a verse indicates that the verse or verses may be omitted without injury to the sense of the hymn.

An asterisk by an author's name indicates that there has been an alteration to the original text. Usually this applies to deceased authors. Where a living author has given permission, or the alterations are of a minor nature, there is no sign.

At the end of most sections, e.g. after 'Evening', there is a *'See also'* list of hymns that are also appropriate to the section, but which appear in the book under another section.

PREFACE

A new hymn book is a significant event in the life of the Church. And the arrival of *Common Praise,* a new edition of *Hymns Ancient and Modern,* is, to those who know and love its previous editions, an important moment. It comes at the end of a turbulent century, rich with the accumulated experience of pain, and sorrow, and hope, and love: it looks forward to the new century, with its future that no one can foretell. It does so at a time of unprecedented change, in society and in church worship, and it gathers up into itself all the hopes and apprehensions of a Church that is visibly changing in an age of experiment and scepticism. It does so with hope and faith, witnessing to the continuing traditions of Christian experience, and responding to new ways of expressing that belief.

Hymns Ancient and Modern was first published in 1860–61. By the end of the nineteenth century, it had become a national, and even imperial, institution, used in most Anglican churches in Great Britain and throughout the British Empire: so much so, that a radical new edition of 1904 was greeted with dismay, because the old 'A and M' had become so familiar and beloved.

Two factors contributed to its success. One was the shrewd decision by the hymn book committee to invite suggestions from the clergy and other interested parties, who were encouraged to write in with their hymns and ideas; another was the editors' sensible following of John Keble's advice to 'make it comprehensive'. In addition to these basic principles, the book had the services of a remarkable music editor, William Henry Monk. Since that time, successive editors have sought to adhere to the same principles of being alert to the needs of the Church, and to a wide variety of in¿uences: *Hymns Ancient and Modern* has never been a book associated with any single tradition. It has become a 'bench-mark' hymn book, widely regarded as sound and sensible, representing the best of traditional hymnody while being open to new ideas and acknowledging change.

The Council of *Hymns Ancient and Modern* sought to respond to the needs of a later time with the publication of the revised edition of 1950 and then with two supplementary volumes, *100 Hymns for Today* (1969) and *More Hymns for Today* (1980). The 1950 volume was an acclaimed hymn book, and the two supplements allowed the addition of much new material, some of it from the vigorous revival of hymn writing which had taken place since 1960. That revival sought to respond, with intelligence and poetic skill, to the rapidly-changing conditions of the time: to new forms of worship, including questions of gender and language and of changing 'thou' to 'you'; to new translations of the Bible (the *New English Bible* inspired Timothy Dudley-Smith's 'Tell out, my soul, the greatness of the Lord'); and to the demands of a modern society, transformed by rapid travel, by television and other media, and by the second industrial revolution of new technologies, including computers. Patterns of worship, also, were changing so rapidly that a new definitive edition did not seem appropriate in the 1980s: accordingly, *Hymns Ancient and Modern New Standard* (1983) was designed to meet those new conditions. It included the core of the 1950 edition, together with the two supplements, bound in one volume.

Inevitably, some of the hymns in the two supplements have proved more successful than others; and at the end of the twentieth century the time has come for a hymn book which will gather up the finest hymns, old and new, and present them for use as material for worship in the twenty-first century. This new edition is therefore a book which looks forward as well as back. It looks back to the great riches of Anglican spirituality, to George Herbert, Charles Wesley, Henry Francis Lyte, Cecil Frances Alexander, and John Ellerton; to the non-conformist hymns of Isaac Watts, Philip Doddridge, and James Montgomery; and to the revival of pre-Reformation hymnody and Catholic spirituality by John Mason Neale and Edward Caswall. It also looks forward to a century in which those traditions will have to engage with social forces and political developments which cannot be foreseen and perhaps cannot even be imagined.

The hymn book committee has made decisions with a strong sense of what is practicable as well as desirable: for example, to produce *Common Praise* in book form rather than rely solely on electronic reproduction, which would have been up-to-date but impossible to use for many churches. The book could not be too large, for obvious reasons of expense and convenience, so that every hymn had to 'earn its place': therefore each hymn which was in *Hymns Ancient and Modern New Standard* (and the other editions) has been re-examined; and a great many other books and single-author collections, in print and in manuscript, have been carefully scrutinized for possible new inclusions. Hymns have been included if they seemed to the committee to be serviceable, well-written, singable, clear, and unaffected: that is, without affectation of diction or sentiment, so that they may be sung without fear of embarrassment and with a full heart by people of good will and good sense. There are many examples of contemporary hymns; but there are also many hymns from previous ages which are contemporary because they are timeless. In compiling this collection, the committee envisaged a worshipping congregation of those who are open-minded, neither too wedded to experiment nor too rigid and set in their ways, who intend to 'keep the mean between two extremes'; remembering that the original sub-title of *Hymns Ancient and Modern* in 1860–61 was 'for the Services of the Church'.

In understanding 'the Church' at the beginning of the twenty-first century, the committee had in mind something very different from the situation of the Victorian editors. This is an age of increasing secularism: two world wars and a host of lesser but no less inhuman con¿icts in the twentieth century have created a climate of uncertainty and danger, while other changes, less dramatic but probably more devastating – global warming, genetic engineering, environmental pollution – contain possibilities and terrors which are only just beginning to be felt. Beside the very real improvements in human life — the eradication of some diseases and the better control of others, easier travel and communication — there is now the fear of the destruction of the planet, either by exhausting its natural resources through greed and carelessness, or through the appalling prospect of nuclear or biological warfare. In the face of this, a Christian hymn book points its users to the Rock of Ages, as the Church continues to affirm the centrality of the Christian faith and the need of the world for the gospel of divine love.

In addition, the Church has become more ecumenical during the last quarter of the twentieth century, so that this is a book which is not for Anglicans only: it contains hymns from many sources and in many modes, and the committee hopes that it will be seen as a book that will be useful everywhere. Hymns have an important part to play in the process of bringing Christians of different traditions closer together: at this time there is much tentative sharing of gifts and of understandings, and it is hoped that a book such as the present one will assist in this process.

Within the Church of England, however, *Common Praise* has its own particular place, connected with the traditional understanding of the Church's year. The committee has benefited greatly from discussions with members of the Liturgical Commission, and this new edition may be used in conjunction with the Revised Common Lectionary, now used in *Common Worship*, to provide coherent worship on particular themes and for special occasions. The book should also be useful for schools and colleges, and for other communities such as prisons and hospitals; for daily worship and for mid-week meetings; and not least for private devotion. In some small worshipping groups, it may be sensible to read some of the hymns, either together or in a responsive reading, rather than attempt to sing them.

Mindful of the needs of the church in today's world, therefore, the committee has carefully looked at the words and music of each hymn. It has developed a conservative editorial policy for hymns written before 1900, respecting the integrity of the text, the author's known intentions, and the poetry of the original. Nevertheless, when words have become obscure, or changed their meaning, the committee has on occasion exercised its discretion and amended archaisms to produce a more accessible text. It has also been aware of the problem of gender-based language, and has gently sought to avoid this where appropriate by 'invisible mending'.

With hymns written after 1900, the problems have been more easily resolved. The texts have not been so hallowed by time and tradition; and often the authors themselves have been sensitive to issues of non-inclusive language, while many recent or contemporary hymns have followed the practice of modern liturgies in using 'you' rather than 'thou'. During the last twenty years, many authors have re-written their hymns to accommodate these concerns. Where older forms or exclusive language have remained, the committee has generally rejected the hymn or verse altogether, or sought amendments to make them acceptable to contemporary worshippers.

A certain number of worship songs have also been included. They represent a very small selection of what is available, but they should enable the book to be useful for those churches who wish to include in their services a song that has become well-tried and widely known. Similarly, the Christmas section includes a number of carols: many more could have been added, but carols are found in many easily-available books, and the present book should contain enough for most churches on the occasion of a representative and traditional carol service.

Much of the success of a good hymn depends on its music. The committee has carefully examined the music of every hymn, with a view to ensuring a marriage of words and tune which will allow it to become a successful and respected part of worship. The music allows the words to reverberate with meaning, to acquire a different and nobler life than when they are read aloud; and in congregational singing members of the Body of Christ are united in praise and thanksgiving by the shared experience of the music and the words. And although it is better, in some situations, to say the words rather than sing them badly, there is no doubt that good hymn-singing can be inspiring and uplifting. One of the great factors in the success of the first edition of *Hymns Ancient and Modern* was Monk's outstanding musical editing, which set tunes to words which have since become inseparable from them. It would be unthinkable, for example, to sing 'O God, our help in ages past' to any tune other than ST ANNE, or

'Abide with me' to anything except EVENTIDE. The present edition follows in a musical tradition which has given to the Church some of its finest hymns, and every tune has been examined to ensure that it is worthy of its place and appropriate to the words to which it is set.

The committee has tried to select the best hymns, those which will last. In the process, it has consulted widely, trying to find out what has become acceptable and valuable to people in worship, and what is loved by them; in addition, it has received submissions from many advisers and potential contributors. It has been conscious of the English-speaking contribution to the spirituality of the Anglican communion, but also of the vigour and freshness which come from other countries. It has also been concerned to provide hymns that will be useful at specific points in a service. It has sought to aid the choice of such hymns by the provision of indexes, which should be used creatively; the suggestions should be taken as helpful pointers rather than as excluding other possibilities. There are many hymns written for a specific time of year, or associated with it, which could be used at other times or as general hymns.

Used imaginatively, therefore, this book should provide a valuable resource, to meet the challenge of the twenty-first century. In making its choice, the committee has been mindful of the practical needs of today's worshipping church as well as the great tradition which the previous editions of this book have represented for almost a century and a half. Sunday by Sunday, in cathedrals, in towns and suburbs, in remote villages, and in churches all over the world, *Hymns Ancient and Modern* has given its people a much-loved and well-used selection of old and new hymns, set to music that has become so familiar as to be an integral part of the living tradition of the Church. To these are now added a wide selection from what we believe to be the best contemporary hymns.

These are hymns and songs that touch the human heart: and that this edition should continue to be of service to the Church, and to the individual believer, is the committee's most earnest and deeply-felt prayer. It offers *Common Praise* in the hope that its use will enrich daily worship, bring closer the kingdom of God upon earth, and give glory to God in the highest.

Hymn Book Committee
Henry Chadwick (Chairman), Lionel Dakers,
Timothy Dudley-Smith, Gordon Knights,
Patricia Nappin, J. Richard Watson,
Allan Wicks, Robert Willis

THE WORDING OF HYMNS

The texts of hymns have often been altered to make them suitable for worship in a later age from the one in which they were written. Isaac Watts and Charles Wesley, for example, often used the word 'bowels' as an image for the mercy of Christ, and this would not be appropriate today. More recently, a word such as 'gay' has, regrettably, acquired a meaning which makes it unsuitable for singing in certain contexts.

More difficult is the question of returning to the author's original text, when it has been superseded for many years. The 1904 edition of *Hymns Ancient and Modern,* with a commendable care for authenticity, changed 'Hark the herald angels sing' to Charles Wesley's original 'Hark, how all the welkin rings', but the change was widely ridiculed at the time.

However, care needs to be taken in alteration, and the compilers of *Common Praise* have been cautious in their practice. As a rule, they have not, for example, altered 'thou' to 'you', or made other changes to hymns written before 1900. These are traditional texts, which have been loved and used by worshippers in their original (or near original) form for generations.

Occasionally, however, it has seemed possible to alter hymns to remove non-inclusive language, as in 'All for Jesus', where the fourth verse reads:

All for Jesus, all for Jesus,
this the Church's song must be;
till, at last, her sons are gathered
one in love and one in thee.

which becomes:

All for Jesus, all for Jesus;
this the Church's song must be;
till, at last, we all are gathered
one in love and one in thee.

Another example would be Fred Pratt Green's hymn, 'When in man's music, God is glorified', which can become 'When in our music, God is glorified'.

These and other alterations have been made, we think, with the need for change balanced against the claims of the original words. In addition, there is the need to respect the text as it had been known for generations. We hope, therefore, that in *Common Praise*, the words of the hymns will speak to the mind and heart with authenticity, and also with relevance to the needs of today.

ACKNOWLEDGEMENT OF COPYRIGHT

The Publishers thank the owners or controllers of copyright for permission to use the hymns throughout this collection. An asterisk denotes that the text has been altered by permission.

Every effort has been made to trace copyright owners to seek permission to use or alter text. The Publishers apologise to those who have not been traced and whose rights have inadvertently not been acknowledged. Any omissions or inaccuracies of permission or copyright details will be corrected in future printings.

A list of copyright owners appears below, and some copyright addresses appear at the at the end of this section, on p. xvi. Further copyright details appear on-page for the equivalent hymn in the Full Music edition, or may be had from the Publishers.

AUTHOR	COPYRIGHT HOLDER	HYMN & COPYRIGHT DATE
Alington, C. A.	Hymns Ancient & Modern Ltd	145, 219, 258, 628
Alington, C. A.	Lady Fiona Mynors	509
Appleford, Patrick	Josef Weinberger Ltd	488 (1965), 505 (1965)
Arlott, John	Trustees of the late John Arlott	271
Bayly, Albert F.	Oxford University Press	210, 263, 272 (1988), 510
Bell, G. K. A.	Oxford University Press	165
Bell, John	WGRG	78 (1987), 348 (1987), 622 (1987)
Bewes, Richard	Richard Bewes / Jubilate Hymns	443
Bowers, John E.	The author	52, 290, 327, 399
Bridge, Basil E.	The author	328, 337, 342
Briggs, G. W.	Oxford University Press	152, 256, 293, 396
Brooks, R. T.	Hope Publishing Co. / CopyCare	584 (1954 renewed 1982)
Burkitt, F. C.	SPCK	39, 194
Burns, Edward J.	The author	612
Caird, George B.	G. B. Caird Fund	528
Caird, George B.	The United Reformed Church	374 (1984)
Carter, Sydney	Stainer & Bell Ltd	468 (1963)
Chesterton, G. K.	Oxford University Press	358
Chisholm, Thomas	Hope Publishing Co. / CopyCare	453 (1923 renewed 1951)
Clare, T. C. Hunter	G. T. Haxby	192
Coelho, Terrye	Maranatha Music / CopyCare	297 (1972)
Cosnett, Elizabeth	Stainer & Bell Ltd	80 (1992)
Cosnett, Elizabeth	The author	201 (1980), 339
Cross, Stewart	Mrs Mary Cross	418
Crum, J. M. C.	Oxford University Press	153 (1928)
Daw, Carl P.	Hope Publishing Co. / CopyCare	185 (1982), 564 (1989), 614 (1994)
Dearmer, Geoffrey	The Revd J. Woollcombe	103
Dearmer, Percy	Oxford University Press	3, 73 (1928), 121, 135, 280, 323, 487
Dix, William Chatterton	Canterbury Press Norwich	74
Dobbie, Robert	Executors of the late Robert Dobbie	336

Dudley-Smith, Timothy	Timothy Dudley-Smith	4, 47, 79, 81, 196, 200, 252, 268, 341, 349, 360, 362, 363, 364, 367, 397, 501, 525, 611
Easter Proclamation	Central Board of Finance of the Church of England	156 (1984, 1986)
Evans, David J.	Kingsway's Thankyou Music	383 (1986)
Farjeon, Eleanor	Gervase Farjeon	35, 260
Fishel, Donald	Word of God Music / CopyCare	136 (1973)
Foley, Brian	Faber Music Ltd	183 (1971), 269 (1971)
Forster, Michael	Kevin Mayhew Ltd	179 (1992)
Fosdick, Harry E.	Dr E. Downs	448
Fox, Adam	Hymns Ancient & Modern Ltd	303
Fox, David	The author	451
Fraser, Ian	Stainer & Bell Ltd	257 (1969)
Gaunt, Alan	Stainer & Bell Ltd	403 (1991), 408 (1997), 463 (1997), 613 (1991)
Gaunt, H. C. A.	Oxford University Press	204, 217, 319, 321, 335
Gillard, Richard	Kingsway's Thankyou Music	393
Green, F. Pratt	Stainer & Bell Ltd	58 (1971), 93 (1980), 124 (1973), 130 (1974), 213 (1969), 227 (1973, 1980), 254 (1970), 301 (1979), 344, 346 (1969), 559 (1982), 618 (1972)
Gurney, Dorothy F.	Oxford University Press	343
Hardy, H. E.	Continuum International Publishing Group Ltd	116
Herklots, Rosamond	Oxford University Press	428
Hine, Stuart K.	Stuart K. Hine / Kingsway's Thankyou Music	262 (1953)
Houghton, Frank	OMF International	72
Housman, Laurence	Oxford University Press	71
Hoyle, Richard	World Student Christian Federation	160
Hughes, Donald Wynn	Mr P. Hughes	410
Hull, Eleanor	Estate of the Editor of The Poem Book of the Gael / Chatto & Windus	386
Humphreys, Charles W.	Oxford University Press	323
Hunter Clare, T. C.	G. T. Haxby	192
Idle, Christopher M.	Christopher Idle / Jubilate Hymns	266, 300, 415, 450, 462, 576
Kaan, Fred	Stainer & Bell Ltd	315 (1968), 427 (1968)
Kendrick, Graham	Kingsway's Thankyou Music	432, 513
Le Grice, Edwin	Kevin Mayhew Ltd	155 (1992)
Liturgy of Malabar	Hymns Ancient & Modern Ltd	303
Lowry, S. C.	Oxford University Press	573
Mansell, David	Word's Spirit of Praise Music / CopyCare	170 (1982)
Martin, Hugh	The Hymn Society / Hope Publishing Co. / CopyCare	535 (1989)
Martin, Marcella	Stanbrook Abbey	8
Maule, Graham	WGRG	78 (1987), 348 (1987), 622 (1987)
Milner-Barry, Alda	The National Society for Promoting Religious Education	146
Morgan, Edmund R.	Hymns Ancient & Modern Ltd	333

Murray, Shirley Erena	Hope Publishing Co. / CopyCare	447 (1992)
Newbolt, M. R.	Hymns Ancient & Modern Ltd	499
O'Neill, Judith Beatrice	The author	340
Oxenham, John	Desmond Dunkerley	477
Peacey, J. R.	The Revd M. J. Hancock	238, 334, 412, 425, 438
Perry, Michael	Mrs B. Perry / Jubilate Hymns	68
Phillips, C. S.	Hymns Ancient & Modern Ltd	234, 246
Quinn, James	Continuum International Publishing Group Ltd	205, 314, 429, 441, 567, 625
Rees, Bryn	Alexander Scott	458, 591
Rees, Timothy	Continuum International Publishing Group Ltd	288, 442
Reid, William Watkins	The Hymn Society / Hope Publishing Co. / CopyCare	460 (1951 renewed 1987)
Riley, Athelstan	Oxford University Press	230
Routley, Erik	Hinshaw Music Inc.	596
Routley, Erik	Hope Publishing Co. / CopyCare	479, 527 (1974)
Routley, Erik	Stainer & Bell Ltd	373 (1969)
Rutt, Richard	The author	131
Saward, Michael	Michael Saward / Jubilate Hymns	398
Schutte, Dan	Daniel L Schutte / New Dawn Music	470 (1981)
Scott, R. B. Y.	Executors of the late R. B. Y. Scott	33
Seddon, James E.	Mrs C. Seddon / Jubilate Hymns	437
Sherlock, Hugh	Trustees for Methodist Church Purposes	514
Sparrow-Simpson, W. J.	Novello and Co. Ltd	277
Stanbrook Abbey	Stanbrook Abbey	115, 365
Struther, Jan (Joyce Placzek)	Oxford University Press	507, 616
Sturch, Richard	Stainer & Bell Ltd	134 (1990)
Temple, Sebastian	OCP Publications	519
Thompson, Colin P.	The author	289, 529, 551
Timms, G. B.	Oxford University Press	241, 568
Troeger, Thomas H.	Oxford University Press Inc.	249, 552
Tucker, F. Bland	Church Pension Fund	92, 102, 298, 372, 588
Turton, William	Hymns Ancient & Modern Ltd	318
Vanstone, W. H.	J. W. Shore	259
Wigmore, Paul	Paul Wigmore / Jubilate Hymns	330
Wilbur, Richard	Faber Music Ltd	42
Willis, Robert	The Very Revd Robert Willis	476, 590
Winslow, Jack C.	Mrs J. Tyrrell	357, 508
Woodward, G. R.	Canterbury Press Norwich	294
Woodward, G. R.	Cathedral Music	161
Wren, Brian A.	Stainer & Bell Ltd	133 (1975 & 1995), 140 (1969 & 1995), 198 (1969, 1985), 305 (1971, 1995)

COPYRIGHT HOLDERS' ADDRESSES

G.B. **Caird** Fund, c/o Nicholas Blinco, Mansfield College, Oxford OX1 3TF

Canterbury Press Norwich, St Mary's Works, St Mary's Plain, Norwich NR3 3BH

Cathedral Music, King Charles Cottage, Racton, Chichester, West Sussex PO18 9DT

Church Pension Fund, 445 Fifth Avenue, New York, NY 10016, USA

Continuum International Publishing Group Limited, The Tower Building, 11 York Road, London SE1 7NZ

CopyCare, PO Box 77, Hailsham BN27 3EF (music@copycare.com)

J. **Curwen & Sons Ltd**, 8/9 Frith Street, London W1D 3JB

Faber Music Ltd, 3 Queen's Square, London WC1N 3AV

Gervase **Farjeon**, c/o David Higham Associates Ltd, 5-8 Lower John Street, Golden Square, London W1R 4HA

GIA Publications Inc., 7404 S. Mason Avenue, Chicago, IL 60638, USA

Hinshaw Music Inc., PO Box 470, Chapel Hill, NC 27514-0470, USA

Hymns Ancient & Modern Ltd, St Mary's Works, St Mary's Plain, Norwich NR3 3BH

Jubilate Hymns, Southwick House, 4 Thorne Park Road, Chelston, Torquay TQ2 6RX

Kingsway Music, PO Box 75, Eastbourne, East Sussex BN23 6NW (tym@kingsway.co.uk)

Kevin **Mayhew** Ltd, Buxhall, Stowmarket, Suffolk IP14 3BW

Trustees for **Methodist Church Purposes**, Methodist Publishing House, 4 John Wesley Road, Werrington, Peterborough. PE4 6ZP

New Dawn Music, 5536 NE Hassalo, Portland, Oregon, OR 97213, USA

Novello and Co. Ltd, 8/9 Frith Street, London W1D 3JB

OCP Publications, 5536 NE Hassalo, Portland, Oregon, OR 97213, USA

OMF International, 2 Cluny Road, Singapore

Oxford University Press, Great Clarendon Street, Oxford OX2 6DP

Oxford University Press Inc., 198 Madison Avenue, New York, NY 10016-4314, USA

SPCK, Holy Trinity Church, Marylebone Road, London NW1 4DU

Stainer & Bell Ltd, PO Box 110, 23 Gruneisen Road, London N3 1DZ

Stanbrook Abbey, Callow End, Worcester WR2 4TD

The **United Reformed Church**, 86 Tavistock Place, London WC1H 9RT

Joseph **Weinberger Ltd**, 12-14 Mortimer Street, London W1N 7RD

WGRG, Iona Community, Glasgow G51 3UU

World Student Christian Federation, 5 Route des Morillons, 1218 Grand-Saconnex, Geneva, Switzerland

MORNING

1

AWAKE, my soul, and with the sun
thy daily stage of duty run;
shake off dull sloth, and joyful rise
to pay thy morning sacrifice.

2 Redeem thy mis-spent time that's past,
and live this day as if thy last;
improve thy talent with due care;
for the great day thyself prepare.

3 Let all thy converse be sincere,
thy conscience as the noon-day clear;
think how all-seeing God thy ways
and all thy secret thoughts surveys.

4 Wake, and lift up thyself, my heart,
and with the angels bear thy part,
who all night long unwearied sing,
high praise to the eternal King.

PART TWO

5 GLORY to thee, who safe hast kept
and hast refreshed me whilst I slept;
grant, Lord, when I from death shall wake,
I may of endless light partake.

6 Lord, I my vows to thee renew;
disperse my sins as morning dew;
guard my first springs of thought and will,
and with thyself my spirit fill.

7 Direct, control, suggest, this day,
all I design or do or say;
that all my powers, with all their might,
in thy sole glory may unite.

DOXOLOGY

To be sung after either part

8 Praise God, from whom all blessings flow,
praise him, all creatures here below,
praise him above, angelic host,
praise Father, Son, and Holy Ghost.

THOMAS KEN * 1637–1711

2

CHRIST, whose glory fills the skies,
Christ, the true, the only light,
Sun of Righteousness, arise,
triumph o'er the shades of night;
Dayspring from on high, be near;
Daystar, in my heart appear.

2 Dark and cheerless is the morn
unaccompanied by thee;
joyless is the day's return,
till thy mercy's beams I see,
till they inward light impart,
glad my eyes, and warm my heart.

3 Visit then this soul of mine,
pierce the gloom of sin and grief;
fill me, radiancy divine,
scatter all my unbelief;
more and more thyself display,
shining to the perfect day.

CHARLES WESLEY 1707–1788

3

FATHER, we praise thee,
now the night is over;
active and watchful,
stand we all before thee;
singing we offer
prayer and meditation:
thus we adore thee.

2 Monarch of all things,
fit us for thy mansions;
banish our weakness,
health and wholeness sending;
bring us to heaven,
where thy saints united
joy without ending.

3 All-holy Father,
Son and equal Spirit,
Trinity blessèd,
send us thy salvation;
thine is the glory,
gleaming and resounding
through all creation.

10th century, or earlier
tr. PERCY DEARMER 1867–1936

4

LORD, as the day begins
lift up our hearts in praise;
take from us all our sins,
guard us in all our ways:
our every step direct and guide
that Christ in all be glorified!

2 Christ be in work and skill,
serving each other's need;
Christ be in thought and will,
Christ be in word and deed:
our minds be set on things above
in joy and peace, in faith and love.

3 Grant us the Spirit's strength,
teach us to walk his way;
so bring us all at length
safe to the close of day:
from hour to hour sustain and bless,
and let our song be thankfulness.

4 Now as the day begins
make it the best of days;
take from us all our sins,
guard us in all our ways:
our every step direct and guide
that Christ in all be glorified!

TIMOTHY DUDLEY-SMITH *b.* 1926

5

MY Father, for another night
of quiet sleep and rest,
for all the joy of morning light,
thy holy name be blest.

2 Now with the new-born day I give
myself anew to thee,
that as thou willest I may live,
and what thou willest be.

3 Whate'er I do, things great or small,
whate'er I speak or frame,
thy glory may I seek in all,
do all in Jesus' name.

4 My Father, for his sake, I pray,
thy child accept and bless;
and lead me by thy grace to-day
in paths of righteousness.

H. W. BAKER 1821–1877

6

NEW every morning is the love
our wakening and uprising prove;
through sleep and darkness safely brought,
restored to life and power and thought.

2 New mercies, each returning day,
hover around us while we pray;
new perils past, new sins forgiven,
new thoughts of God, new hopes of heaven.

3 If on our daily course our mind
be set to hallow all we find,
new treasures still, of countless price,
God will provide for sacrifice.

4 The trivial round, the common task,
will furnish all we need to ask,
room to deny ourselves, a road
to bring us daily nearer God.

5 Only, O Lord, in thy dear love
fit us for perfect rest above;
and help us, this and every day,
to live more nearly as we pray.

JOHN KEBLE * 1792–1866

7

O SPLENDOUR of God's glory bright,
who bringest forth the light from Light;
O Light, of light the fountain-spring;
O Day, our days illumining;

2 Come, very Sun of truth and love,
come in thy radiance from above,
and shed the Holy Spirit's ray
on all we think or do to-day.

3 Teach us to work with all our might;
put Satan's fierce assaults to flight;
turn all to good that seems most ill;
help us our calling to fulfil.

4 O joyful be the livelong day,
our thoughts as pure as morning ray,
our faith like noonday's glowing height,
our souls undimmed by shades of night.

5 All praise to God the Father be,
all praise, eternal Son, to thee,
whom with the Spirit we adore
for ever and for evermore.

St Ambrose *c.* 340–397
tr. compilers of *Hymns Ancient and Modern* 1904

8

THE day is filled with splendour,
when God brings light from Light,
and all renewed creation
rejoices in his sight.

2 The Father gives his children
the wonders of the world
in which his power and glory
like banners are unfurled.

3 With every living creature,
awaking with the day,
we turn to God our Father,
lift up our hearts and pray:

4 O Father, Son and Spirit,
your grace and mercy send,
that we may live to praise you
today and to the end.

Marcella Martin *b.* 1908

9

THIS is the day the Lord hath made,
he calls the hours his own;
let heaven rejoice, let earth be glad,
and praise surround the throne.

2 To-day he rose and left the dead,
and Satan's empire fell;
to-day the saints his triumphs spread,
and all his wonders tell.

3 Hosanna to the anointed King,
to David's holy Son.
O help us, Lord, descend and bring
salvation from thy throne.

4 Blest be the Lord, who comes to men
with messages of grace;
who comes, in God his Father's name,
to save our sinful race.

5 Hosanna in the highest strains
the Church on earth can raise;
the highest heavens in which he reigns
shall give him nobler praise.

Isaac Watts 1674–1748
Psalm 118. 24–26

See also

382 Awake, our souls! Away, our fears!
142 Come, let us with our Lord arise
619 When morning gilds the skies

EVENING

10

ABIDE with me; fast falls the eventide;
the darkness deepens; Lord, with me abide!
when other helpers fail, and comforts flee,
help of the helpless, O abide with me.

2 Swift to its close ebbs out life's little day;
earth's joys grow dim, its glories pass away;
change and decay in all around I see;
O thou who changest not, abide with me.

3 I need thy presence every passing hour;
what but thy grace can foil the tempter's power?
who like thyself my guide and stay can be?
through cloud and sunshine, O abide with me.

4 I fear no foe with thee at hand to bless;
ills have no weight, and tears no bitterness.
Where is death's sting? Where, grave, thy victory?
I triumph still, if thou abide with me.

5 Hold thou thy cross before my closing eyes;
shine through the gloom, and point me to the skies:
Heaven's morning breaks, and earth's vain shadows flee;
in life, in death, O Lord, abide with me!

H. F. LYTE 1793–1847

11

AS now the sun's declining rays
  at eventide descend,
so life's brief day is sinking down
  to its appointed end.

2 Lord, on the cross thine arms were stretched
  to draw thy people nigh:
O grant us then that cross to love,
  and in those arms to die.

3 All glory to the Father be,
  all glory to the Son,
all glory, Holy Ghost, to thee,
  while endless ages run.

Latin, CHARLES COFFIN 1676–1749
tr. JOHN CHANDLER * 1806–1876

12

AT even, ere the sun was set,
  the sick, O Lord, around thee lay;
O in what divers pains they met!
  O with what joy they went away!

2 Once more 'tis eventide, and we
oppressed with various ills draw near;
what if thy form we cannot see?
we know and feel that thou art here.

3 O Saviour Christ, our woes dispel;
for some are sick, and some are sad,
and some have never loved thee well,
and some have lost the love they had;

4 And some have found the world is vain,
yet from the world they break not free;
and some have friends who give them pain,
yet have not sought a friend in thee;

5 And none, O Lord, have perfect rest,
for none are wholly free from sin;
and they who fain would serve thee best
are conscious most of wrong within.

6 O Saviour Christ, thou too art man;
thou hast been troubled, tempted, tried;
thy kind but searching glance can scan
the very wounds that shame would hide.

7 Thy touch has still its ancient power;
no word from thee can fruitless fall:
Hear, in this solemn evening hour,
and in thy mercy heal us all.

HENRY TWELLS 1823–1900

13

BEFORE the ending of the day,
Creator of the world, we pray,
that with thy wonted favour thou
wouldst be our guard and keeper now.

2 From all ill dreams defend our eyes,
from nightly fears and fantasies;
tread under foot our ghostly foe,
that no pollution we may know.

3 O Father, that we ask be done,
through Jesus Christ thine only Son,
who, with the Holy Ghost and thee,
doth live and reign eternally. Amen.

Latin, before 11th century
tr. J. M. NEALE 1818–1866

14

GLORY to thee, my God, this night
for all the blessings of the light;
keep me, O keep me, King of kings,
beneath thy own almighty wings.

2 Forgive me, Lord, for thy dear Son,
the ill that I this day have done,
that with the world, myself, and thee,
I, ere I sleep, at peace may be.

3 Teach me to live, that I may dread
the grave as little as my bed;
teach me to die, that so I may
rise glorious at the aweful day.

4 O may my soul on thee repose,
and with sweet sleep my eyelids close,
sleep that may me more vigorous make
to serve my God when I awake.

5 When in the night I sleepless lie,
my soul with heavenly thoughts supply;
let no ill dreams disturb my rest,
no powers of darkness me molest.

6 Praise God from whom all blessings flow,
praise him, all creatures here below,
praise him above, angelic host,
praise Father, Son, and Holy Ghost.

THOMAS KEN 1637–1711

15

GOD, that madest earth and heaven,
darkness and light;
who the day for toil hast given,
for rest the night;
may thine angel-guards defend us,
slumber sweet thy mercy send us,
holy dreams and hopes attend us,
this livelong night.

2 Guard us waking, guard us sleeping,
and, when we die,
may we in thy mighty keeping
all peaceful lie:
when the last dread call shall wake us,
do not thou our God forsake us,
but to reign in glory take us
with thee on high.

v. 1 Reginald Heber 1783–1826
v. 2 Richard Whately 1787–1863

16

HAIL, gladdening Light, of his pure glory poured
who is the immortal Father, heavenly, blest,
holiest of holies, Jesus Christ our Lord.

2 Now we are come to the sun's hour of rest,
the lights of evening round us shine,
we hymn the Father, Son, and Holy Spirit divine.

3 Worthiest art thou at all times to be sung
with undfilèd tongue,
Son of our God, giver of life, alone:
therefore in all the world thy glories, Lord, they own.

Greek, 3rd century or earlier
tr. John Keble 1792–1866

17

O GLADSOME light, O grace
of God the Father's face,
the eternal splendour wearing;
celestial, holy, blest,
our Saviour Jesus Christ,
joyful in thine appearing.

2 Now, ere day fadeth quite,
we see the evening light,
our wonted hymn outpouring;
Father of might unknown,
thee, his incarnate Son,
and Holy Spirit adoring.

3 To thee of right belongs
all praise of holy songs,
O Son of God, lifegiver;
thee therefore, O most high,
the world doth glorify
and shall exalt for ever.

Greek, 3rd century or earlier
tr. ROBERT BRIDGES 1844–1930

18

O STRENGTH and stay upholding all creation,
who ever dost thyself unmoved abide,
yet day by day the light in due gradation
from hour to hour through all its changes guide;

2 Grant to life's day a calm unclouded ending,
an eve untouched by shadows of decay,
the brightness of a holy death-bed blending
with dawning glories of the eternal day.

3 Hear us, O Father, gracious and forgiving,
through Jesus Christ thy co-eternal Word,
who with the Holy Ghost by all things living
now and to endless ages art adored.

ST AMBROSE c. 340–397
tr. JOHN ELLERTON 1826–1893 and F. J. A. HORT 1828–1892

19

ROUND me falls the night;
Saviour, be my light;
through the hours in darkness shrouded
let me see thy face unclouded;
let thy glory shine
in this heart of mine.

2 Earthly work is done,
earthly sounds are none;
rest in sleep and silence seeking,
let me hear thee softly speaking;
in my spirit's ear
whisper, 'I am near.'

3 Blessèd, heavenly Light,
shining through earth's night;
voice, that oft of love hast told me;
arms, so strong to clasp and hold me;
thou thy watch wilt keep,
Saviour, o'er my sleep.

WILLIAM ROMANIS 1824–1899

20

SAVIOUR, again to thy dear name we raise
with one accord our parting hymn of praise;
we stand to bless thee ere our worship cease;
then, lowly kneeling, wait thy word of peace.

2 Grant us thy peace upon our homeward way;
with thee began, with thee shall end, the day:
guard thou the lips from sin, the hearts from shame,
that in this house have called upon thy name.

3 Grant us thy peace, Lord, through the coming night;
turn thou for us its darkness into light;
from harm and danger keep thy children free,
for dark and light are both alike to thee.

4 Grant us thy peace throughout our earthly life,
our balm in sorrow, and our stay in strife;
then, when thy voice shall bid our conflict cease,
call us, O Lord, to thine eternal peace.

JOHN ELLERTON 1826–1893

21

SUN of my soul, thou Saviour dear,
it is not night if thou be near:
O may no earth-born cloud arise
to hide thee from thy servant's eyes.

2 When the soft dews of kindly sleep
my wearied eyelids gently steep,
be my last thought, how sweet to rest
for ever on my Saviour's breast.

3 Abide with me from morn till eve,
for without thee I cannot live;
abide with me when night is nigh,
for without thee I dare not die.

4 If some poor wandering child of thine
have spurned to-day the voice divine,
now, Lord, the gracious work begin;
let him no more lie down in sin.

5 Watch by the sick; enrich the poor
with blessings from thy boundless store;
be every mourner's sleep to-night
like infant's slumbers, pure and light.

6 Come near and bless us when we wake,
ere through the world our way we take;
till in the ocean of thy love
we lose ourselves in heaven above.

JOHN KEBLE 1792–1866

22

THE day thou gavest, Lord, is ended,
the darkness falls at thy behest;
to thee our morning hymns ascended,
thy praise shall sanctify our rest.

2 We thank thee that thy Church unsleeping,
while earth rolls onward into light,
through all the world her watch is keeping,
and rests not now by day or night.

3 As o'er each continent and island
the dawn leads on another day,
the voice of prayer is never silent,
nor dies the strain of praise away.

4 The sun that bids us rest is waking
our brethren 'neath the western sky,
and hour by hour fresh lips are making
thy wondrous doings heard on high.

5 So be it, Lord: thy throne shall never,
like earth's proud empires, pass away;
thy kingdom stands, and grows for ever,
till all thy creatures own thy sway.

JOHN ELLERTON 1826–1893

23

THE duteous day now closeth,
each flower and tree reposeth,
shade creeps o'er wild and wood:
let us, as night is falling,
on God our maker calling,
give thanks to him, the giver good.

2 Now all the heavenly splendour
breaks forth in starlight tender
  from myriad worlds unknown;
and man, the marvel seeing,
forgets his selfish being,
  for joy of beauty not his own.

3 His care he drowneth yonder,
lost in the abyss of wonder;
  to heaven his soul doth steal:
this life he disesteemeth,
the day it is that dreameth,
  that doth from truth his vision seal.

4 Awhile his mortal blindness
may miss God's loving-kindness,
  and grope in faithless strife:
  but when life's day is over
shall death's fair night discover
  the fields of everlasting life.

ROBERT BRIDGES 1844–1930
based on *Nun ruhen alle Wälder,*
PAUL GERHARDT 1607–1676

ADVENT

24

COME, thou long-expected Jesus,
  born to set thy people free;
from our fears and sins release us;
  let us find our rest in thee.

2 Israel's strength and consolation,
  hope of all the earth thou art;
dear desire of every nation,
  joy of every longing heart.

3 Born thy people to deliver;
  born a child and yet a king;
born to reign in us for ever;
  now thy gracious kingdom bring.

4 By thy own eternal Spirit,
rule in all our hearts alone:
by thy all-sufficient merit,
raise us to thy glorious throne.

CHARLES WESLEY * 1707–1788

25

CREATOR of the starry height,
thy people's everlasting light,
Jesu, redeemer of us all,
hear thou thy servants when they call.

2 Thou, sorrowing at the helpless cry
of all creation doomed to die,
didst come to save our fallen race
by healing gifts of heavenly grace.

3 When earth was near its evening hour,
thou didst, in love's redeeming power,
like bridegroom from his chamber, come
forth from a virgin-mother's womb.

*4 At thy great name, exalted now,
all knees in lowly homage bow;
all things in heaven and earth adore,
and own thee King for evermore.

5 To thee, O Holy One, we pray,
our judge in that tremendous day,
ward off, while yet we dwell below,
the weapons of our crafty foe.

6 To God the Father, God the Son,
and God the Spirit, Three in One,
praise, honour, might, and glory be
from age to age eternally. Amen.

Latin
tr. J. M. NEALE 1818–1866

26

HARK, a thrilling voice is sounding;
  'Christ is nigh,' it seems to say;
'cast away the dreams of darkness,
  O ye children of the day.'

2 Wakened by the solemn warning,
  let the earth-bound soul arise;
Christ, her Sun, all ill dispelling,
  shines upon the morning skies.

3 Lo, the Lamb, so long expected,
  comes with pardon down from heaven;
let us haste, with tears of sorrow,
  one and all to be forgiven;

4 That when next he comes with glory,
  and the world is wrapped in fear,
with his mercy he may shield us,
  and with words of love draw near.

5 Honour, glory, might, and blessing
  to the Father and the Son,
with the everlasting Spirit,
  while eternal ages run.

Latin
tr. EDWARD CASWALL * 1814–1878

27

HARK the glad sound! the Saviour comes,
  the Saviour promised long:
Let every heart prepare a throne,
  and every voice a song.

2 He comes, the prisoners to release
  in Satan's bondage held;
the gates of brass before him burst,
  the iron fetters yield.

3 He comes, the broken heart to bind,
the bleeding soul to cure,
and with the treasures of his grace
to enrich the humble poor.

4 Our glad hosannas, Prince of peace,
thy welcome shall proclaim;
and heaven's eternal arches ring
with thy belovèd name.

Luke 4. 18–19
PHILIP DODDRIDGE 1702–1751

28

HARK what a sound, and too divine for hearing,
stirs on the earth and trembles in the air!
Is it the thunder of the Lord's appearing?
Is it the music of his people's prayer?

2 Surely he cometh, and a thousand voices
shout to the saints, and to the deaf are dumb;
surely he cometh, and the earth rejoices,
glad in his coming who hath sworn: I come!

3 This hath he done, and shall we not adore him?
This shall he do, and can we still despair?
come, let us quickly fling ourselves before him,
cast at his feet the burden of our care.

4 Yea through life, death, through sorrow
and through sinning,
he shall suffice me, for he hath sufficed:
Christ is the end, for Christ was the beginning,
Christ the beginning, for the end is Christ.

FREDERIC W. H. MYERS 1843–1901

29

HILLS of the North, rejoice,
  river and mountain-spring,
hark to the advent voice;
  valley and lowland, sing.
Christ comes in righteousness and love,
he brings salvation from above.

2 Isles of the Southern seas,
  sing to the listening earth,
carry on every breeze
  hope of a world's new birth:
In Christ shall all be made anew,
his word is sure, his promise true.

3 Lands of the East, arise,
  he is your brightest morn,
greet him with joyous eyes,
  praise shall his path adorn:
your seers have longed to know their Lord;
to you he comes, the final word.

4 Shores of the utmost West,
  lands of the setting sun,
welcome the heavenly guest
  in whom the dawn has come:
he brings a never-ending light
who triumphed o'er our darkest night.

5 Shout, as you journey home,
  songs be in every mouth,
lo, from the North they come,
  from East and West and South:
in Jesus all shall find their rest,
in him the universe be blest.

Editors of *English Praise* 1975 *
based on CHARLES E. OAKLEY 1832–1865

30

LIFT up your heads, you mighty gates,
behold, the King of Glory waits,
the King of kings is drawing near,
the Saviour of the world is here.

2 O blest the land, the city blest
where Christ the ruler is confessed.
O happy hearts and happy homes
to whom this King in triumph comes.

3 Fling wide the portals of your heart,
make it a temple set apart
from earthly use for heaven's employ,
adorned with prayer and love and joy.

4 Come, Saviour, come, with us abide;
our hearts to thee we open wide:
Thy Holy Spirit guide us on,
until our glorious goal is won.

GEORG WEISSEL 1590–1635
tr. CATHERINE WINKWORTH 1827–1878

31

LO, he comes with clouds descending,
once for favoured sinners slain;
thousand thousand saints attending
swell the triumph of his train:
Alleluia!
God appears on earth to reign.

2 Every eye shall now behold him
robed in dreadful majesty;
those who set at naught and sold him,
pierced and nailed him to the Tree,
deeply wailing,
shall the true Messiah see.

3 Those dear tokens of his passion
still his dazzling body bears,
cause of endless exultation
to his ransomed worshippers:
with what rapture
gaze we on those glorious scars!

4 Yea, Amen, let all adore thee,
high on thine eternal throne;
Saviour, take the power and glory,
claim the kingdom for thine own:
Alleluia!
Thou shalt reign, and thou alone.

CHARLES WESLEY 1707–1788
and JOHN CENNICK 1718–1755

32

O COME, O come, Emmanuel,
and ransom captive Israel,
that mourns in lonely exile here,
until the Son of God appear:
Rejoice! rejoice! Emmanuel
shall come to thee, O Israel.

2 O come, thou Rod of Jesse, free
thine own from Satan's tyranny;
from depths of hell thy people save,
and give them victory o'er the grave:

3 O come, thou Dayspring, come and cheer
our spirits by thine advent here;
disperse the gloomy clouds of night,
and death's dark shadows put to flight:

4 O come, thou Key of David, come,
and open wide our heavenly home;
make safe the way that leads on high,
and close the path to misery:

5 O come, O come, thou Lord of Might,
who to thy tribes, on Sinai's height,
in ancient times didst give the law
in cloud and majesty and awe:
Rejoice! rejoice! Emmanuel
shall come to thee, O Israel.

Latin Advent Antiphons
tr. J. M. NEALE * 1818–1866

33

O DAY of God, draw nigh
in beauty and in power,
come with thy timeless judgement now
to match our present hour.

2 Bring to our troubled minds,
uncertain and afraid,
the quiet of a steadfast faith,
calm of a call obeyed.

3 Bring justice to our land,
that all may dwell secure,
and finely build for days to come
foundations that endure.

4 Bring to our world of strife
thy sovereign word of peace,
that war may haunt the earth no more
and desolation cease.

5 O Day of God, draw nigh;
as at creation's birth
let there be light again, and set
thy judgements in the earth.

R. B. Y. SCOTT 1899–1987

34

ON Jordan's bank the Baptist's cry
announces that the Lord is nigh;
awake and hearken, for he brings
glad tidings from the King of kings.

2 Then cleansed be every breast from sin;
make straight the way for God within;
prepare we in our hearts a home,
where such a mighty guest may come.

3 For thou art our salvation, Lord,
our refuge and our great reward;
without thy grace we waste away,
like flowers that wither and decay.

4 To heal the sick stretch out thine hand,
and bid the fallen sinner stand;
shine forth, and let thy light restore
earth's own true loveliness once more.

5 All praise, eternal Son, to thee
whose advent doth thy people free,
whom with the Father we adore,
and Holy Ghost for evermore.

CHARLES COFFIN 1676–1749
tr. JOHN CHANDLER 1808–1876
altered by compilers of
Hymns Ancient and Modern

35

PEOPLE, look East. The time is near
of the crowning of the year.
Make your house fair as you are able,
trim the hearth and set the table.
People, look East and sing to-day:
Love, the Guest, is on the way.

2 Furrows, be glad. Though earth is bare,
one more seed is planted there:
give up your strength the seed to nourish,
that in course the flower may flourish.
People, look East, and sing today:
Love, the Rose, is on the way.

3 Stars, keep the watch. When night is dim,
one more light the bowl shall brim,
shining beyond the frosty weather,
bright as sun and moon together.
People, look East, and sing today:
Love, the Star, is on the way.

4 Angels, announce with shouts of mirth
him who brings new life to earth.
Set every peak and valley humming
with the word, the Lord is coming.
People, look East, and sing today:
Love, the Lord, is on the way.

ELEANOR FARJEON * 1881–1965

36

THE advent of our King
our prayers must now employ,
and we must hymns of welcome sing
in strains of holy joy.

2 The everlasting Son
incarnate deigns to be;
himself a servant's form puts on,
to set his servants free.

3 Daughter of Sion, rise
to meet thy lowly King;
nor let thy faithless heart despise
the peace he comes to bring.

4 As judge, on clouds of light,
he soon will come again,
and his true members all unite
with him in heaven to reign.

5 All glory to the Son
who comes to set us free,
with Father, Spirit, ever One,
through all eternity.

CHARLES COFFIN 1676–1749
tr. JOHN CHANDLER 1808–1876

37

THE Lord will come and not be slow,
his footsteps cannot err;
before him righteousness shall go,
his royal harbinger.

2 Truth from the earth, like to a flower,
shall bud and blossom then;
and justice, from her heavenly bower,
look down on mortal men.

3 Rise, God, judge thou the earth in might,
this wicked earth redress;
for thou art he who shalt by right
the nations all possess.

4 The nations all whom thou hast made
shall come, and all shall frame
to bow them low before thee, Lord,
and glorify thy name.

5 For great thou art, and wonders great
by thy strong hand are done:
thou in thy everlasting seat
remainest God alone.

Psalms 82, 85, 86
JOHN MILTON 1608–1674

38

THE people that in darkness sat
  a glorious light have seen;
the light has shined on them who long
  in shades of death have been.

2 To hail thee, Sun of Righteousness,
  the gathering nations come;
they joy as when the reapers bear
  their harvest treasures home.

*3 For thou their burden dost remove,
  and break the tyrant's rod,
as in the day when Midian fell
  before the sword of God.

4 For unto us a child is born,
  to us a Son is given,
and on his shoulder ever rests
  all power in earth and heaven.

5 His name shall be the Prince of Peace,
  the everlasting Lord,
the Wonderful, the Counsellor,
  the God by all adored.

6 His righteous government and power
  shall over all extend;
on judgement and on justice based,
  his reign shall have no end.

7 Lord Jesus, reign in us, we pray,
  and make us thine alone,
who with the Father ever art
  and Holy Spirit One.

Isaiah 9. 2–7
as in *Scottish Paraphrases* 1781
JOHN MORRISON * 1750–1798

39

WAKE, O wake! With tidings thrilling
the watchmen all the air are filling,
arise, Jerusalem, arise!
Midnight strikes! No more delaying,
'The hour has come!' we hear them saying,
'where are ye all, ye virgins wise?
The Bridegroom comes in sight,
raise high your torches bright!'
Alleluia!
The wedding song swells loud and strong:
go forth and join the festal throng.

2 Zion hears the watchmen shouting,
her heart leaps up with joy undoubting,
she stands and waits with eager eyes;
see her Friend from heaven descending,
adorned with truth and grace unending!
Her light burns clear, her star doth rise.
Now come, thou precious Crown,
Lord Jesus, God's own Son!
Alleluia!
Let us prepare to follow there,
where in thy supper we may share.

3 Every soul in thee rejoices;
from earth and from angelic voices
be glory given to thee alone!
Now the gates of pearl receive us,
thy presence never more shall leave us,
we stand with angels round thy throne.
Earth cannot give below
the bliss thou dost bestow.
Alleluia!
Grant us to raise, to length of days,
the triumph-chorus of thy praise.

PHILIPP NICOLAI 1556–1608
tr. F. C. BURKITT 1864–1935
based on Matthew 25. 1–13 and Revelation 19. 6–9

40

YE servants of the Lord,
each in his office wait,
observant of his heavenly word,
and watchful at his gate.

2 Let all your lamps be bright,
and trim the golden flame;
gird up your loins as in his sight,
for aweful is his name.

3 Watch! 'tis your Lord's command,
and while we speak, he's near;
mark the first signal of his hand,
and ready all appear.

4 O happy servant he
in such a posture found!
he shall his Lord with rapture see,
and be with honour crowned.

5 Christ shall the banquet spread
with his own royal hand,
and raise that faithful servant's head
amid the angelic band.

Luke 12. 35–38
PHILIP DODDRIDGE * 1702–1751

See also

476 In a world where people walk in darkness
590 The Kingdom is upon you!
591 The Kingdom of God is justice
607 Thy Kingdom come, O God
608 Thy Kingdom come! On bended knee

41

A GREAT and mighty wonder,
a full and holy cure!
the Virgin bears the Infant
with virgin-honour pure:
Repeat the hymn again:
'To God on high be glory,
and peace on earth to men.'

2 The Word becomes incarnate,
and yet remains on high;
and cherubim sing anthems
to shepherds from the sky:

3 While thus they sing your Monarch,
those bright angelic bands,
rejoice, ye vales and mountains,
ye oceans, clap your hands:

4 Since all he comes to ransom,
by all be he adored,
the Infant born in Bethl'em,
the Saviour and the Lord:
Repeat the hymn again:
'To God on high be glory,
and peace on earth to men.'

St Germanus c. 639–c. 734
tr. J. M. Neale 1818–1866

42

A STABLE lamp is lighted
  whose glow shall wake the sky;
the stars shall bend their voices,
  and every stone shall cry.
  And every stone shall cry,
  and straw like gold shall shine;
a barn shall harbour heaven,
  a stall become a shrine.

2 This Child through David's city
  shall ride in triumph by;
the palm shall strew its branches,
  and every stone shall cry.
  And every stone shall cry,
  though heavy, dull and dumb,
and lie within the roadway
  to pave God's kingdom come.

3 Yet he shall be forsaken
  and yielded up to die;
the sky shall groan and darken,
  and every stone shall cry.
  And every stone shall cry,
  for stony hearts he's slain;
God's blood upon the spear-head,
  God's love refused again.

4 But now as at the ending
  the low is lifted high:
the stars shall bend their voices,
  and every stone shall cry.
  And every stone shall cry,
  in praises of the Child
by whose descent among us
  the worlds are reconciled.

RICHARD WILBUR *b.* 1921

43

ALL my heart this night rejoices,
as I hear,
far and near,
sweetest angel voices:
'Christ is born!' their choirs are singing,
'till the air
everywhere
now with joy is ringing.

2 Hark, a voice from yonder manger,
soft and sweet,
doth entreat,
'flee from woe and danger;
children, come; from all doth grieve you
you are freed,
all you need
I will surely give you.'

3 Come then, let us hasten yonder;
here let all,
great and small,
kneel in awe and wonder;
love him who with love is yearning;
hail the star
that from far
bright with hope is burning!

4 Thee, O Lord, with heed I'll cherish,
live to thee,
and with thee
dying, shall not perish;
but shall dwell with thee for ever,
far on high,
in the joy
that can alter never.

PAUL GERHARDT 1607–1676
tr. CATHERINE WINKWORTH 1827–1878

44

ANGELS from the realms of glory,
wing your flight o'er all the earth;
ye who sang creation's story
now proclaim Messiah's birth:
Come and worship Christ the new-born King.

2 Shepherds in the field abiding,
watching o'er your flocks by night,
God with us is now residing;
yonder shines the infant Light:

3 Sages, leave your contemplations;
brighter visions beam afar;
seek the great Desire of Nations;
ye have seen his natal star:

4 Saints before the altar bending,
watching long in hope and fear,
suddenly the Lord, descending,
in his temple shall appear:

5 Though an infant now we view him,
he shall fill his Father's throne,
gather all the nations to him;
every knee shall then bow down:
Come and worship Christ the new-born King.

from *Iris* 1816 and *The Christmas Box* 1825
vv. 1–4, JAMES MONTGOMERY 1771–1854

45

AWAY in a manger, no crib for a bed,
the little Lord Jesus laid down his sweet head;
the stars in the bright sky looked down where he lay,
the little Lord Jesus asleep on the hay.

2 The cattle are lowing, the baby awakes,
but little Lord Jesus no crying he makes.
I love thee, Lord Jesus! Look down from the sky,
and stay by my side until morning is nigh.

3 Be near me, Lord Jesus; I ask thee to stay
close by me for ever, and love me, I pray.
Bless all the dear children in thy tender care,
and fit us for heaven, to live with thee there.

Little children's book Philadelphia 1885
ANONYMOUS

46

BEHOLD, the great Creator makes
himself a house of clay,
a robe of virgin flesh he takes
which he will wear for aye.

2 Hark, hark! the wise eternal Word
like a weak infant cries;
in form of servant is the Lord,
and God in cradle lies.

3 This wonder struck the world amazed,
it shook the starry frame;
squadrons of spirits stood and gazed,
then down in troops they came.

4 Glad shepherds ran to view this sight;
a choir of angels sings,
and eastern sages with delight
adore this King of kings.

5 Join then, all hearts that are not stone,
and all our voices prove,
to celebrate this Holy One,
the God of peace and love.

THOMAS PESTEL 1585–1659

47

CHILD of the stable's secret birth,
the Lord by right of the lords of earth,
let angels sing of a King new-born,
the world is weaving a crown of thorn:
  A crown of thorn for that infant head
  cradled soft in the manger bed.

2 Eyes that shine in the lantern's ray;
a face so small in its nest of hay,
face of a child who is born to scan
the world he made through the eyes of man:
  And from that face in the final day
  earth and heaven shall flee away.

3 Voice that rang through the courts on high
contracted now to a wordless cry,
a voice to master the wind and wave,
the human heart and the hungry grave:
  The voice of God through the cedar trees
  rolling forth as the sound of seas.

4 Infant hands in a mother's hand,
for none but Mary may understand
whose are the hands and the fingers curled
but his who fashioned and made our world;
  and through these hands in the hour of death
  nails shall strike to the wood beneath.

5 Child of the stable's secret birth,
the Father's gift to a wayward earth,
to drain the cup in a few short years
of all our sorrows, our sins and tears;
  ours the prize for the road he trod:
  Risen with Christ; at peace with God.

TIMOTHY DUDLEY-SMITH *b.* 1926

48

CHRISTIANS, awake! salute the happy morn,
whereon the Saviour of the world was born;
rise to adore the mystery of love,
which hosts of angels chanted from above:
with them the joyful tidings first begun
of God incarnate and the Virgin's Son.

2 Then to the watchful shepherds it was told,
who heard the angelic herald's voice, 'Behold,
I bring good tidings of a Saviour's birth
to you and all the nations upon earth:
this day hath God fulfilled his promised word,
this day is born a Saviour, Christ the Lord.'

*3 He spake; and straightway the celestial choir
in hymns of joy, unknown before, conspire;
the praises of redeeming love they sang,
and heaven's whole orb with alleluias rang:
God's highest glory was their anthem still,
peace upon earth, and unto men good will.

*4 To Bethl'em straight the enlightened shepherds ran,
to see the wonder God had wrought for man,
and found, with Joseph and the blessèd Maid,
her Son, the Saviour, in a manger laid:
then to their flocks, still praising God, return,
and their glad hearts with holy rapture burn.

5 O may we keep and ponder in our mind
God's wondrous love in saving lost mankind;
trace we the babe, who hath retrieved our loss,
from his poor manger to his bitter cross;
tread in his steps, assisted by his grace,
till man's first heavenly state again takes place.

6 Then may we hope, the angelic hosts among,
to sing, redeemed, a glad triumphal song:
he that was born upon this joyful day
around us all his glory shall display;
saved by his love, incessant we shall sing
eternal praise to heaven's almighty King.

JOHN BYROM * 1692–1763

49

COME, thou Redeemer of the earth,
and manifest thy virgin-birth:
let every age adoring fall;
such birth befits the God of all.

2 Begotten of no human will,
but of the Spirit, thou art still
the Word of God, in flesh arrayed,
the Saviour, now to us displayed.

3 From God the Father he proceeds,
to God the Father back he speeds,
runs out his course to death and hell,
returns on God's high throne to dwell.

*4 O equal to thy Father, thou!
Gird on thy fleshly mantle now,
the weakness of our mortal state
with deathless might invigorate.

5 Thy cradle here shall glitter bright,
and darkness glow with new-born light,
no more shall night extinguish day,
where love's bright beams their power display.

6 O Jesu, virgin-born, to thee
eternal praise and glory be,
whom with the Father we adore
and Holy Spirit, evermore. Amen.

ST AMBROSE c. 340–397
tr. J. M. NEALE 1818–1866
and others

50

DOST thou in a manger lie,
  who hast all created,
stretching infant hands on high,
  Saviour, long awaited?
If a monarch, where thy state,
where thy court on thee to wait,
  sceptre, crown and sphere?
Here no regal pomp we see,
naught but need and penury:
  why thus cradled here?

2 'For the world a love supreme
  brought me to this stable;
all creation to redeem
  I alone am able.
By this lowly birth of mine,
sinner, riches shall be thine,
  matchless gifts and free;
willingly this yoke I take,
and this sacrifice I make,
  heaping joys for thee.'

3 Christ we praise with voices bold,
  laud and honour raising;
for these mercies manifold
  join the hosts in praising:
Father, glory be to thee
for the wondrous charity
  of thy Son, our Lord.
Better witness to thy worth,
purer praise than ours on earth,
  angels' songs afford.

JEAN MAUBURN 1460–1503
tr. ELIZABETH RUNDLE CHARLES 1828–1896
and others

51

FROM heaven high I come to you,
I bring you tidings good and new;
glad tidings of great joy I bring,
whereof I now will say and sing.

2 To you this night is born a child
of Mary, chosen Virgin mild;
this little child, of lowly birth,
shall be the joy of all the earth.

3 This is the Christ, our God and Lord,
who in all need shall aid afford;
he will himself your Saviour be
from all your sins to set you free.

4 These are the tokens ye shall mark:
the swaddling clothes and manger dark;
there ye shall find the infant laid
by whom the heavens and earth were made.

5 Now let us all with gladsome cheer
go with the shepherds and draw near
to see the precious gift of God,
who hath his own dear Son bestowed.

6 Welcome to earth, thou noble guest,
through whom the sinful world is blest!
in my distress thou com'st to me;
what thanks shall I return to thee?

MARTIN LUTHER 1483–1546
tr. CATHERINE WINKWORTH * 1827–1878

52

'GLORY to God!' all heav'n with joy is ringing;
angels proclaim the gospel of Christ's birth,
'Glory to God!', and still their song is bringing
good news of God incarnate here on earth.

2 Lowly in wonder shepherds kneel before him,
no gift to bring save love of heart and mind:
come like those shepherds, sing his praise, adore him,
a babe so weak, yet Saviour of mankind.

3 Humble, yet regal, wise men kneel before him,
gold, incense, myrrh, their gifts to Christ they bring:
come like those wise men, sing his praise, adore him
a babe so poor and modest, yet a King.

4 Though now no crib or cradle is concealing
Jesus our Lord in that far-distant shrine,
Christ at each eucharist is still revealing
his very self in forms of bread and wine.

JOHN E. BOWERS *b.* 1923

53

HARK! the herald angels sing
glory to the new-born King,
peace on earth and mercy mild,
God and sinners reconciled.
Joyful, all ye nations rise,
join the triumph of the skies;
with the angelic host proclaim,
'Christ is born in Bethlehem.'
Hark, the herald angels sing
glory to the new-born King.

2 Christ, by highest heaven adored,
Christ, the everlasting Lord,
late in time behold him come,
offspring of a Virgin's womb!
Veiled in flesh the Godhead see:
Hail, the incarnate Deity,
pleased as man with man to dwell,
Jesus, our Emmanuel.
Hark, the herald angels sing
glory to the new-born King.

3 Hail, the heaven-born Prince of Peace!
Hail, the Sun of Righteousness!
Light and life to all he brings,
risen with healing in his wings.
Mild he lays his glory by,
born that man no more may die,
born to raise the sons of earth,
born to give them second birth.
Hark, the herald angels sing
glory to the new-born King.

CHARLES WESLEY 1707–1788 and others

54

I CANNOT tell why he, whom angels worship,
should set his love upon the sons of men,
or why, as Shepherd, he should seek the wanderers,
to bring them back, they know not how or when.
But this I know, that he was born of Mary
when Bethl'em's manger was his only home,
and that he lived at Nazareth and laboured,
and so the Saviour, Saviour of the world, is come.

2 I cannot tell how silently he suffered,
as with his peace he graced this place of tears,
or how his heart upon the cross was broken,
the crown of pain to three and thirty years.
But this I know, he heals the broken-hearted
and stays our sin and calms our lurking fear
and lifts the burden from the heavy laden;
for still the Saviour, Saviour of the world is here.

3 I cannot tell how he will win the nations,
how he will claim his earthly heritage,
how satisfy the needs and aspirations
of east and west, of sinner and of sage.
But this I know, all flesh shall see his glory,
and he shall reap the harvest he has sown,
and some glad day his sun will shine in splendour
when he the Saviour, Saviour of the world, is known.

4 I cannot tell how all the lands shall worship,
when at his bidding every storm is stilled,
or who can say how great the jubilation
when every heart with love and joy is filled.
But this I know, the skies will thrill with rapture,
and myriad myriad human voices sing,
and earth to heav'n, and heav'n to earth, will answer,
'at last the Saviour, Saviour of the world, is King!'

WILLIAM YOUNG FULLERTON 1857–1932

55

IN the bleak mid-winter.
Frosty wind made moan,
earth stood hard as iron,
water like a stone;
snow had fallen, snow on snow,
snow on snow,
in the bleak mid-winter,
long ago.

2 Our God, heaven cannot hold him,
nor earth sustain;
heaven and earth shall flee away
when he comes to reign:
in the bleak mid-winter
a stable-place sufficed
the Lord God Almighty,
Jesus Christ.

3 Enough for him whom cherubim
worship night and day,
a breastful of milk
and a mangerful of hay;
enough for him whom angels
fall down before,
the ox and ass and camel
which adore.

4 Angels and archangels
may have gathered there,
cherubim and seraphim
thronged the air;
but only his mother
in her maiden bliss
worshipped the Belovèd
with a kiss.

5 What can I give him,
poor as I am?
If I were a shepherd,
I would bring a lamb,
if I were a wise man
I would do my part;
yet what I can I give him,
give my heart.

CHRISTINA ROSSETTI 1830–1894

56

IT came upon the midnight clear,
that glorious song of old,
from angels bending near the earth
to touch their harps of gold:
'Peace on the earth, good will to men,
from heaven's all-gracious King!'
the world in solemn stillness lay
to hear the angels sing.

2 Still through the cloven skies they come,
with peaceful wings unfurled;
and still their heavenly music floats
o'er all the weary world:
above its sad and lowly plains
they bend on hovering wing;
and ever o'er its Babel-sounds
the blessèd angels sing.

3 Yet with the woes of sin and strife
the world has suffered long;
beneath the angel strain have rolled
two thousand years of wrong;
and man, at war with man, hears not
the love-song which they bring:
O hush the noise, ye men of strife,
and hear the angels sing.

*4 And ye, beneath life's crushing load,
whose forms are bending low,
who toil along the climbing way
with painful steps and slow,
look, now! for glad and golden hours
come swiftly on the wing;
O rest beside the weary road,
and hear the angels sing.

5 For lo, the days are hastening on,
by prophet-bards foretold,
when, with the ever-circling years,
comes round the age of gold;
when peace shall over all the earth
its ancient splendours fling,
and the whole world give back the song
which now the angels sing.

EDMUND H. SEARS 1810–1876

57

JOY to the world, the Lord is come!
let earth receive her King;
let every heart prepare him room,
and heaven and nature sing,
and heaven and nature sing,
and heaven, and heaven and nature sing.

2 Joy to the world, the Saviour reigns!
let all their songs employ;
while fields and floods, rocks, hills and plains
repeat the sounding joy,
repeat the sounding joy,
repeat, repeat the sounding joy.

3 He rules the world with truth and grace,
and makes the nations prove
the glories of his righteousness
and wonders of his love,
and wonders of his love,
and wonders, wonders of his love.

ISAAC WATTS 1674–1748

58

LONG ago, prophets knew
Christ would come, born a Jew,
come to make all things new,
bear his people's burden,
freely love and pardon.
Ring, bells, ring, ring, ring!
sing, choirs, sing, sing, sing!
when he comes,
when he comes,
who will make him welcome?

2 God in time, God in man,
this is God's timeless plan:
he will come, as a man,
born himself of woman,
God divinely human:

3 Mary, hail! Though afraid,
she believed, she obeyed.
In her womb God is laid:
till the time expected,
nurtured and protected:

4 Journey ends! Where afar
Bethl'em shines, like a star,
stable door stands ajar.
Unborn Son of Mary,
Saviour, do not tarry!
Ring, bells, ring, ring, ring!
sing, choirs, sing, sing, sing!
Jesus comes!
Jesus comes!
We will make him welcome!

F. PRATT GREEN 1903–2000

59

LOVE came down at Christmas,
love all lovely, Love divine;
love was born at Christmas,
star and angels gave the sign.

2 Worship we the Godhead,
love incarnate, Love divine;
worship we our Jesus:
but wherewith for sacred sign?

3 Love shall be our token,
love be yours and love be mine,
Love to God and all men,
love for plea and gift and sign.

CHRISTINA ROSSETTI 1830–1894

60

LULLY, lulla,
thou little tiny child,
by by, lully lullay.

2 O sisters too,
how may we do
for to preserve this day
this poor youngling,
for whom we do sing
by by, lully lullay?

3 Herod the king,
in his raging,
chargèd he hath this day
his men of might,
in his own sight,
all young childrèn to slay.

4 That woe is me,
poor child for thee!
and ever morn and day,
for thy parting
neither say nor sing
by by, lully lullay!

Lully, lulla,
thou little tiny child,
by by, lully lullay.

English, 15th century

61, 62

O COME, all ye faithful,
joyful and triumphant,
O come ye, O come ye to Bethlehem;
come and behold him
born the King of Angels:
O come, let us adore him,
O come, let us adore him,
O come, let us adore him,
Christ the Lord!

2 God of God,
Light of Light,
lo! he abhors not the Virgin's womb;
very God,
begotten, not created:

*3 See how the shepherds,
summoned to his cradle,
leaving their flocks, draw nigh with lowly fear;
we too will thither
bend our joyful footsteps:

*4 Lo! star-led chieftains,
Magi, Christ adoring,
offer him incense, gold, and myrrh;
we to the Christ child
bring our heart's oblations:

5 Child, for us sinners
poor and in the manger,
fain we embrace thee, with awe and love;
who would not love thee,
loving us so dearly?

6 Sing, choirs of angels,
sing in exultation,
sing, all ye citizens of heaven above;
glory to God
in the highest:

On Christmas Day

7 Yea, Lord, we greet thee,
born this happy morning,
Jesu, to thee be glory given;
Word of the Father,
now in flesh appearing:
O come, let us adore him,
O come, let us adore him,
O come, let us adore him,
Christ the Lord!

Latin, 18th century
tr. FREDERICK OAKELEY 1802–1880 and others

63

O LITTLE town of Bethlehem,
  how still we see thee lie!
above thy deep and dreamless sleep
  the silent stars go by:
yet in thy dark streets shineth
  the everlasting Light;
the hopes and fears of all the years
  are met in thee tonight.

2 O morning stars, together
  proclaim the holy birth,
and praises sing to God the King,
  and peace to men on earth.
For Christ is born of Mary;
  and, gathered all above,
while mortals sleep, the angels keep
  their watch of wondering love.

3 How silently, how silently,
  the wondrous gift is given!
so God imparts to human hearts
  the blessings of his heaven.
No ear may hear his coming;
  but in this world of sin,
where meek souls will receive him, still
  the dear Christ enters in.

4 O holy Child of Bethlehem,
  descend to us, we pray;
cast out our sin, and enter in:
  be born in us today.
We hear the Christmas angels
  the great glad tidings tell:
O come to us, abide with us,
  our Lord Emmanuel.

PHILLIPS BROOKS 1835–1893

64

OF the Father's love begotten
ere the worlds began to be,
he is Alpha and Omega,
he the source, the ending he,
of the things that are, that have been,
and that future years shall see,
evermore and evermore.

2 O that birth for ever blessèd,
when the Virgin, full of grace,
by the Holy Ghost conceiving,
bare the Saviour of our race,
and the babe, the world's Redeemer,
first revealed his sacred face,
evermore and evermore.

3 O ye heights of heaven, adore him;
angel hosts, his praises sing;
powers, dominions, bow before him,
and extol our God and King:
let no tongue on earth be silent,
every voice in concert ring,
evermore and evermore.

PRUDENTIUS 348–*c.* 413
tr. J. M. NEALE 1818–1866

65

OF the Father's love begotten
ere the worlds began to be,
he is Alpha and Omega,
he the source, the ending he,
of the things that are, that have been,
and that future years shall see,
evermore and evermore.

*2 At his word they were created;
he commanded; it was done:
heaven and earth and depths of ocean
in their threefold order one;
all that grows beneath the shining
of the light of moon and sun,
evermore and evermore.

3 O that birth for ever blessèd
when the Virgin, full of grace,
by the Holy Ghost conceiving,
bare the Saviour of our race,
and the babe, the world's Redeemer,
first revealed his sacred face,
evermore and evermore.

4 O ye heights of heaven, adore him;
angel-hosts, his praises sing;
powers, dominions, bow before him,
and extol our God and King:
let no tongue on earth be silent,
every voice in concert ring,
evermore and evermore.

5 This is he whom seers and sages
sang of old with one accord;
whom the writings of the prophets
promised in their faithful word;
now he shines, the long-expected:
let creation praise its Lord,
evermore and evermore.

*6 Hail, thou Judge of souls departed!
Hail, thou King of them that live!
On the Father's throne exalted
none in might with thee may strive;
who at last in judgement coming
sinners from thy face shalt drive,
evermore and evermore.

7 Christ, to thee, with God the Father,
and, O Holy Ghost, to thee,
hymn and chant and high thanksgiving
and unwearied praises be,
honour, glory, and dominion,
and eternal victory,
evermore and evermore.

PRUDENTIUS 348–c. 413
tr. J. M. NEALE 1818–1866
H. W. BAKER 1821–1877
and others

66

ONCE in royal David's city
stood a lowly cattle shed,
where a mother laid her baby
in a manger for his bed:
Mary was that mother mild,
Jesus Christ her little child.

2 He came down to earth from heaven
who is God and Lord of all,
and his shelter was a stable,
and his cradle was a stall;
with the poor and mean and lowly
lived on earth our Saviour holy.

3 And through all his wondrous childhood
he would honour and obey,
love and watch the lowly maiden,
in whose gentle arms he lay:
Christian children all must be
mild, obedient, good as he.

4 For he is our childhood's pattern,
day by day like us he grew,
he was little, weak, and helpless,
tears and smiles like us he knew;
and he feeleth for our sadness,
and he shareth in our gladness.

5 And our eyes at last shall see him,
through his own redeeming love,
for that child so dear and gentle
is our Lord in heaven above;
and he leads his children on
to the place where he is gone.

6 Not in that poor lowly stable,
with the oxen standing by,
we shall see him; but in heaven,
set at God's right hand on high;
where like stars his children crowned
all in white shall wait around.

CECIL FRANCES ALEXANDER 1818–1895

67

SEE, amid the winter's snow,
born for us on earth below,
see, the Lamb of God appears,
promised from eternal years!
Hail, thou ever-blessèd morn!
Hail, redemption's happy dawn!
Sing through all Jerusalem:
Christ is born in Bethlehem!

2 Lo, within a manger lies
he who built the starry skies,
he who, throned in height sublime,
sits amid the cherubim!

3 Say, ye holy shepherds, say,
what your joyful news today;
wherefore have ye left your sheep
on the lonely mountain steep?

4 'As we watched at dead of night,
lo, we saw a wondrous light;
angels, singing "Peace on earth",
told us of a Saviour's birth.'

5 Sacred Infant, all divine,
what a tender love was thine,
thus to come from highest bliss
down to such a world as this!
Hail, thou ever-blessèd morn!
Hail, redemption's happy dawn!
Sing through all Jerusalem:
Christ is born in Bethlehem!

EDWARD CASWALL * 1814–1878

68

SEE him lying on a bed of straw,
a draughty stable with an open door;
Mary cradling the babe she bore —
the Prince of glory is his name.
O now carry me to Bethlehem
to see the Lord of love again:
just as poor as was the stable then,
the Prince of glory when he came!

2 Star of silver, sweep across the skies,
show where Jesus in the manger lies;
shepherds, swiftly from your stupor rise
to see the Saviour of the world!

3 Angels, sing again the song you sang,
sing the glory of God's gracious plan;
sing that Bethl'em's little baby can
be salvation to the soul.

4 Mine are riches, from your poverty;
from your innocence, eternity;
mine, forgiveness by your death for me,
child of sorrow for my joy.
O now carry me to Bethlehem
to see the Lord of love again:
just as poor as was the stable then,
the Prince of glory when he came!

MICHAEL PERRY 1942–1996

69

VERSION ONE

SILENT night, holy night:
sleeps the world; hid from sight,
Mary and Joseph in stable bare
watch o'er the child belovèd and fair
sleeping in heavenly rest.

2 Silent night, holy night:
shepherds first saw the light,
heard resounding clear and long,
far and near, the angel-song:
'Christ the Redeemer is here!'

3 Silent night, holy night:
Son of God, O how bright
love is smiling from thy face;
strikes for us now the hour of grace,
Saviour, since thou art born!

JOSEPH MOHR 1792–1848
tr. S. A. BROOKE 1832–1916

VERSION TWO

SILENT night, holy night.
All is calm, all is bright,
round yon virgin mother and child;
holy infant, so tender and mild,
sleep in heavenly peace.

2 Silent night, holy night.
Shepherds quake at the sight,
glories stream from heaven afar,
heav'nly hosts sing alleluia:
Christ the Saviour is born.

3 Silent night, holy night.
Son of God, love's pure light
radiant beams from thy holy face,
with the dawn of redeeming grace,
Jesus, Lord at thy birth.

JOSEPH MOHR 1792–1848
tr. J. F. YOUNG 1820–1885

70

THE great God of heaven is come down to earth,
his mother a virgin, and sinless his birth;
the Father eternal his Father alone:
he sleeps in the manger; he reigns on the throne:
Then let us adore him, and praise his great love:
to save us poor sinners he came from above.

2 A babe on the breast of a maiden he lies,
yet sits with the Father on high in the skies;
before him their faces the seraphim hide,
while Joseph stands waiting, unscared, by his side:

3 Lo! here is Emmanuel, here is the child,
the Son that was promised to Mary so mild;
whose power and dominion shall ever increase,
the Prince that shall rule o'er a kingdom of peace:

4 The Wonderful Counsellor, boundless in might,
the Father's own image, the beam of his light;
behold him now wearing the likeness of man,
weak, helpless, and speechless, in measure a span:

5 O wonder of wonders, which none can unfold:
The Ancient of Days is an hour or two old;
the Maker of all things is made of the earth,
man is worshipped by angels, and God comes to birth:
Then let us adore him, and praise his great love:
to save us poor sinners he came from above.

H. R. BRAMLEY 1833–1917

71

THE maker of the sun and moon,
the maker of our earth,
lo! late in time, a fairer boon,
himself is brought to birth.

2 How blest was all creation then,
when God so gave increase;
and Christ to heal our hearts of sin
brought righteousness and peace.

3 No star in all the heights of heaven
but burned to see him go;
yet unto earth alone was given
his human form to know.

4 His human form, by earth denied,
took death for human sin;
his endless love, through faith descried,
still lives the world to win.

5 O perfect love, outpassing sight,
O light beyond our ken,
come down through all the world tonight,
and heal our hearts again!

LAURENCE HOUSMAN * 1865–1959

72

THOU who wast rich beyond all splendour,
all for love's sake becamest poor;
thrones for a manger didst surrender,
sapphire-paved courts for stable floor.
Thou who wast rich beyond all splendour,
all for love's sake becamest poor.

2 Thou who art God beyond all praising,
all for love's sake becamest man;
stooping so low, but sinners raising
heavenwards by thine eternal plan.
Thou who art God beyond all praising,
all for love's sake becamest man.

3 Thou who art love beyond all telling,
Saviour and King, we worship thee.
Emmanuel, within us dwelling,
make us what thou wouldst have us be.
Thou who art love, beyond all telling,
Saviour and King, we worship thee.

FRANK HOUGHTON 1894–1972

73

UNTO us a boy is born!
King of all creation,
came he to a world forlorn,
the Lord of every nation.

2 Cradled in a stall was he
with sleepy cows and asses;
but the very beasts could see
that he all men surpasses.

3 Herod then with fear was filled:
'A prince', he said, 'in Jewry!'
all the little boys he killed
at Bethl'em in his fury.

4 Now may Mary's son, who came
so long ago to love us,
lead us all with hearts aflame
unto the joys above us.

5 Omega and Alpha he!
let the organ thunder,
while the choir with peals of glee
doth rend the air asunder.

Latin, 15th century
tr. PERCY DEARMER 1867–1936

74

WHAT child is this, who, laid to rest
on Mary's lap is sleeping?
whom angels greet with anthems sweet,
while shepherds watch are keeping?
this, this is Christ the King,
whom shepherds worship and angels sing:
haste, haste to bring him praise
the babe, the son of Mary.

2 Why lies he in such mean estate,
where ox and ass are feeding?
come, have no fear, God's Son is here,
his love all loves exceeding:
nails, spear, shall pierce him through,
the cross be borne for me, for you:
hail, hail, the Saviour comes,
the babe, the son of Mary.

3 So bring him incense, gold and myrrh,
all tongues and peoples own him,
the King of kings salvation brings,
let every heart enthrone him:
raise, raise your song on high
while Mary sings a lullaby,
joy, joy, for Christ is born,
the babe, the son of Mary.

WILLIAM CHATTERTON DIX 1837–1898
and editors of *New English Hymnal* 1986

75

WHERE is this stupendous stranger?
prophets, shepherds, kings, advise:
lead me to my Master's manger,
show me where my Saviour lies.

2 O most mighty, O most holy,
far beyond the seraph's thought!
Art thou then so mean and lowly
as unheeded prophets taught?

3 O the magnitude of meekness,
worth from worth immortal sprung!
O the strength of infant weakness,
if eternal is so young!

4 God all-bounteous, all-creative,
whom no ills from good dissuade,
is incarnate, and a native
of the very world he made.

CHRISTOPHER SMART * 1722–1771

76

WHILE shepherds watched their flocks by night,
all seated on the ground,
the angel of the Lord came down,
and glory shone around.

2 'Fear not,' said he (for mighty dread
had seized their troubled mind);
'glad tidings of great joy I bring
to you and all mankind.

3 'To you in David's town this day
is born of David's line
a Saviour, who is Christ the Lord;
and this shall be the sign:

4 'the heavenly babe you there shall find
to human view displayed,
all meanly wrapped in swathing bands,
and in a manger laid.'

5 Thus spake the seraph; and forthwith
appeared a shining throng
of angels praising God, who thus
addressed their joyful song:

6 'All glory be to God on high,
and to the earth be peace;
good will henceforth from heaven to men
begin and never cease.'

NAHUM TATE 1652–1715

77

WHO is he, in yonder stall,
at whose feet the shepherds fall?
'Tis the Lord! O wondrous story!
'Tis the Lord, the King of glory!
At his feet we humbly fall;
crown him, crown him Lord of all!
At his feet we humbly fall — the Lord of all:
crown him, crown him, crown him, crown him,
crown him, Lord of all!

2 Who is he, in deep distress,
fasting in the wilderness?

3 Who is he that stands and weeps
at the grave where Lazarus sleeps?

4 Lo! at midnight, who is he,
prays in dark Gethsemane?

5 Who is he, in Calvary's throes,
asks for blessings on his foes?

6 Who is he that from the grave
comes to heal and help and save?

7 Who is he that from his throne
rules through all the world alone?
'Tis the Lord! O wondrous story!
'Tis the Lord, the King of glory!
At his feet we humbly fall;
crown him, crown him Lord of all!
At his feet we humbly fall — the Lord of all:
crown him, crown him, crown him, crown him,
crown him, Lord of all!

B. R. Hanby 1833–1867

78

WHO would think that what was needed
   to transform and save the earth
might not be a plan or army
   proud in purpose, proved in worth?
who would think, despite derision,
   that a child should lead the way?
God surprises earth with heaven,
   coming here on Christmas Day.

2 Shepherds watch and wise men wonder,
   monarchs scorn and angels sing;
such a place as none would reckon
   hosts a holy, helpless thing;
stabled beasts and passing strangers
   watch a baby laid in hay:
God surprises earth with heaven,
   coming here on Christmas Day.

JOHN BELL *b.* 1949
and GRAHAM MAULE * *b.* 1958

See also

595 The Son of God his glory hides

CHRISTINGLE

79

GOD whose love is everywhere
made our earth and all things fair,
ever keeps them in his care;
   praise the God of love!
He who hung the stars in space
holds the spinning world in place;
   praise the God of love!

2 Come with thankfulness to sing
of the gifts the seasons bring,
summer, winter, autumn, spring;
praise the God of love!
He who gave us breath and birth
gives us all the fruitful earth;
praise the God of love!

3 Mark what love the Lord displayed,
all our sins upon him laid,
by his blood our ransom paid;
praise the God of love!
Circled by that scarlet band,
all the world is in his hand;
praise the God of love!

4 See the sign of love appear,
flame of glory, bright and clear,
light for all the world is here;
praise the God of love!
Gloom and darkness, get you gone!
Christ the Light of life has shone;
praise the God of love!

TIMOTHY DUDLEY-SMITH *b.* 1926

80

WHEN candles are lighted on Candlemas Day
the dark is behind us, and spring's on the way.
A glory dawns in every dark place,
the light of Christ, the fullness of grace.

2 The kings have departed, the shepherds have gone,
the child and his parents are left on their own.
A glory dawns ...

3 They go to the temple, obeying the law,
and offer two pigeons, the gift of the poor.
A glory dawns ...

4 But Anna and Simeon recognise there
the Christ-child who came at the turn of the year.
A glory dawns ...

5 The old who have suffered and waited so long
see hope for the world as they welcome the young.
A glory dawns ...

6 They gaze at God's wonderful answer to prayer,
the joy of the Jews and the Gentiles' desire.
A glory dawns ...

*7 The light is increasing and spring's in the air.
Look back with thanksgiving! Look forward with awe!
A glory dawns ...

*8 They see before Mary a heart-piercing grief,
but trust is complete at the end of their life.
A glory dawns ...

*9 For Mary will follow, with tears in her eyes,
her Saviour and Son to the foot of the cross.
A glory dawns ...

*10 Great Spirit of Jahweh, with courage inspire
your everyday saints who face up to despair.
A glory dawns ...

*11 They pass through temptation, through failure, through death.
When darkness descends they plod onward in faith.
A glory dawns ...

*12 Like Anna, like Simeon, may they have trust,
the eyes to see Jesus, and peace at the last.
A glory dawns ...

13 The candles invite us to praise and to pray
when Christmas greets Easter on Candlemas Day.
A glory dawns in every dark place,
the light of Christ, the fullness of grace.

ELIZABETH COSNETT *b.* 1936

See also

476 In a world where people walk in darkness
513 Lord, the light of your love is shining

NEW YEAR

81

LORD, for the years your love has kept and guided,
urged and inspired us, cheered us on our way,
sought us and saved us, pardoned and provided,
Lord of the years, we bring our thanks today.

2 Lord, for that word, the word of life which fires us,
speaks to our hearts and sets our souls ablaze,
teaches and trains, rebukes us and inspires us,
Lord of the word, receive your people's praise.

3 Lord, for our land, in this our generation,
spirits oppressed by pleasure, wealth and care;
for young and old, for commonwealth and nation,
Lord of our land, be pleased to hear our prayer.

4 Lord, for our world; when we disown and doubt him,
loveless in strength, and comfortless in pain;
hungry and helpless, lost indeed without him,
Lord of the world, we pray that Christ may reign.

5 Lord, for ourselves; in living power remake us,
self on the cross and Christ upon the throne;
past put behind us, for the future take us,
Lord of our lives, to live for Christ alone.

TIMOTHY DUDLEY-SMITH *b.* 1926

82

O GOD, whom neither time nor space
can limit, hold, or bind,
look down from heaven, thy dwelling-place,
with love for humankind.

2 Another year its course has run;
thy loving care renew:
forgive the ill that we have done,
the good we failed to do.

3 In doubt or danger, all our days,
be near to guard us still;
let all our thoughts and all our ways
be governed by thy will.

4 O help us here on earth to live
from selfish passions free;
to us at last in mercy give
eternal life with thee.

HORACE SMITH 1836–1922
and others

See also

444 God is working his purpose out
548 One more step along the world I go
562 Put thou thy trust in God

EPIPHANY

83

AS with gladness men of old
did the guiding star behold,
as with joy they hailed its light,
leading onward, beaming bright;
so, most gracious Lord, may we
evermore be led to thee.

2 As with joyful steps they sped,
Saviour, to thy lowly bed,
there to bend the knee before
thee whom heaven and earth adore;
so may we with willing feet
ever seek thy mercy-seat.

3 As they offered gifts most rare
at thy cradle rude and bare,
so may we with holy joy,
pure and free from sin's alloy,
all our costliest treasures bring,
Christ, to thee our heavenly King.

4 Holy Jesus, every day
keep us in the narrow way,
and, when earthly things are past,
bring our ransomed souls at last
where they need no star to guide,
where no clouds thy glory hide.

5 In the heavenly country bright
need they no created light;
thou its light, its joy, its crown,
thou its sun which goes not down;
there for ever may we sing
alleluias to our King.

WILLIAM CHATTERTON DIX 1837–1898

84

BRIGHTEST and best of the sons of the morning,
dawn on our darkness, and lend us thine aid;
star of the east, the horizon adorning,
guide where our infant Redeemer is laid.

2 Cold on his cradle the dew-drops are shining;
low lies his head with the beasts of the stall;
angels adore him in slumber reclining,
Maker and Monarch and Saviour of all.

3 Say, shall we yield him, in costly devotion,
odours of Edom, and offerings divine,
gems of the mountain, and pearls of the ocean,
myrrh from the forest, or gold from the mine?

4 Vainly we offer each ample oblation,
vainly with gifts would his favour secure:
richer by far is the heart's adoration,
dearer to God are the prayers of the poor.

5 Brightest and best of the sons of the morning,
dawn on our darkness, and lend us thine aid;
star of the east, the horizon adorning,
guide where our infant Redeemer is laid.

REGINALD HEBER 1783–1826

85

EARTH has many a noble city;
Bethl'em, thou dost all excel:
out of thee the Lord from heaven
came to rule his Israel.

2 Fairer than the sun at morning
was the star that told his birth,
to the world its God announcing
seen in fleshly form on earth.

3 Eastern sages at his cradle
make oblations rich and rare;
see them give in deep devotion
gold and frankincense and myrrh.

4 Sacred gifts of mystic meaning:
incense doth their God disclose,
gold the King of kings proclaimeth,
myrrh his sepulchre foreshows.

5 Jesu, whom the Gentiles worshipped
at thy glad Epiphany,
unto thee with God the Father
and the Spirit glory be.

PRUDENTIUS 348–c. 413
tr. EDWARD CASWALL 1814–1878

86

FROM the eastern mountains
pressing on they come,
wise men in their wisdom,
to his humble home;
stirred by deep devotion,
hasting from afar,
ever journeying onward,
guided by a star.

2 There their Lord and Saviour
meek and lowly lay,
wondrous light that led them
onward on their way,
ever now to lighten
nations from afar,
as they journey homeward
by that guiding star.

3 Thou who in a manger
once hast lowly lain,
who dost now in glory
o'er all kingdoms reign,
gather in the peoples,
who in lands afar
ne'er have seen the brightness
of thy guiding star.

*4 Gather in the outcasts,
all who've gone astray;
throw thy radiance o'er them,
guide them on their way:
those who never knew thee,
those who've wandered far,
guide them by the brightness
of thy guiding star.

*5 Onward through the darkness
of the lonely night,
shining still before them
with thy kindly light,
guide them, Jew and Gentile,
homeward from afar,
young and old together,
by thy guiding star.

6 Until every nation,
whether bond or free,
'neath thy star-lit banner,
Jesu, follow thee
o'er the distant mountains
to that heavenly home,
where nor sin nor sorrow
evermore shall come.

Godfrey Thring 1823–1903

87

HAIL to the Lord's Anointed,
great David's greater Son!
hail, in the time appointed,
his reign on earth begun!
He comes to break oppression,
to set the captive free,
to take away transgression,
and rule in equity.

2 He comes with succour speedy
to those who suffer wrong;
to help the poor and needy,
and bid the weak be strong;
to give them songs for sighing,
their darkness turn to light,
whose souls, condemned and dying,
were precious in his sight.

3 He shall come down like showers
upon the fruitful earth,
and love, joy, hope, like flowers,
spring in his path to birth:
before him on the mountains
shall peace, the herald, go;
and righteousness in fountains
from hill to valley flow.

4 Arabia's desert-ranger
to him shall bow the knee;
the Ethiopian stranger
his glory come to see;
with offerings of devotion
ships from the isles shall meet,
to pour the wealth of ocean
in tribute at his feet.

5 Kings shall bow down before him,
and gold and incense bring;
all nations shall adore him,
his praise all people sing:
to him shall prayer unceasing
and daily vows ascend;
his kingdom still increasing,
a kingdom without end.

6 O'er every foe victorious,
he on his throne shall rest;
from age to age more glorious,
all-blessing and all-blest:
the tide of time shall never
his covenant remove;
his name shall stand for ever,
his changeless name of love.

Psalm 72
JAMES MONTGOMERY * 1771–1854

88

HOW brightly shines the morning star!
The nations see and hail afar
   the light in Judah shining.
Thou David's son of Jacob's race,
the bridegroom, and the King of grace,
   for thee our hearts are pining!
      Lowly, holy,
great and glorious, thou victorious
      Prince of graces,
filling all the heavenly places!

2 Though circled by the hosts on high,
he deigns to cast a pitying eye
   upon his helpless creature;
the whole creation's Head and Lord,
by highest seraphim adored,
   assumes our very nature.
      Jesu, grant us,
through thy merit, to inherit
      thy salvation;
hear, O hear our supplication.

3 Rejoice, ye heav'ns; thou earth, reply;
with praise, ye sinners, fill the sky,
   for this his Incarnation.
Incarnate God, put forth thy power,
ride on, ride on, great Conqueror,
   till all know thy salvation.
      Amen, amen!
Alleluia, alleluia!
      Praise be given
evermore by earth and heaven.

Wie schön leuchtet der Morgenstern
PHILIPP NICOLAI 1556–1608
and JOHANN ADOLF SCHLEGEL 1721–1793
tr. WILLIAM MERCER 1811–1873

89

O WORSHIP the Lord in the beauty of holiness;
bow down before him, his glory proclaim;
with gold of obedience, and incense of lowliness,
kneel and adore him: the Lord is his name.

2 Low at his feet lay thy burden of carefulness:
high on his heart he will bear it for thee,
comfort thy sorrows, and answer thy prayerfulness,
guiding thy steps as may best for thee be.

3 Fear not to enter his courts in the slenderness
of the poor wealth thou wouldst reckon as thine:
truth in its beauty, and love in its tenderness,
these are the offerings to lay on his shrine.

4 These, though we bring them in trembling and fearfulness,
he will accept for the name that is dear;
mornings of joy give for evenings of tearfulness,
trust for our trembling and hope for our fear.

5 O worship the Lord in the beauty of holiness;
bow down before him, his glory proclaim;
with gold of obedience, and incense of lowliness,
kneel and adore him: the Lord is his name.

J. S. B. MONSELL 1811–1875

90

SONGS of thankfulness and praise,
Jesu, Lord, to thee we raise,
manifested by the star
to the sages from afar;
branch of royal David's stem
in thy birth at Bethlehem:
anthems be to thee addrest,
God in man made manifest.

2 Manifest at Jordan's stream,
Prophet, Priest, and King supreme;
and at Cana wedding-guest
in thy Godhead manifest;
manifest in power divine,
changing water into wine:
anthems be to thee addrest,
God in man made manifest.

3 Manifest in making whole
palsied limbs and fainting soul;
manifest in valiant fight,
quelling all the devil's might;
manifest in gracious will,
ever bringing good from ill:
anthems be to thee addrest,
God in man made manifest.

4 Sun and moon shall darkened be,
stars shall fall, the heavens shall flee;
Christ will then like lightning shine,
all will see his glorious sign;
all will then the trumpet hear,
all will see the Judge appear:
thou by all wilt be confest,
God in man made manifest.

5 Grant us grace to see thee, Lord,
mirrored in thy holy word;
may we imitate thee now,
and be pure, as pure art thou;
that we like to thee may be
at thy great Epiphany;
and may praise thee, ever blest,
God in man made manifest.

CHRISTOPHER WORDSWORTH 1807–1885

91

WE three kings of Orient are,
bearing gifts we traverse afar
field and fountain, moor and mountain,
following yonder star:
O star of wonder, star of night,
star with royal beauty bright,
westward leading, still proceeding,
guide us to thy perfect light.

2 Born a king on Bethlehem plain,
gold I bring to crown him again,
king for ever, ceasing never
over us all to reign:
O star of wonder ...

3 Frankincense to offer have I,
incense owns a deity nigh;
prayer and praising, all men raising,
worship him, God most high:
O star of wonder ...

4 Myrrh is mine, its bitter perfume
breathes a life of gathering gloom;
sorrowing, sighing, bleeding, dying,
sealed in the stone-cold tomb:
O star of wonder ...

5 Glorious now behold him arise,
king and God and sacrifice.
Heaven sings: 'Alleluia';
'Alleluia,' the earth replies:
O star of wonder, star of night,
star with royal beauty bright,
westward leading, still proceeding,
guide us to thy perfect light.

J. H. HOPKINS * 1820–1891

See also

52 'Glory to God!' all heav'n with joy is ringing

BAPTISM OF JESUS

92

CHRIST, when for us you were baptized
God's Spirit on you came,
as peaceful as a dove, and yet
as urgent as a flame.

2 God called you his belovèd Son,
called you his servant too;
his kingdom you were called to preach,
his holy will to do.

3 Straightway and steadfast until death
you then obeyed his call,
freely as Son of Man to serve,
and give your life for all.

4 Baptize us with your Spirit, Lord,
your cross on us be signed,
that likewise in God's service, we
may perfect freedom find.

F. BLAND TUCKER 1895–1984

93

WHEN Jesus came to Jordan
to be baptized by John,
he did not come for pardon,
but as his Father's Son.
He came to share repentance
with all who mourn their sins,
to speak the vital sentence
with which good news begins.

2 He came to share temptation,
our utmost woe and loss;
for us and our salvation
to die upon the cross.
So when the Dove descended
on him, the Son of Man,
the hidden years had ended,
the age of grace began.

3 Come, Holy Spirit, aid us
to keep the vows we make,
this very day invade us,
and every bondage break.
Come, give our lives direction,
the gift we covet most:
to share the resurrection
that leads to Pentecost.

F. Pratt Green 1903–2000

CANDLEMAS

94

HAIL to the Lord who comes,
comes to his temple gate,
not with his angel host,
not in his kingly state:
no shouts proclaim him nigh,
no crowds his coming wait.

2 But borne upon the throne
of Mary's gentle breast,
watched by her duteous love,
in her fond arms at rest;
thus to his Father's house
he comes, the heavenly guest.

3 There Joseph at her side
in reverent wonder stands;
and, filled with holy joy,
old Simeon in his hands
takes up the promised child,
the glory of all lands.

*4 Hail to the great First-born,
whose ransom-price they pay,
the Son before all worlds,
the child of man to-day,
that he might ransom us
who still in bondage lay.

5 O Light of all the earth,
thy children wait for thee:
come to thy temples here,
that we, from sin set free,
before thy Father's face
may all presented be.

JOHN ELLERTON 1826–1893

See also

44 Angels from the realms of glory
360 Faithful vigil ended
238 For Mary, Mother of the Lord
476 In a world where people walk in darkness
513 Lord the light of your love is shining
244 Virgin-born, we bow before thee
80 When candles are lighted on Candlemas Day
231 Ye who own the faith of Jesus

LENT

95

FORTY days and forty nights
thou wast fasting in the wild;
forty days and forty nights
tempted, and yet undefiled:

2 Sunbeams scorching all the day;
chilly dew-drops nightly shed;
prowling beasts about thy way;
stones thy pillow, earth thy bed.

3 Shall not we thy sorrows share,
and from earthly joys abstain,
fasting with unceasing prayer,
glad with thee to suffer pain?

4 And if Satan, vexing sore,
flesh or spirit should assail,
thou, his vanquisher before,
grant we may not faint nor fail.

5 So shall we have peace divine;
holier gladness ours shall be;
round us too shall angels shine,
such as ministered to thee.

6 Keep, O keep us, Saviour dear,
ever constant by thy side;
that with thee we may appear
at the eternal Eastertide.

G. H. SMYTTAN 1822–1870
and FRANCIS POTT 1832–1909

96

JESU, lover of my soul,
let me to thy bosom fly,
while the nearer waters roll,
while the tempest still is high:
hide me, O my Saviour, hide,
till the storm of life is past;
safe into the haven guide,
O receive my soul at last.

2 Other refuge have I none,
hangs my helpless soul on thee;
leave, ah, leave me not alone,
still support and comfort me.
All my trust on thee is stayed,
all my help from thee I bring;
cover my defenceless head
with the shadow of thy wing.

3 Thou, O Christ, art all I want;
more than all in thee I find;
raise the fallen, cheer the faint,
heal the sick, and lead the blind.
Just and holy is thy name,
I am all unrighteousness;
false and full of sin I am,
thou art full of truth and grace.

4 Plenteous grace with thee is found,
grace to cover all my sin;
let the healing streams abound,
make and keep me pure within.
Thou of life the fountain art:
freely let me take of thee,
spring thou up within my heart,
rise to all eternity.

CHARLES WESLEY 1707–1788

97

LORD Jesus, think on me,
and purge away my sin;
from earthborn passions set me free,
and make me pure within.

2 Lord Jesus, think on me
with many a care opprest;
let me thy loving servant be,
and taste thy promised rest.

3 Lord Jesus, think on me,
nor let me go astray;
through darkness and perplexity
point thou the heavenly way.

4 Lord Jesus, think on me,
that, when the flood is past,
I may the eternal brightness see,
and share thy joy at last.

SYNESIUS OF CYRENE *c.* 365–*c.* 414
tr. A. W. CHATFIELD 1808–1896

98

LORD, teach us how to pray aright
with reverence and with fear;
though dust and ashes in thy sight,
we may, we must, draw near.

2 We perish if we cease from prayer:
O grant us power to pray;
and, when to meet thee we prepare,
Lord, meet us by the way.

3 God of all grace, we bring to thee
a broken, contrite heart;
give what thine eye delights to see,
truth in the inward part;

4 Faith in the only sacrifice
that can for sin atone,
to cast our hopes, to fix our eyes,
on Christ, on Christ alone;

5 Patience to watch and wait and weep,
though mercy long delay;
courage our fainting souls to keep,
and trust thee though thou slay.

6 Give these, and then thy will be done;
thus, strengthened with all might,
we, through thy Spirit and thy Son,
shall pray, and pray aright.

JAMES MONTGOMERY 1771–1854

99

MY spirit longs for thee
within my troubled breast,
though I unworthy be
of so divine a guest.

2 Of so divine a guest
unworthy though I be,
yet has my heart no rest
unless it come from thee.

3 Unless it come from thee,
in vain I look around;
in all that I can see
no rest is to be found.

4 No rest is to be found
but in thy blessèd love:
O let my wish be crowned,
and send it from above!

JOHN BYROM 1692–1763

See also

385 Be thou my guardian and my guide
402 Come let us to the Lord our God
404 Come, my soul, thy suit prepare
411 Dear Lord and Father of mankind
428 Forgive our sins as we forgive
496 Lead us, heavenly Father, lead us
500 Lift up your hearts! We lift them, Lord, to thee
532 O for a closer walk with God
547 Oft in danger, oft in woe
571 Soldiers of Christ arise
582 Take up thy Cross, the Saviour said

PASSIONTIDE and HOLY WEEK

100

AH, holy Jesu, how hast thou offended,
that we to judge thee have in hate pretended!
By foes derided, by thine own rejected,
O most afflicted.

2 Who was the guilty? Who brought this upon thee?
Alas, my treason, Jesu, hath undone thee.
'Twas I, Lord Jesu, I it was denied thee:
I crucified thee.

3 Lo, the good Shepherd for the sheep is offered:
the slave hath sinnèd, and the Son hath suffered:
for our atonement, while we nothing heeded,
God interceded.

4 For me, kind Jesu, was thy incarnation,
thy mortal sorrow, and thy life's oblation;
thy death of anguish and thy bitter passion,
for my salvation.

5 Therefore, kind Jesu, since I cannot pay thee,
I do adore thee, and will ever pray thee,
think on thy pity and thy love unswerving,
not my deserving.

ROBERT BRIDGES 1844–1930
from JOHANN HEERMANN 1585–1647
based on an 11th-century Latin meditation

101

ALL ye who seek for sure relief
in trouble and distress,
whatever sorrow vex the mind,
or guilt the soul oppress;

2 Jesus, who gave himself for you
upon the cross to die,
opens to you his sacred heart:
O to that heart draw nigh.

3 Ye hear how kindly he invites;
ye hear his words so blest:
'All ye that labour come to me,
and I will give you rest.'

4 O Jesus, joy of saints on high,
thou hope of sinners here,
attracted by those loving words
to thee we lift our prayer.

5 Wash thou our wounds in that dear blood
which from thy heart doth flow;
a new and contrite heart on all
who cry to thee bestow.

Latin, 18th century
tr. EDWARD CASWALL * 1814–1878

102

ALONE thou goest forth, O Lord,
in sacrifice to die;
is this thy sorrow naught to us
who pass unheeding by?

2 Our sins, not thine, thou bearest, Lord,
make us thy sorrow feel,
till through our pity and our shame
love answers love's appeal.

3 This is earth's darkest hour, but thou
dost light and life restore;
then let all praise be given thee
who livest evermore.

4 Grant us with thee to suffer, Lord,
that, as we share this hour,
thy cross may bring us to thy joy
and resurrection power.

PETER ABELARD 1079-1142
tr. F. BLAND TUCKER * 1895–1984

103

AND didst thou travel light, dear Lord,
was thine so smooth a road
that thou upon thy shoulders broad
could hoist our heavy load?
Too frail each other's woes to bear
without thy help are we;
can we each other's burdens share
if we not burden thee?

2 O wonder of the world withstood!
That night of prayer and doom
was not the sunset red with blood,
the dawn pale as a tomb?
In agony and bloody sweat,
in tears of love undried,
O undespairing Lord, and yet
with us identified.

3 As in dark drops the pitting rain,
falls on a dusty street,
so tears shall fall and fall again
to wash thy wounded feet.
But thy quick hands to heal are strong,
O Love, thy patients we,
who sing with joy the pilgrims' song
and walk, dear Lord, with thee.

GEOFFREY DEARMER * 1893–1996

104

AT the cross her station keeping
stood the mournful Mother weeping,
  where he hung, the dying Lord;
for her soul, of joy bereavèd,
bowed with anguish, deeply grievèd,
  felt the sharp and piercing sword.

2 O how sad and sore distressèd
now was she, that Mother blessèd
  of the sole-begotten one!
Deep the woe of her affliction,
when she saw the crucifixion
  of her ever-glorious Son.

3 Who, on Christ's dear Mother gazing
pierced by anguish so amazing,
  born of woman, would not weep?
Who, on Christ's dear Mother thinking
such a cup of sorrow drinking,
  would not share her sorrows deep?

4 For his people's sins chastisèd,
she beheld her Son despisèd,
  scourged, and crowned with thorns entwined;
saw him then from judgement taken,
and in death by all forsaken,
  till his spirit he resigned.

5 O good Jesu, let me borrow
something of thy Mother's sorrow,
  fount of love, Redeemer kind,
that my heart fresh ardour gaining,
and a purer love attaining,
  may with thee acceptance find.

ascribed to JACOPONE DA TODI *d.* 1306
tr. EDWARD CASWALL * 1814–1878

105

BENEATH the cross of Jesus
I fain would take my stand,
the shadow of a mighty rock
within a weary land;
a home within a wilderness,
a rest upon the way,
from the burning of the noontide heat,
and the burden of the day.

2 Upon that cross of Jesus
mine eye at times can see
the very dying form of one
who suffered there for me;
and from my smitten heart, with tears,
two wonders I confess:
the wonders of his glorious love,
and my own worthlessness.

3 I take, O cross, thy shadow,
for my abiding place;
I ask no other sunshine than
the sunshine of his face;
content to let the world go by,
to know no gain nor loss;
my sinful self my only shame,
my glory all, the cross.

ELIZABETH CLEPHANE 1830–1869

106

DROP, drop, slow tears,
  and bathe those beauteous feet,
which brought from heaven
  the news and Prince of Peace.

2 Cease not, wet eyes,
his mercies to entreat;
to cry for vengeance
sin doth never cease.

3 In your deep floods
drown all my faults and fears;
nor let his eye
see sin, but through my tears.

PHINEAS FLETCHER 1582–1650

107

FATHER, whose everlasting love
thy only Son for sinners gave,
whose grace to all did freely move,
and sent him down the world to save:

2 Help us thy mercy to extol,
immense, unfathomed, unconfined;
to praise the Lamb who died for all,
the general Saviour of mankind.

3 Thy undistinguishing regard
was cast on Adam's fallen race;
for all thou hast in Christ prepared
sufficient, sovereign, saving grace.

4 The world he suffered to redeem;
for all he hath th' atonement made;
for those that will not come to him
the ransom of his life was paid.

5 Arise, O God, maintain thy cause,
the fullness of the nations call;
lift up the standard of thy cross
and all shall own thou diedst for all.

CHARLES WESLEY 1707–1788

108

GLORY be to Jesus,
who, in bitter pains,
poured for me the life-blood
from his sacred veins.

2 Grace and life eternal
in that blood I find;
blest be his compassion
infinitely kind.

3 Blest through endless ages
be the precious stream,
which from endless torments
did the world redeem.

4 Abel's blood for vengeance
pleaded to the skies;
but the blood of Jesus
for our pardon cries.

5 Oft as it is sprinkled
on our guilty hearts,
Satan in confusion
terror-struck departs.

6 Oft as earth exulting
wafts its praise on high,
angel-hosts rejoicing
make their glad reply.

7 Lift ye then your voices;
swell the mighty flood;
louder still and louder
praise the precious blood.

Italian
tr. EDWARD CASWALL * 1814–1878

109

IT is a thing most wonderful,
almost too wonderful to be,
that God's own Son should come from heaven,
and die to save a child like me.

2 And yet I know that it is true:
he chose a poor and humble lot,
and wept and toiled and mourned and died
for love of those who loved him not.

3 I cannot tell how he could love
a child so weak and full of sin;
his love must be most wonderful,
if he could die my love to win.

4 I sometimes think about the cross,
and shut my eyes, and try to see
the cruel nails and crown of thorns,
and Jesus crucified for me.

5 But even could I see him die,
I could but see a little part
of that great love which, like a fire,
is always burning in his heart.

6 It is most wonderful to know
his love for me so free and sure;
but 'tis more wonderful to see
my love for him so faint and poor.

7 And yet I want to love thee, Lord;
O light the flame within my heart,
and I will love thee more and more,
until I see thee as thou art.

W. Walsham How 1823–1897

110

JESU, grant me this, I pray,
ever in thy heart to stay;
let me evermore abide
hidden in thy wounded side.

2 If the world or Satan lay
tempting snares about my way,
I am safe when I abide
in thy heart and wounded side.

3 If the flesh, more dangerous still,
tempt my soul to deeds of ill,
naught I fear when I abide
in thy heart and wounded side.

4 Death will come one day to me;
Jesu, cast me not from thee:
dying let me still abide
in thy heart and wounded side.

Latin, 17th century
tr. H. W. Baker 1821–1877

111

JESU, thy blood and righteousness
my beauty are, my glorious dress;
midst flaming worlds, in these arrayed,
with joy shall I lift up my head.

2 Bold shall I stand in that great day
for to my charge who aught shall lay?
Fully absolved through thee I am
from sin and fear, from guilt and shame.

3 Jesu, be endless praise to thee,
whose boundless mercy hath for me,
for me, a full atonement made,
an everlasting ransom paid.

4 Ah! give to all thy servants, Lord,
with power to speak thy gracious word,
that all who to thy wounds will flee
may find eternal life in thee.

5 O let the dead now hear thy voice!
Now bid thy banished ones rejoice!
Their beauty this, their glorious dress,
Jesu, thy blood and righteousness.

N. L. VON ZINZENDORF 1700-1760
tr. JOHN WESLEY * 1703–1791

112

MY song is love unknown,
  my Saviour's love to me,
love to the loveless shown,
  that they might lovely be.
  O who am I,
    that for my sake
    my Lord should take
  frail flesh, and die?

2 He came from his blest throne,
  salvation to bestow;
but men made strange, and none
  the longed-for Christ would know.
  But O, my Friend,
    my Friend indeed,
    who at my need
  his life did spend!

3 Sometimes they strew his way,
  and his sweet praises sing;
resounding all the day
  hosannas to their King.
  Then 'Crucify!'
    is all their breath,
    and for his death
  they thirst and cry.

4 Why, what hath my Lord done?
What makes this rage and spite?
He made the lame to run,
he gave the blind their sight.
Sweet injuries!
yet they at these
themselves displease,
and 'gainst him rise.

5 They rise, and needs will have
my dear Lord made away;
a murderer they save,
the Prince of Life they slay.
Yet cheerful he
to suffering goes,
that he his foes
from thence might free.

6 In life, no house, no home
my Lord on earth might have;
in death, no friendly tomb
but what a stranger gave.
What may I say?
Heaven was his home;
but mine the tomb
wherein he lay.

7 Here might I stay and sing:
no story so divine;
never was love, dear King,
never was grief like thine!
This is my Friend,
in whose sweet praise
I all my days
could gladly spend.

SAMUEL CROSSMAN 1624–1683

113

NATURE with open volume stands
to spread her Maker's praise abroad,
and every labour of his hands
shows something worthy of our God.

2 But in the grace that rescued man
his brightest form of glory shines;
here on the cross 'tis fairest drawn
in precious blood and crimson lines.

3 Here his whole name appears complete;
nor wit can guess, nor reason prove
which of the letters best is writ,
the power, the wisdom, or the love.

4 O the sweet wonders of that cross
where God the Saviour loved and died;
her noblest life my spirit draws
from his dear wounds and bleeding side.

5 I would for ever speak his name
in sounds to mortal ears unknown,
with angels join to praise the Lamb,
and worship at his Father's throne.

ISAAC WATTS * 1674–1748

114

O COME and mourn with me awhile;
O come ye to the Saviour's side;
O come, together let us mourn:
Jesus, our Lord, is crucified!

2 Seven times he spoke, seven words of love;
and all three hours his silence cried
for mercy on the souls of all:
Jesus, our Lord, is crucified!

3 O break, O break, hard heart of mine!
Thy weak self-love and guilty pride
his Pilate and his Judas were:
Jesus, our Lord, is crucified!

4 O love of God! O sin of man!
In this dread act your strength is tried;
and victory remains with Love:
for he, our Lord, is crucified!

F. W. FABER * 1814–1863

115

O CROSS of Christ, immortal tree
on which our Saviour died,
the world is sheltered by your arms
that bore the crucified.

2 From bitter death and barren wood
the tree of life is made;
its branches bear unfailing fruit
and leaves that never fade.

3 O faithful cross, you stand unmoved
while ages run their course:
foundation of the universe,
creation's binding force.

4 Give glory to the risen Christ
and to his cross give praise,
the sign of God's unfathomed love,
the hope of all our days.

from STANBROOK ABBEY

116

O DEAREST Lord, thy sacred head
with thorns was pierced for me;
O pour thy blessing on my head
that I may think for thee.

2 O dearest Lord, thy sacred hands
with nails were pierced for me;
O shed thy blessing on my hands
that they may work for thee.

3 O dearest Lord, thy sacred feet
with nails were pierced for me;
O pour thy blessing on my feet
that they may follow thee.

4 O dearest Lord, thy sacred heart
with spear was pierced for me;
O pour thy Spirit in my heart
that I may live for thee.

H. E. HARDY
(FATHER ANDREW SDC) 1869–1946

117

O LOVE divine, what hast thou done!
The immortal God hath died for me!
The Father's co-eternal Son
bore all my sins upon the tree;
the immortal God for me hath died!
My Lord, my Love is crucified:

2 Is crucified for me and you,
to bring us rebels back to God;
believe, believe the record true,
we all are bought with Jesu's blood,
pardon for all flows from his side:
my Lord, my Love is crucified.

3 Then let us sit beneath the cross,
and gladly catch the healing stream,
all things for him account but loss,
and give up all our hearts to him;
of nothing think or speak beside:
my Lord, my Love is crucified.

CHARLES WESLEY * 1708–1788

118

O LOVE, how deep, how broad, how high!
It fills the heart with ecstasy,
that God, the Son of God, should take
our mortal form for mortals' sake.

2 He sent no angel to our race
of higher or of lower place,
but wore the robe of human frame
himself, and to this lost world came.

3 For us he was baptized, and bore
his holy fast, and hungered sore;
for us temptations sharp he knew;
for us the tempter overthrew.

4 For us to wicked men betrayed,
scourged, mocked, in purple robe arrayed,
he bore the shameful cross and death;
for us at length gave up his breath.

5 For us he rose from death again,
for us he went on high to reign,
for us he sent his Spirit here
to guide, to strengthen, and to cheer.

6 To him whose boundless love has won
salvation for us through his Son,
to God the Father, glory be
both now and through eternity.

ascribed to THOMAS À KEMPIS *c.* 1379–1471
tr. BENJAMIN WEBB * 1819–1885

119

O SACRED head, sore wounded,
defiled and put to scorn;
O kingly head, surrounded
with mocking crown of thorn:
what sorrow mars thy grandeur?
Can death thy bloom deflower?
O countenance whose splendour
the hosts of heaven adore.

2 Thy beauty, long-desirèd,
hath vanished from our sight;
thy power is all expirèd,
and quenched the Light of light.
Ah me! for whom thou diest,
hide not so far thy grace:
show me, O Love most highest,
the brightness of thy face.

3 I pray thee, Jesus, own me,
me, Shepherd good, for thine;
who to thy fold hast won me,
and fed with truth divine.
Me guilty, me refuse not,
incline thy face to me,
this comfort that I lose not,
on earth to comfort thee.

4 In thy most bitter passion
my heart to share doth cry,
with thee for my salvation
upon the cross to die.
Ah, keep my heart thus movèd
to stand thy cross beneath,
to mourn thee, well-belovèd,
yet thank thee for thy death.

5 My days are few, O fail not,
with thine immortal power,
to hold me that I quail not
in death's most fearful hour:
that I may fight befriended,
and see in my last strife
to me thine arms extended
upon the cross of life.

PAUL GERHARDT 1607–1676 from a 14th-century
Latin hymn *tr.* ROBERT BRIDGES 1844–1930

120

O SACRED head, surrounded
by crown of piercing thorn!
O bleeding head, so wounded,
so shamed and put to scorn!
Death's pallid hue comes o'er thee,
the glow of life decays;
yet angel-hosts adore thee,
and tremble as they gaze.

2 Thy comeliness and vigour
is withered up and gone,
and in thy wasted figure
I see death drawing on.
O agony and dying!
O love to sinners free!
Jesu, all grace supplying,
turn thou thy face on me.

3 In this thy bitter passion,
good Shepherd, think of me
with thy most sweet compassion,
unworthy though I be:
beneath thy cross abiding
for ever would I rest,
in thy dear love confiding,
and with thy presence blest.

PAUL GERHARDT 1607–1676 from a 14th-century
Latin hymn *tr.* H. W. BAKER 1821–1877

121

SING, my tongue, the glorious battle,
sing the ending of the fray,
o'er the cross, the victor's trophy,
sound the loud triumphant lay:
tell how Christ, the world's Redeemer,
as a victim won the day.

2 God in pity saw man fallen,
shamed and sunk in misery,
when he fell on death by tasting
fruit of the forbidden tree:
then another tree was chosen
which the world from death should free.

3 Therefore when the appointed fullness
of the holy time was come,
he was sent who maketh all things
forth from God's eternal home:
thus he came to earth, incarnate,
offspring of a maiden's womb.

4 Thirty years among us dwelling,
now at length his hour fulfilled,
born for this, he meets his Passion,
for that this he freely willed,
on the cross the Lamb is lifted,
where his life-blood shall be spilled.

5 To the Trinity be glory,
to the Father and the Son,
with the co-eternal Spirit,
ever Three and ever One,
one in love and one in splendour,
while unending ages run. Amen.

Latin, VENANTIUS FORTUNATUS 530–609
tr. mainly by PERCY DEARMER 1867–1936

122

THE royal banners forward go,
the cross shines forth in mystic glow;
where he in flesh, our flesh who made,
our sentence bore, our ransom paid.

2 There whilst he hung, his sacred side
by soldier's spear was opened wide,
to cleanse us in the precious flood
of water mingled with his blood.

3 Fulfilled is now what David told
in true prophetic song of old,
how God the nations' King should be;
for God is reigning from the tree.

4 O tree of glory, tree most fair,
ordained those holy limbs to bear,
how bright in purple robe it stood,
the purple of a Saviour's blood!

5 Upon its arms, like balance true,
he weighed the price for sinners due,
the price which none but he could pay,
and spoiled the spoiler of his prey.

6 To thee, eternal Three in One,
let homage meet by all be done:
as by the cross thou dost restore,
so rule and guide us evermore. Amen.

Latin, VENANTIUS FORTUNATUS 530–609
tr. J. M. NEALE * 1818–1866

123

THERE is a green hill far away,
without a city wall,
where the dear Lord was crucified,
who died to save us all.

2 We may not know, we cannot tell,
what pains he had to bear,
but we believe it was for us
he hung and suffered there.

3 He died that we might be forgiven,
he died to make us good,
that we might go at last to heaven,
saved by his precious blood.

4 There was no other good enough
to pay the price of sin;
he only could unlock the gate
of heaven, and let us in.

5 O dearly, dearly has he loved,
and we must love him too,
and trust in his redeeming blood,
and try his works to do.

C. F. ALEXANDER 1818–1895

124

TO mock your reign, O dearest Lord,
they made a crown of thorns;
set you with taunts along that road
from which no one returns.
They could not know, as we do now,
how glorious is that crown:
that thorns would flower upon your brow,
your sorrows heal our own.

2 In mock acclaim, O gracious Lord,
they snatched a purple cloak,
your passion turned, for all they cared,
into a soldier's joke.
They could not know, as we do now,
that, though we merit blame,
you will your robe of mercy throw
around our naked shame.

3 A sceptred reed, O patient Lord,
they thrust into your hand,
and acted out their grim charade
to its appointed end.
They could not know, as we do now,
though empires rise and fall,
your kingdom shall not cease to grow
till love embraces all.

F. Pratt Green 1903–2000

125

WE sing the praise of him who died,
of him who died upon the cross;
the sinner's hope let men deride,
for this we count the world but loss.

2 Inscribed upon the cross we see
in shining letters, 'God is love';
he bears our sins upon the tree;
he brings us mercy from above.

3 The cross! It takes our guilt away:
it holds the fainting spirit up;
it cheers with hope the gloomy day,
and sweetens every bitter cup.

4 It makes the coward spirit brave,
and nerves the feeble arm for fight;
it takes its terror from the grave,
and gilds the bed of death with light:

5 The balm of life, the cure of woe,
the measure and the pledge of love,
the sinner's refuge here below,
the angels' theme in heaven above.

Thomas Kelly 1769–1855

126

WERE you there when they crucified my Lord?
Were you there when they crucified my Lord?
Oh, sometimes it causes me to tremble,
tremble, tremble;
were you there when they crucified my Lord?

2 Were you there when they nailed him to the tree?
Were you there when they nailed him to the tree?
Oh, sometimes it causes me to tremble,
tremble, tremble;
were you there when they nailed him to the tree?

3 Were you there when they laid him in the tomb?
Were you there when they laid him in the tomb?
Oh, sometimes it causes me to tremble,
tremble, tremble;
were you there when they laid him in the tomb?

AMERICAN FOLK HYMN

127

WHEN I survey the wondrous cross
on which the Prince of glory died,
my richest gain I count but loss,
and pour contempt on all my pride.

2 Forbid it, Lord, that I should boast
save in the cross of Christ my God;
all the vain things that charm me most,
I sacrifice them to his blood.

3 See from his head, his hands, his feet,
sorrow and love flow mingled down;
did e'er such love and sorrow meet,
or thorns compose so rich a crown!

4 His dying crimson, like a robe,
spreads o'er his body on the tree:
then am I dead to all the globe,
and all the globe is dead to me.

5 Were the whole realm of nature mine,
that were a present far too small;
love so amazing, so divine,
demands my soul, my life, my all.

Galatians 6. 14
ISAAC WATTS 1674–1748

See also

432 From heaven you came
468 I danced in the morning
480 In the cross of Christ I glory
499 Lift high the Cross
524 My God, I love thee not because
525 Name of all majesty
557 Praise to the Holiest
582 Take up thy cross

PALM SUNDAY

128

ALL glory, laud, and honour
to thee, Redeemer, King,
to whom the lips of children
made sweet hosannas ring.

2 Thou art the King of Israel,
thou David's royal Son,
who in the Lord's name comest,
the King and blessèd one:
All glory, laud, and honour ...

3 The company of angels
are praising thee on high,
and mortal men and all things
created make reply:
All glory, laud, and honour ...

4 The people of the Hebrews
with palms before thee went:
our praise and prayer and anthems
before thee we present:
All glory, laud, and honour ...

5 To thee before thy passion
they sang their hymns of praise:
to thee now high exalted
our melody we raise:
All glory, laud, and honour ...

6 Thou didst accept their praises,
accept the prayers we bring,
who in all good delightest,
thou good and gracious King:
All glory, laud, and honour ...

*7 Thy sorrow and thy triumph
grant us, O Christ, to share,
that to the holy city
together we may fare:
All glory, laud, and honour ...

*8 For homage may we bring thee
our victory o'er the foe,
that in the Conqueror's triumph
this strain may ever flow:

9 *All glory, laud, and honour
to thee, Redeemer, King,
to whom the lips of children
made sweet hosannas ring.*

THEODULPH OF ORLEANS *d.* 821
tr. J. M. NEALE 1818–1866

129

RIDE on, ride on in majesty!
Hark, all the tribes hosanna cry:
O Saviour meek, pursue thy road
with palms and scattered garments strowed.

2 Ride on, ride on in majesty!
In lowly pomp ride on to die:
O Christ, thy triumphs now begin
o'er captive death and conquered sin.

3 Ride on, ride on in majesty!
The wingèd squadrons of the sky
look down with sad and wondering eyes
to see the approaching sacrifice.

4 Ride on, ride on in majesty!
The last and fiercest strife is nigh:
the Father on his sapphire throne
awaits his own anointed Son.

5 Ride on, ride on in majesty!
In lowly pomp ride on to die;
bow thy meek head to mortal pain,
then take, O God, thy power, and reign.

H. H. MILMAN * 1791–1868

See also

433 Give me joy in my heart

MAUNDY THURSDAY

130

AN Upper Room did our Lord prepare
for those he loved until the end:
and his disciples still gather there,
to celebrate their Risen Friend.

2 A lasting gift Jesus gave his own,
to share his bread, his loving cup.
Whatever burdens may bow us down,
he by his Cross shall lift us up.

3 And after Supper he washed their feet,
for service, too, is sacrament.
In him our joy shall be made complete
sent out to serve, as he was sent.

4 No end there is! We depart in peace.
He loves beyond our uttermost:
in every room in our Father's house
he will be there, as Lord and host.

F. PRATT GREEN 1903–2000

131

BLEST by the sun, the olive tree
brought clusters of fair fruit to birth,
whose ripeness now we bring with prayer,
Lord Christ, redeemer of the earth.

2 Eternal King, look down and bless
the oil your servants offer here,
and may it be a lively sign
which all the powers of darkness fear.

3 From those washed in the sacred font
let Satan's influence depart,
and when this oil the brow shall seal
transforming grace invade the heart.

4 Our wounded nature thus be healed
by your anointing grace, O Lord;
in men and women so renewed
shall God's own image be restored.

5 Lord Christ, the Father's only Son,
who took our flesh in Mary's womb,
give light to your anointed ones,
and break the power of death's dark tomb.

6 So may this joyous Paschal feast,
the time when saving grace is given,
fill every Christian soul with praise,
and raise our minds from earth to heaven.

from an early Latin hymn
tr. RICHARD RUTT *b.* 1925

132

GO to dark Gethsemane,
ye that feel the tempter's power;
your Redeemer's conflict see,
watch with him one bitter hour;
turn not from his griefs away;
learn of Jesus Christ to pray.

2 See him at the judgement-hall;
beaten, bound, reviled, arraigned.
O the wormwood and the gall!
O the pangs his soul sustained!
Shun not suffering, shame, or loss:
learn of Christ to bear the cross.

3 Calvary's mournful mountain climb;
there, adoring at his feet,
mark that miracle of time,
God's own sacrifice complete.
'It is finished!' hear him cry;
learn of Jesus Christ to die.

4 Early hasten to the tomb
where they laid his breathless clay;
all is solitude and gloom:
who has taken him away?
Christ is risen! He meets our eyes;
Saviour, teach us so to rise.

JAMES MONTGOMERY * 1771–1854

133

GREAT God, your love has called us here,
as we, by love, for love were made.
Your living likeness still we bear,
though marred, dishonoured, disobeyed.
We come, with all our heart and mind
your call to hear, your love to find.

2 We come with self-inflicted pains
of broken trust and chosen wrong,
half-free, half-bound by inner chains,
by social forces swept along,
by powers and systems close confined,
yet seeking hope for humankind.

3 Great God, in Christ you call our name,
and then receive us as your own,
not through some merit, right or claim,
but by your gracious love alone.
We strain to glimpse your mercy-seat,
and find you kneeling at our feet.

4 Then take the towel, and break the bread,
and humble us, and call us friends.
Suffer and serve till all are fed,
and show how grandly love intends
to work till all creation sings,
to fill all worlds, to crown all things.

5 Great God, in Christ you set us free
your life to live, your joy to share.
Give us your Spirit's liberty
to turn from guilt and dull despair
and offer all that faith can do,
while love is making all things new.

Brian A. Wren *b.* 1936

134

THIS is the night, dear friends, the night for weeping,
when powers of darkness overcome the day,
the night the faithful mourn the weight of evil
whereby our sins the Son of Man betray.

2 This night the traitor, wolf within the sheepfold,
betrays himself into his victim's will;
the Lamb of God for sacrifice preparing,
sin brings about the cure for sin's own ill.

3 This night Christ institutes his holy supper,
blest food and drink for heart and soul and mind;
this night injustice joins its hand to treason's,
and buys the ransom-price of humankind.

4 This night the Lord by slaves shall be arrested,
he who destroys our slavery to sin;
accused of crime, to criminals be given,
that judgement on the righteous Judge begin.

5 O make us sharers, Saviour, of your Passion,
that we may share your glory that shall be;
let us pass through these three dark nights of sorrow
to Easter's laughter and its liberty.

Latin, PETER ABELARD 1079–1142
tr. RICHARD STURCH *b.* 1936

See also

441 God is love, and where true love is
316 Now my tongue, the mystery telling
318 O thou, who at thy Eucharist didst pray
326 The heavenly Word, proceeding forth
559 Pray for the church afflicted

135

A BRIGHTER dawn is breaking,
and earth with praise is waking;
for thou, O King most highest,
the power of death defiest;

2 And thou hast come victorious,
with risen body glorious,
who now for ever livest,
and life abundant givest.

3 O free the world from blindness,
and fill the world with kindness,
give sinners resurrection,
bring striving to perfection.

4 In sickness give us healing,
in doubt thy clear revealing,
that praise to thee be given
in earth as in thy heaven.

PERCY DEARMER 1867–1936

136

ALLELUIA, alleluia,
give thanks to the risen Lord.
Alleluia, alleluia,
give praise to his name.

2 Jesus is Lord of all the earth:
he is the King of creation:
Alleluia, alleluia ...

3 Spread the good news o'er all the earth:
Jesus has died and has risen:
Alleluia, alleluia ...

4 We have been crucified with Christ:
now we shall live for ever:
Alleluia, alleluia ...

5 God has proclaimed the just reward:
Life for all men, alleluia:
Alleluia, alleluia ...

6 Come, let us praise the living God,
joyfully sing to our Saviour:
Alleluia, alleluia,
give thanks to the risen Lord.
Alleluia, alleluia,
give praise to his name.

DONALD FISHEL *b.* 1950

137

ALLELUIA! Alleluia!
Hearts to heaven and voices raise;
sing to God a hymn of gladness,
sing to God a hymn of praise:
he who on the cross a victim
for the world's salvation bled,
Jesus Christ, the King of glory,
now is risen from the dead.

2 Christ is risen, Christ the first-fruits
of the holy harvest field,
which will all its full abundance
at his second coming yield;
then the golden ears of harvest
will their heads before him wave,
ripened by his glorious sunshine,
from the furrows of the grave.

3 Christ is risen, we are risen;
shed upon us heavenly grace,
rain, and dew, and gleams of glory
from the brightness of thy face;
that we, with our hearts in heaven,
here on earth may fruitful be,
and by angel-hands be gathered,
and be ever, Lord, with thee.

4 Alleluia! Alleluia!
Glory be to God on high;
Alleluia to the Saviour,
who has gained the victory;
Alleluia to the Spirit,
fount of love and sanctity;
Alleluia! Alleluia!
to the Triune Majesty.

CHRISTOPHER WORDSWORTH 1807–1885

138

AT the Lamb's high feast we sing
praise to our victorious King,
who hath washed us in the tide
flowing from his piercèd side;
praise we him, whose love divine
gives his sacred blood for wine,
gives his body for the feast,
Christ the victim, Christ the priest.

*2 Where the Paschal blood is poured,
death's dark angel sheathes his sword;
Israel's hosts triumphant go
through the wave that drowns the foe.
Praise we Christ, whose blood was shed,
Paschal victim, Paschal bread;
with sincerity and love
eat we manna from above.

3 Mighty victim from the sky,
hell's fierce powers beneath thee lie;
thou hast conquered in the fight,
thou hast brought us life and light.
Now no more can death appal,
now no more the grave enthral:
thou hast opened paradise,
and in thee thy saints shall rise.

4 Easter triumph, Easter joy,
sin alone can this destroy;
from sin's power do thou set free
souls new-born, O Lord, in thee.
Hymns of glory and of praise,
risen Lord, to thee we raise;
holy Father, praise to thee,
with the Spirit, ever be.

Latin Breviary hymn
tr. Robert Campbell 1814–1868

139

BLEST be the everlasting God,
the Father of our Lord!
Be his abounding mercy praised,
his majesty adored!

2 When from the dead he raised his Son,
and called him to the sky,
he gave our souls a lively hope
that they should never die.

3 There's an inheritance divine
reserved against that day;
'tis uncorrupted, undefiled,
and cannot fade away.

4 Saints by the power of God are kept,
till that salvation come:
we walk by faith as strangers here,
till Christ shall call us home.

I Peter 1. 3–5, Isaac Watts 1674–1748

140

CHRIST is alive! Let Christians sing.
The cross stands empty to the sky.
Let streets and homes with praises ring.
Love, drowned in death, shall never die.

2 Christ is alive! No longer bound
to distant years in Palestine,
but saving, healing, here and now,
and touching every place and time.

3 In every insult, rift and war,
where colour, scorn or wealth divide,
Christ suffers still, yet loves the more,
and lives, where even hope has died.

4 Women and men, in age and youth,
can feel the Spirit, hear the call,
and find the way, the life, the truth,
revealed in Jesus, freed for all.

5 Christ is alive, and comes to bring
good news to this and every age,
till earth and sky and ocean ring
with joy, with justice, love and praise.

BRIAN A. WREN *b.* 1936

141

CHRIST the Lord is risen again,
Christ hath broken every chain.
Hark, angelic voices cry,
singing evermore on high,
Alleluia!

2 He who gave for us his life,
who for us endured the strife,
is our Paschal Lamb to-day;
we too sing for joy, and say
Alleluia!

3 He who bore all pain and loss
comfortless upon the cross,
lives in glory now on high,
pleads for us, and hears our cry:
Alleluia!

*4 He whose path no records tell,
who descended into hell,
who the strong man armed hath bound,
now in highest heaven is crowned.
Alleluia!

5 He who slumbered in the grave
is exalted now to save;
now through Christendom it rings
that the Lamb is King of kings.
Alleluia!

6 Now he bids us tell abroad
how the lost may be restored,
how the penitent forgiven,
how we too may enter heaven.
Alleluia!

7 Thou, our Paschal Lamb indeed,
Christ, thy ransomed people feed;
take our sins and guilt away:
let us sing by night and day
Alleluia!

MICHAEL WEISSE *c.* 1480–1534
tr. CATHERINE WINKWORTH 1827–1878

142

COME, let us with our Lord arise,
our Lord, who made both earth and skies:
who died to save the world he made,
and rose triumphant from the dead;
he rose, the Prince of life and peace,
and stamped the day for ever his.

2 This is the day the Lord has made,
that all may see his love displayed,
may feel his resurrection's power,
and rise again, to fall no more,
in perfect righteousness renewed,
and filled with all the life of God.

3 Then let us render him his own,
with solemn prayer approach his throne,
with meekness hear the gospel word,
with thanks his dying love record,
our joyful hearts and voices raise,
and fill his courts with songs of praise.

4 Honour and praise to Jesus pay
throughout his consecrated day;
be all in Jesu's praise employed,
nor leave a single moment void;
with utmost care the time improve,
and only breathe his praise and love.

CHARLES WESLEY 1707–1788

143

COME, ye faithful, raise the strain
of triumphant gladness!
God hath brought his Israel
into joy from sadness;
loosed from Pharaoh's bitter yoke
Jacob's sons and daughters;
led them with unmoistened foot
through the Red Sea waters.

2 'Tis the spring of souls to-day;
Christ hath burst his prison,
and from three days' sleep in death
as a sun hath risen:
all the winter of our sins,
long and dark, is flying
from his light, to whom we give
laud and praise undying.

3 Now the queen of seasons, bright
with the day of splendour,
with the royal feast of feasts,
comes its joy to render;
comes to glad Jerusalem,
who with true affection
welcomes in unwearied strains
Jesu's resurrection.

4 Alleluia now we cry
to our King immortal,
who triumphant burst the bars
of the tomb's dark portal;
Alleluia, with the Son
God the Father praising;
Alleluia yet again
to the Spirit raising.

ST JOHN OF DAMASCUS *d. c.* 754
tr. J. M. NEALE * 1818–1866

144

FINISHED the strife of battle now,
gloriously crowned the Victor's brow:
sing with gladness, hence with sadness:
Alleluia, alleluia.

2 After the death that him befell,
Jesus Christ has harrowed hell:
songs of praising we are raising:
Alleluia, alleluia.

3 On the third morning he arose,
shining with victory o'er his foes;
earth is singing, heaven is ringing:
Alleluia, alleluia.

4 Lord, by your wounds on you we call:
now that from death you've freed us all:
may our living be thanksgiving:
Alleluia, alleluia.

Latin, probably 17th century
tr. J. M. NEALE * 1818–1866

145

GOOD Christians all, rejoice and sing!
Now is the triumph of our King.
To all the world glad news we bring:
Alleluia.

2 The Lord of Life is risen for ay:
bring flowers of song to strew his way;
let all the earth rejoice and say
Alleluia.

3 Praise we in songs of victory
that Love, that Life, which cannot die,
and sing with hearts uplifted high
Alleluia.

4 Thy name we bless, O risen Lord,
and sing to-day with one accord
the life laid down, the life restored:
Alleluia.

C. A. ALINGTON * 1872–1955

146

GOOD Joseph had a garden,
close by that sad green hill
where Jesus died a bitter death
to save mankind from ill.

2 One evening in that garden,
their faces dark with gloom,
they laid the Saviour's body
within good Joseph's tomb.

*3 There came the holy women
with spices and with tears;
the angels tried to comfort them,
but could not calm their fears.

4 Came Mary to that garden:
and sobbed with heart forlorn;
she thought she heard the gardener ask:
'whom seekest thou this morn?'

5 She heard her own name spoken,
and then she lost her care:
all in his strength and beauty
the risen Lord stood fair!

*6 Good Joseph had a garden;
amid its trees so tall
the Lord Christ rose on Easter Day:
he lives to save us all.

7 And as he rose at Easter
he is alive for aye,
the very same Lord Jesus Christ
who hears us sing today.

8 Go tell the Lord Christ's message,
the Easter triumph sing,
till all his waiting children know
that Jesus is their King.

ALDA M. MILNER-BARRY 1875–1940

147

JESUS Christ is risen to-day, *Alleluia,*
our triumphant holy day, *Alleluia,*
who did once, upon the cross, *Alleluia,*
suffer to redeem our loss. *Alleluia.*

2 Hymns of praise then let us sing *Alleluia,*
unto Christ, our heavenly King, *Alleluia,*
who endured the cross and grave, *Alleluia,*
sinners to redeem and save. *Alleluia.*

3 But the pains that he endured *Alleluia,*
our salvation have procured; *Alleluia,*
now above the sky he's King, *Alleluia,*
where the angels ever sing *Alleluia.*

Lyra Davidica 1708 and others

148

JESUS lives! thy terrors now
can, O death, no more appal us;
Jesus lives! by this we know
thou, O grave, canst not enthral us.
Alleluia.

2 Jesus lives! henceforth is death
but the gate of life immortal:
this shall calm our trembling breath,
when we pass its gloomy portal.
Alleluia.

3 Jesus lives! for us he died;
then, alone to Jesus living,
pure in heart may we abide,
glory to our Saviour giving.
Alleluia.

4 Jesus lives! our hearts know well
naught from us his love shall sever;
life nor death nor powers of hell
tear us from his keeping ever.
Alleluia.

5 Jesus lives! to him the throne
over all the world is given:
may we go where he is gone,
rest and reign with him in heaven.
Alleluia.

C. F. GELLERT 1715–1769
tr. FRANCES ELIZABETH COX * 1812–1897

149

PART ONE

LIGHT'S glittering morn bedecks the sky;
heaven thunders forth its victor-cry:
Alleluia.
The glad earth shouts her triumph high,
and groaning hell makes wild reply:
Alleluia.

2 While he, the King, the mighty King,
despoiling death of all its sting,
and trampling down the powers of night,
brings forth his ransomed saints to light:

3 His tomb of late the threefold guard
of watch and stone and seal had barred;
but now, in pomp and triumph high,
he comes from death to victory:

4 The pains of hell are loosed at last,
the days of mourning now are past;
an angel robed in light hath said,
'The Lord is risen from the dead':

PART TWO

5 O BITTER the apostles' pain
for their dear Lord so lately slain,
by rebel servants doomed to die
a death of cruel agony:

6 With gentle voice the angel gave
the women tidings at the grave:
'Fear not, your Master shall ye see;
he goes before to Galilee':

7 Then, hastening on their eager way
the joyful tidings to convey,
their Lord they met, their living Lord,
and falling at his feet adored:

8 His faithful followers with speed
to Galilee forthwith proceed,
that there once more they may behold
the Lord's dear face, as he foretold:

PART THREE

9 THAT Eastertide with joy was bright,
the sun shone out with fairer light,
when, to their longing eyes restored,
the glad apostles saw their Lord:

10 He bade them see his hands, his side,
where yet the glorious wounds abide;
the tokens true which made it plain
their Lord indeed was risen again:

11 Jesu, the King of gentleness,
do thou thyself our hearts possess,
that we may give thee all our days
the tribute of our grateful praise:

DOXOLOGY

*To be sung at the end of any part,
or of the whole hymn*

12 O Lord of all, with us abide
in this our joyful Eastertide;
from every weapon death can wield
thine own redeemed for ever shield:

13 All praise be thine, O risen Lord,
from death to endless life restored;
Alleluia.
all praise to God the Father be
and Holy Ghost eternally:
Alleluia.

Latin, 4th century
tr. J. M. NEALE * 1818–1866

150

LOVE'S redeeming work is done;
fought the fight, the battle won:
lo, our Sun's eclipse is o'er,
lo, he sets in blood no more.

2 Vain the stone, the watch, the seal;
Christ has burst the gates of hell;
death in vain forbids his rise;
Christ has opened paradise.

3 Lives again our glorious King;
where, O death, is now thy sting?
dying once, he all doth save;
where thy victory, O grave?

4 Soar we now where Christ has led,
following our exalted Head;
made like him, like him we rise;
ours the cross, the grave, the skies.

5 Hail the Lord of earth and heaven!
Praise to thee by both be given:
thee we greet triumphant now;
hail, the Resurrection Thou!

CHARLES WESLEY * 1707–1788

151

MOST glorious Lord of life, that on this day
didst make thy triumph over death and sin,
and having harrowed hell, didst bring away
captivity thence captive, us to win:

2 This joyous day, dear Lord, with joy begin,
and grant that we for whom thou diddest die,
being with thy dear blood clean washed from sin,
may live for ever in felicity:

3 And that thy love we weighing worthily,
may likewise love thee for the same again;
and for thy sake, who dost all grace supply,
with love may one another entertain;

4 So let us love, dear Love, like as we ought;
love is the lesson which the Lord us taught.

EDMUND SPENSER * 1552–1599

152

NOW is eternal life,
if ris'n with Christ we stand,
in him to life reborn,
and held within his hand;
no more we fear death's ancient dread,
in Christ arisen from the dead.

2 Man long in bondage lay,
brooding o'er life's brief span;
was it, O God, for naught,
for naught, thou madest man?
Thou art our hope, our vital breath;
shall hope undying end in death?

3 And God, the living God,
stooped down to man's estate;
by death destroying death,
Christ opened wide life's gate.
He lives, who died; he reigns on high;
who lives in him shall never die.

4 Unfathomed love divine,
reign thou within my heart;
from thee nor depth nor height,
nor life nor death can part;
my life is hid in God with thee,
now and through all eternity.

G. W. BRIGGS * 1875–1959

153

NOW the green blade riseth from the buried grain,
wheat that in dark earth many days has lain;
love lives again, that with the dead has been:
Love is come again, like wheat that springeth green.

2 In the grave they laid him, Love whom men had slain,
thinking that never he would wake again,
laid in the earth like grain that sleeps unseen:
Love is come again, like wheat that springeth green.

3 Forth he came at Easter, like the risen grain,
he that for three days in the grave had lain,
quick from the dead my risen Lord is seen:
Love is come again, like wheat that springeth green.

4 When our hearts are wintry, grieving, or in pain,
thy touch can call us back to life again,
fields of our hearts that dead and bare have been:
Love is come again, like wheat that springeth green.

J. M. C. CRUM 1872–1958

154

ALLELUIA! Alleluia! Alleluia!

O SONS and daughters, let us sing!
The King of heaven, the glorious King,
o'er death to-day rose triumphing.
Alleluia!

2 That Easter morn, at break of day,
the faithful women went their way
to seek the tomb where Jesus lay.
Alleluia!

3 An angel clad in white they see,
who sat, and spake unto the three,
'Your Lord doth go to Galilee.'
Alleluia!

4 That night the apostles met in fear;
amidst them came their Lord most dear,
and said, 'My peace be on all here.'
Alleluia!

*5 When Thomas first the tidings heard,
how they had seen the risen Lord,
he doubted the disciples' word.
Alleluia!

*6 'My piercèd side, O Thomas, see;
my hands, my feet I show to thee;
not faithless, but believing be.'
Alleluia!

*7 No longer Thomas then denied;
he saw the feet, the hands, the side;
'Thou art my Lord and God,' he cried.
Alleluia!

8 How blest are they who have not seen,
and yet whose faith hath constant been,
for they eternal life shall win.
Alleluia!

9 On this most holy day of days,
to God your hearts and voices raise
in laud and jubilee and praise,
Alleluia!

JEAN TISSERAND *d.* 1419
tr. J. M. NEALE * 1818–1866

155

PASCHAL Feast! Upon the cross
Jesus gave himself to save us.
Sin's sad leaven throw away:
break the bread of life he gave us.
Alleluia!

2 Risen again, our living Lord
death's dominion now has shattered.
Now we share his risen life,
hell's dread powers for ever scattered.
Alleluia!

3 Christ is risen from the grave,
all who sleep in death awaking.
First fruit of the harvest field:
now our Easter dawn is breaking.
Alleluia!

4 As through man death comes to all,
so has man unlocked death's prison.
As in Adam all are dead,
so in Christ shall all be risen.
Alleluia!

EDWIN LE GRICE 1911–1992

156

SING choirs of heaven! Let saints and angels sing!
Around God's throne exult in harmony.
Now Jesus Christ is risen from the grave.
Salute your King in glorious symphony.

2 Sing choirs of earth! Behold, your light has come!
The glory of the Lord shines radiantly.
Lift up your hearts, for Christ has conquered death.
The night is past; the day of life is here.

3 Sing Church of God! Exult with joy outpoured!
The gospel trumpets tell of victory won.
Your Saviour lives: he's with you evermore.
Let all God's people shout the long Amen.

THE EASTER PROCLAMATION

157

THE day of resurrection!
  Earth, tell it out abroad;
the Passover of gladness,
  the Passover of God;
from death to life eternal,
  from earth unto the sky,
our God hath brought us over
  with hymns of victory.

2 Our hearts be pure from evil,
  that we may see aright
the Lord in rays eternal
  of resurrection-light;
and, listening to his accents,
  may hear so calm and plain
his own 'All hail', and, hearing,
  may raise the victor strain.

3 Now let the heavens be joyful,
  and earth her song begin,
the round world keep high triumph,
  and all that is therein;
let all things seen and unseen
  their notes of gladness blend,
for Christ the Lord is risen,
  our joy that hath no end.

ST JOHN OF DAMASCUS *d. c.* 754
tr. J. M. NEALE * 1818–1866

158

THE Lord is risen indeed:
  now is his work performed;
now is the mighty captive freed,
  and death's strong castle stormed.

2 The Lord is risen indeed:
  then hell has lost its prey;
with him is risen the ransomed seed
  to reign in endless day.

3 The Lord is risen indeed:
he lives, to die no more;
he lives, the sinner's cause to plead,
whose curse and shame he bore.

4 The Lord is risen indeed:
attending angels, hear!
Up to the courts of heaven with speed
the joyful tidings bear.

5 Then take your golden lyres,
and strike each cheerful chord;
join, all ye bright celestial choirs,
to sing our risen Lord.

THOMAS KELLY * 1769–1855

159

THE strife is o'er, the battle done;
now is the Victor's triumph won;
O let the song of praise be sung:
Alleluia.

2 Death's mightiest powers have done their worst,
and Jesus hath his foes dispersed;
let shouts of praise and joy outburst:
Alleluia.

3 On the third morn he rose again
glorious in majesty to reign;
O let us swell the joyful strain:
Alleluia.

4 Lord, by the stripes which wounded thee
from death's dread sting thy servants free,
that we may live, and sing to thee
Alleluia.

Latin, probably 17th century
tr. FRANCIS POTT 1832–1909

160

THINE be the glory, risen, conquering Son,
endless is the victory thou o'er death hast won;
angels in bright raiment rolled the stone away,
kept the folded grave-clothes where thy body lay.
Thine be the glory, risen, conquering Son,
endless is the victory thou o'er death hast won.

2 Lo, Jesus meets us, risen from the tomb;
lovingly he greets us, scatters fear and gloom;
let the church with gladness hymns of triumph sing,
for her Lord now liveth, death hath lost its sting:
Thine be the glory ...

3 No more we doubt thee, glorious Prince of Life;
life is naught without thee: aid us in our strife;
make us more than conquerors through thy deathless love;
bring us safe through Jordan to thy home above:
Thine be the glory, risen, conquering Son,
endless is the victory thou o'er death hast won.

French, 19th century, EDMOND BUDRY 1854–1932
tr. RICHARD HOYLE 1875–1939

161

THIS joyful Eastertide,
away with sin and sorrow.
My Love, the Crucified,
hath sprung to life this morrow:
Had Christ, that once was slain,
ne'er burst his three-day prison,
our faith had been in vain:
but now hath Christ arisen.

2 My flesh in hope shall rest,
and for a season slumber:
till trump from east to west
shall wake the dead in number:
Had Christ, that once was slain ...

3 Death's flood hath lost its chill,
since Jesus crossed the river:
Lover of souls, from ill
my passing soul deliver:
Had Christ, that once was slain,
ne'er burst his three-day prison,
our faith had been in vain:
but now hath Christ arisen.

G. R. WOODWARD * 1848–1934

162

YE choirs of new Jerusalem,
your sweetest notes employ,
the Paschal victory to hymn
in strains of holy joy.

2 How Judah's Lion burst his chains,
and crushed the serpent's head;
and brought with him, from death's domains,
the long-imprisoned dead.

*3 From hell's devouring jaws the prey
alone our Leader bore;
his ransomed hosts pursue their way
where he hath gone before.

4 Triumphant in his glory now
his sceptre ruleth all,
earth, heaven, and hell before him bow,
and at his footstool fall.

5 While joyful thus his praise we sing,
his mercy we implore,
into his palace bright to bring
and keep us evermore.

6 All glory to the Father be,
all glory to the Son,
all glory, Holy Ghost, to thee,
while endless ages run.

Alleluia! Amen.

St Fulbert of Chartres *d.* 1028
tr. Robert Campbell 1814–1868

ASCENSION

163

ALL hail the power of Jesu's name;
let angels prostrate fall;
bring forth the royal diadem
to crown him Lord of all.

*2 Crown him, ye morning stars of light,
who fixed this floating ball;
now hail the Strength of Israel's might,
and crown him Lord of all.

3 Crown him, ye martyrs of your God,
who from his altar call;
praise him whose way of pain ye trod,
and crown him Lord of all.

4 Ye seed of Israel's chosen race,
ye ransomed of the fall,
hail him who saves you by his grace,
and crown him Lord of all.

5 Sinners, whose love can ne'er forget
the wormwood and the gall,
go spread your trophies at his feet,
and crown him Lord of all.

6 Let every tribe and every tongue
to him their hearts enthral,
lift high the universal song
and crown him Lord of all.

EDWARD PERRONET 1726–1792
and others

164

CHRIST, above all glory seated,
King triumphant, strong to save,
dying, thou hast death defeated;
buried, thou hast spoiled the grave.

2 Thou art gone where now is given,
what no mortal might could gain,
on the eternal throne of heaven
in thy Father's power to reign.

*3 There thy kingdoms all adore thee,
heaven above and earth below;
while the depths of hell before thee
trembling and defeated bow.

4 We, O Lord, with hearts adoring,
follow thee above the sky;
hear our prayers thy grace imploring,
lift our souls to thee on high.

5 So when thou again in glory
on the clouds of heaven shalt shine
we thy flock may stand before thee,
owned for evermore as thine.

6 Hail! All hail! In thee confiding,
Jesus, thee shall all adore,
in thy Father's might abiding
with one Spirit evermore.

Latin, 5th century
tr. J. R. WOODFORD 1820–1885

165

CHRIST is the King! O friends rejoice;
brothers and sisters with one voice
tell all the world he is your choice.
Alleluia.

2 O magnify the Lord, and raise
anthems of joy and holy praise
for Christ's brave saints of ancient days.
Alleluia.

3 They with a faith for ever new
followed the King, and round him drew
thousands of faithful hearts and true.
Alleluia.

4 O Christian women, Christian men,
all the world over, seek again
the Way disciples followed then.
Alleluia.

5 Christ through all ages is the same:
place the same hope in his great name,
with the same faith his word proclaim.
Alleluia.

6 Let love's unconquerable might
your scattered companies unite
in service to the Lord of light.
Alleluia.

7 So shall God's will on earth be done,
new lamps be lit, new tasks begun,
and the whole church at last be one.
Alleluia.

G. K. A. BELL * 1883–1958

166

CROWN him with many crowns,
the Lamb upon his throne;
hark, how the heavenly anthem drowns
all music but its own!
Awake, my soul, and sing
of him who died for thee,
and hail him as thy matchless King
through all eternity.

2 Crown him the Virgin's Son,
the God incarnate born,
whose arm those crimson trophies won
which now his brow adorn:
Fruit of the mystic Rose,
as of that Rose the Stem;
the Root whence mercy ever flows,
the Babe of Bethlehem.

3 Crown him the Lord of love;
behold his hands and side,
those wounds yet visible above
in beauty glorified:
no angel in the sky
can fully bear that sight,
but downward bends his burning eye
at mysteries so bright.

4 Crown him the Lord of peace,
whose power a sceptre sways
from pole to pole, that wars may cease,
and all be prayer and praise:
his reign shall know no end,
and round his piercèd feet
fair flowers of paradise extend
their fragrance ever sweet.

5 Crown him the Lord of years,
the Potentate of time,
creator of the rolling spheres,
ineffably sublime:
all hail, Redeemer, hail!
for thou hast died for me;
thy praise shall never, never fail
throughout eternity.

MATTHEW BRIDGES * 1800–1894
Revelation 19. 12

The expression 'mystic Rose' in v.2, l.5, is a mediaeval title for the Blessed Virgin, and is combined here with a reference to Isaiah 11. 1

167

HAIL the day that sees him rise,
Alleluia,
to his throne above the skies;
Alleluia,
Christ, the Lamb for sinners given,
Alleluia,
enters now the highest heaven.
Alleluia!

2 There for him high triumph waits;
lift your heads, eternal gates.
He hath conquered death and sin;
take the King of Glory in.

3 Lo, the heaven its Lord receives,
yet he loves the earth he leaves;
though returning to his throne,
still he calls mankind his own.

4 See, he lifts his hands above;
see, he shews the prints of love;
hark, his gracious lips bestow
blessings on his church below.

5 Still for us he intercedes,
his prevailing death he pleads;
near himself prepares our place,
he the first-fruits of our race.

6 Lord, though parted from our sight,
far above the starry height,
grant our hearts may thither rise,
seeking thee above the skies.

CHARLES WESLEY 1707–1788
THOMAS COTTERILL 1779–1823 and others

168

HAIL, thou once despisèd Jesus!
Hail, thou Galilean King!
Thou didst suffer to release us;
thou didst free salvation bring.
Hail, thou universal Saviour,
bearer of our sin and shame!
By thy merit we find favour;
life is given through thy name.

2 Paschal Lamb by God appointed,
all our sins on thee were laid;
by almighty love anointed,
thou hast full atonement made.
All thy people are forgiven
through the virtue of thy blood;
opened is the gate of heaven;
reconciled are we with God.

3 Jesus, hail! Enthroned in glory,
there for ever to abide;
all the heavenly host adore thee,
seated at thy Father's side.
There for sinners thou art pleading,
there thou dost our place prepare,
ever for us interceding,
till in glory we appear.

JOHN BAKEWELL 1721-1819
MARTIN MADAN * 1726–1790

169

JESU, our hope, our heart's desire,
thy work of grace we sing;
Redeemer of the world art thou,
its Maker and its King.

2 How vast the mercy and the love
which laid our sins on thee,
and led thee to a cruel death,
to set thy people free!

3 But now the bonds of death are burst,
the ransom has been paid;
and thou art on thy Father's throne,
in glorious robes arrayed.

4 O may thy mighty love prevail
our sinful souls to spare;
O may we stand around thy throne,
and see thy glory there.

5 Jesu, our only joy be thou,
as thou our prize wilt be;
in thee be all our glory now
and through eternity.

6 All praise to thee who art gone up
triumphantly to heaven;
all praise to God the Father's name,
and Holy Ghost be given.

Latin, c. 8th century
tr. JOHN CHANDLER * 1806–1876

170

JESUS is Lord! Creation's voice proclaims it,
for by his power each tree and flower was planned and made.
Jesus is Lord! The universe declares it;
sun, moon and stars in heaven cry: Jesus is Lord!
Jesus is Lord! Jesus is Lord!
praise him with Halleluias, for Jesus is Lord!

2 Jesus is Lord! Yet from his throne eternal
in flesh he came to die in pain on Calvary's tree.
Jesus is Lord! From him all life proceeding,
yet gave his life a ransom, thus setting us free:
Jesus is Lord! ...

3 Jesus is Lord! O'er sin the mighty conqueror,
from death he rose; and all his foes shall own his name.
Jesus is Lord! God sends his Holy Spirit
to show by works of power that Jesus is Lord:
Jesus is Lord! Jesus is Lord!
praise him with Halleluias, for Jesus is Lord!

DAVID MANSELL *b.* 1936

171

LOOK, ye saints, the sight is glorious.
See the Man of Sorrows now,
from the fight returned victorious.
Every knee to him shall bow:
Crown him! crown him! crown him! crown him!
Crowns become the victor's brow.

2 Crown the Saviour; angels, crown him;
rich the trophies Jesus brings;
in the seat of power enthrone him,
while the vault of heaven rings:
Crown him! crown him! crown him! crown him!
Crown the Saviour, King of kings!

3 Sinners in derision crowned him,
mocking thus the Saviour's claim;
saints and angels crowd around him,
own his title, praise his name:
Crown him! crown him! crown him! crown him!
Spread abroad the victor's fame!

4 Hark! those bursts of acclamation,
hark! those loud triumphant chords!
Jesus takes the highest station:
O what joy the sight affords.
Crown him! crown him! crown him! crown him!
King of kings and Lord of lords!

THOMAS KELLY 1769–1855

172

THE head that once was crowned with thorns
is crowned with glory now:
a royal diadem adorns
the mighty Victor's brow.

2 The highest place that heaven affords
is his, is his by right,
the King of kings, and Lord of lords,
and heaven's eternal Light;

3 The joy of all who dwell above,
the joy of all below,
to whom he manifests his love,
and grants his name to know.

4 To them the cross, with all its shame,
with all its grace, is given:
their name, an everlasting name,
their joy, the joy of heaven.

5 They suffer with their Lord below,
they reign with him above;
their profit and their joy to know
the mystery of his love.

6 The cross he bore is life and health,
though shame and death to him;
his people's hope, his people's wealth,
their everlasting theme.

THOMAS KELLY 1769–1855
Hebrews 2. 10

173

THE Lord ascendeth up on high,
loud anthems round him swelling;
the Lord hath triumphed gloriously,
in power and might excelling:
hell and the grave are captive led;
lo, he returns, our glorious Head,
to his eternal dwelling.

2 The heavens with joy receive their Lord;
O day of exultation!
By saints, by angel-hosts, adored
for his so great salvation:
O earth, adore thy glorious King,
his rising, his ascension sing
with grateful adoration.

3 By saints in earth and saints in heaven,
with songs for ever blended,
all praise to Christ our King be given,
who hath to heaven ascended:
To Father, Son, and Holy Ghost,
the God of heaven's resplendent host,
in bright array extended.

ARTHUR RUSSELL 1806–1874 and others

See also

372 All praise to thee
380 At the name of Jesus
398 Christ triumphant
490 Jesus shall reign
563 Rejoice! The Lord is King
592 The Lord is King!
612 We have a gospel to proclaim

174

BREATHE on me, Breath of God,
fill me with life anew,
that I may love what thou dost love,
and do what thou wouldst do.

2 Breathe on me, Breath of God,
until my heart is pure;
until with thee I will one will,
to do and to endure.

3 Breathe on me, Breath of God,
till I am wholly thine;
until this earthly part of me
glows with thy fire divine.

4 Breathe on me, Breath of God:
so shall I never die,
but live with thee the perfect life
of thine eternity.

EDWIN HATCH 1835–1889

175

COME down, O Love divine,
seek thou this soul of mine,
and visit it with thine own ardour glowing;
O Comforter, draw near,
within my heart appear,
and kindle it, thy holy flame bestowing.

2 O let it freely burn,
till earthly passions turn
to dust and ashes in its heat consuming;
and let thy glorious light
shine ever on my sight,
and clothe me round, the while my path illuming.

3 Let holy charity
mine outward vesture be,
and lowliness become mine inner clothing:
true lowliness of heart,
which takes the humbler part,
and o'er its own shortcomings weeps with loathing.

4 And so the yearning strong,
with which the soul will long,
shall far outpass the power of human telling;
for none can guess its grace,
till he become the place
wherein the Holy Spirit makes his dwelling.

BIANCO DA SIENA *d.* 1434
tr. R. F. LITTLEDALE 1833–1890

176

COME, gracious Spirit, heavenly Dove,
with light and comfort from above;
be thou our guardian, thou our guide,
o'er every thought and step preside.

2 The light of truth to us display,
and make us know and choose thy way;
plant holy fear in every heart,
that we from God may ne'er depart.

3 Lead us to Christ, the living Way,
nor let us from his pastures stray;
lead us to holiness, the road
that we must take to dwell with God.

4 Lead us to heaven, that we may share
fullness of joy for ever there;
lead us to God, our final rest,
to be with him for ever blest.

S. BROWNE 1680–1732 and others

177

COME Holy Ghost, our hearts inspire,
let us thine influence prove;
source of the old prophetic fire,
fountain of life and love.

2 Come, Holy Ghost, for, moved by thee,
thy prophets wrote and spoke:
unlock the truth, thyself the key,
unseal the sacred book.

3 Expand thy wings, celestial Dove,
brood o'er our nature's night;
on our disordered spirits move,
and let there now be light.

4 God, through himself, we then shall know,
if thou within us shine;
and sound, with all thy saints below,
the depths of love divine.

CHARLES WESLEY 1707–1788

178

COME, Holy Ghost, our souls inspire,
and lighten with celestial fire;
thou the anointing Spirit art,
who dost thy sevenfold gifts impart:

2 Thy blessèd unction from above
is comfort, life, and fire of love;
enable with perpetual light
the dullness of our blinded sight:

3 Anoint and cheer our soilèd face
with the abundance of thy grace:
keep far our foes, give peace at home;
where thou art guide no ill can come.

4 Teach us to know the Father, Son,
and thee, of both, to be but One;
that through the ages all along
this may be our endless song,

5 Praise to thy eternal merit,
Father, Son, and Holy Spirit. Amen.

JOHN COSIN 1594–1672
based on *Veni, Creator Spiritus*

179

COME, Holy Spirit, come!
Inflame our souls with love,
transforming every heart and home
with wisdom from above.
O let us not despise
the humble path Christ trod,
but choose, to shame the worldly-wise,
the foolishness of God.

2 Come with the gift to heal
the wounds of guilt and fear,
and to oppression's face reveal
the kingdom drawing near.
Where chaos longs to reign,
descend, O holy Dove,
and free us all to work again
the miracles of love.

3 Spirit of truth, arise;
inspire the prophet's voice:
expose to scorn the tyrant's lies,
and bid the poor rejoice.
O Spirit, clear our sight,
all prejudice remove,
and help us to discern the right,
and covet only love.

*4 Give us the tongues to speak,
in every time and place,
to rich and poor, to strong and weak,
the word of love and grace.
Enable us to hear
the words that others bring,
interpreting with open ear
the special song they sing.

5 Come, Holy Spirit, dance
within our hearts today,
our earthbound spirits to entrance,
our mortal fears allay.
And teach us to desire,
all other things above,
that self-consuming holy fire,
the perfect gift of love!

I Corinthians 12
MICHAEL FORSTER *b.* 1946

180

COME, thou Holy Spirit, come,
and from thy celestial home
shed a ray of light divine;
come, thou Father of the poor,
come, thou source of all our store,
come, within our bosoms shine.

2 Thou of comforters the best,
thou the soul's most welcome guest,
sweet refreshment here below;
in our labour rest most sweet,
grateful coolness in the heat,
solace in the midst of woe.

3 O most blessèd Light divine,
shine within these hearts of thine,
and our inmost being fill;
where thou art not, man hath naught,
nothing good in deed or thought,
nothing free from taint of ill.

4 Heal our wounds; our strength renew;
on our dryness pour thy dew;
wash the stains of guilt away;
bend the stubborn heart and will;
melt the frozen, warm the chill;
guide the steps that go astray.

5 On the faithful, who adore
and confess thee, evermore
in thy sevenfold gifts descend:
Give them virtue's sure reward,
give them thy salvation, Lord,
give them joys that never end.

STEPHEN LANGTON *d.* 1228
tr. EDWARD CASWALL 1814–1878 and others

181

ETERNAL Ruler of the ceaseless round
of circling planets singing on their way;
guide of the nations from the night profound
into the glory of the perfect day;
rule in our hearts, that we may ever be
guided and strengthened and upheld by thee.

2 We are of thee, the children of thy love,
the brothers of thy well-belovèd Son;
descend, O Holy Spirit, like a dove,
into our hearts, that we may be as one:
as one with thee, to whom we ever tend;
as one with him, our Brother and our Friend.

3 We would be one in hatred of all wrong,
one in our love of all things sweet and fair,
one with the joy that breaketh into song,
one with the grief that trembles into prayer,
one in the power that makes thy children free
to follow truth, and thus to follow thee.

4 O clothe us with thy heavenly armour, Lord,
thy trusty shield, thy sword of love divine;
our inspiration be thy constant word;
we ask no victories that are not thine:
give or withhold, let pain or pleasure be;
enough to know that we are serving thee.

J. W. CHADWICK 1840–1904

182

GRACIOUS Spirit, Holy Ghost,
taught by thee, we covet most
of thy gifts at Pentecost,
holy, heavenly love.

2 Love is kind, and suffers long,
love is meek, and thinks no wrong,
love than death itself more strong;
therefore give us love.

3 Prophecy will fade away,
melting in the light of day;
love will ever with us stay;
therefore give us love.

4 Faith will vanish into sight;
hope be emptied in delight;
love in heaven will shine more bright;
therefore give us love.

5 Faith and hope and love we see
joining hand in hand agree;
but the greatest of the three,
and the best, is love.

6 From the overshadowing
of thy gold and silver wing
shed on us, who to thee sing,
holy, heavenly love.

CHRISTOPHER WORDSWORTH 1807–1885
1 Corinthians 13; Psalm 68. 13

183

HOLY Spirit, come, confirm us
in the truth that Christ makes known;
we have faith and understanding
through your helping gifts alone.

2 Holy Spirit, come, console us,
come as Advocate to plead,
loving Spirit from the Father,
grant in Christ the help we need.

3 Holy Spirit, come, renew us,
come yourself to make us live,
holy through your loving presence,
holy through the gifts you give.

4 Holy Spirit, come, possess us,
you the love of Three in One,
Holy Spirit of the Father,
Holy Spirit of the Son.

BRIAN FOLEY 1919–2000

184

HOLY Spirit, truth divine,
dawn upon this soul of mine;
voice of God, and inward light,
wake my spirit, clear my sight.

2 Holy Spirit, love divine,
glow within this heart of mine;
kindle every high desire;
perish self in thy pure fire.

3 Holy Spirit, power divine,
fill and nerve this will of mine;
by thee may I strongly live,
bravely bear and nobly strive.

4 Holy Spirit, law divine,
reign within this soul of mine;
be my law, and I shall be
firmly bound, for ever free.

5 Holy Spirit, peace divine,
still this restless heart of mine;
speak to calm this tossing sea,
stayed in thy tranquillity.

6 Holy Spirit, joy divine,
gladden thou this heart of mine;
in the desert ways I sing,
spring, O well, for ever spring!

SAMUEL LONGFELLOW 1819–1892

185

LIKE the murmur of the dove's song,
like the challenge of her flight,
like the vigour of the wind's rush,
like the new flame's eager might:
come, Holy Spirit, come.

2 To the members of Christ's Body,
to the branches of the vine,
to the church in faith assembled,
to her midst as gift and sign:
come, Holy Spirit, come.

3 With the healing of division,
with the ceaseless voice of prayer,
with the power to love and witness,
with the peace beyond compare:
come, Holy Spirit, come.

CARL P. DAW JR *b.* 1944

186

LOVE of the Father, Love of God the Son,
from whom all came, in whom was all begun;
who formest heavenly beauty out of strife,
creation's whole desire and breath of life:

2 Thou the all-holy, thou supreme in might,
thou dost give peace, thy presence maketh right;
thou with thy favour all things dost enfold,
with thine all-kindness free from harm wilt hold.

3 Hope of all comfort, splendour of all aid,
that dost not fail nor leave the heart afraid:
to all that cry thou dost all help accord,
the angels' armour, and the saints' reward.

4 Purest and highest, wisest and most just,
there is no truth save only in thy trust;
thou dost the mind from earthly dreams recall,
and bring, through Christ, to him for whom are all.

5 Eternal glory, all men thee adore,
who art and shalt be worshipped evermore:
us whom thou madest, comfort with thy might,
and lead us to enjoy thy heavenly light.

ROBERT BRIDGES 1844–1930
based on *Amor Patris et Filii,* 12th century

187

O HOLY Ghost, thy people bless
who long to feel thy might,
and fain would grow in holiness
as children of the light.

2 To thee we bring, who art the Lord,
our selves to be thy throne;
let every thought and deed and word
thy pure dominion own.

3 Life-giving Spirit, o'er us move,
as on the formless deep;
give life and order, light and love,
where now is death or sleep.

4 Great gift of our ascended King,
his saving truth reveal;
our tongues inspire his praise to sing,
our hearts his love to feel.

5 True wind of heaven, from south or north,
for joy or chastening, blow;
the garden-spices shall spring forth
if thou wilt bid them flow.

6 O Holy Ghost, of sevenfold might,
all graces come from thee;
grant us to know and serve aright
one God in Persons Three.

H. W. BAKER 1821–1877

188

O HOLY Spirit, Lord of grace,
eternal fount of love,
inflame, we pray, our inmost hearts
with fire from heaven above.

2 As thou in bond of love dost join
the Father and the Son,
so fill us all with mutual love,
and knit our hearts in one.

3 All glory to the Father be,
all glory to the Son,
all glory, Holy Ghost, to thee,
while endless ages run.

CHARLES COFFIN 1676–1749
tr. JOHN CHANDLER 1808–1876

189

O KING enthroned on high,
thou Comforter divine,
blest Spirit of all truth, be nigh
and make us thine.

2 Thou art the source of life,
thou art our treasure-store;
give us thy peace and end our strife
for evermore.

3 Descend, O heavenly Dove,
abide with us alway;
and in the fullness of thy love
cleanse us, we pray.

Greek, c. 8th century
tr. JOHN BROWNLIE 1857–1925

190

O SPIRIT of the living God,
in all the fullness of thy grace,
wherever human foot hath trod,
descend on our rebellious race.

2 Give tongues of fire and hearts of love
to preach the reconciling word;
give power and unction from above
whene'er the joyful sound is heard.

3 Be darkness, at thy coming, light;
confusion, order in thy path;
souls without strength inspire with might;
bid mercy triumph over wrath.

4 O Spirit of the Lord, prepare
the whole round earth her God to meet;
breathe thou abroad like morning air,
till hearts of stone begin to beat.

5 Baptize the nations; far and nigh
the triumphs of the cross record;
the name of Jesus glorify
till every kindred call him Lord.

JAMES MONTGOMERY * 1771–1854

191

O THOU who camest from above
the fire celestial to impart,
kindle a flame of sacred love
on the mean altar of my heart!

2 There let it for thy glory burn
with inextinguishable blaze,
and trembling to its source return
in humble prayer and fervent praise.

3 Jesus, confirm my heart's desire
to work, and speak, and think for thee;
still let me guard the holy fire,
and still stir up the gift in me.

4 Ready for all thy perfect will,
my acts of faith and love repeat;
till death thy endless mercies seal,
and make the sacrifice complete.

CHARLES WESLEY * 1707–1788
Leviticus 6. 13

192

ON the day of Pentecost,
when the twelve assembled,
came on them the Holy Ghost
in fire that tongues resembled.

2 In the power of God he came,
as the Lord had told them,
in his blessèd, holy name
with wisdom to uphold them.

3 In the Spirit then they stood
to proclaim Christ dying,
and that he for all men's good
doth live, true strength supplying.

4 Still the might by which we live
from our God descendeth;
still his Spirit Christ doth give,
who guideth and defendeth.

5 Praise, O praise our heavenly King
for his grace toward us;
gladly now his glory sing,
who doth his power afford us.

T. C. Hunter Clare 1910–1984

The fourth line of text of each verse is repeated.

193

OUR blest Redeemer, ere he breathed
his tender last farewell,
a guide, a Comforter, bequeathed
with us to dwell.

2 He came sweet influence to impart,
a gracious willing guest,
while he can find one humble heart
wherein to rest.

3 And his that gentle voice we hear,
soft as the breath of even,
that checks each fault, that calms each fear,
and speaks of heaven.

4 And every virtue we possess,
and every conquest won,
and every thought of holiness,
are his alone.

5 Spirit of purity and grace,
our weakness, pitying, see:
O make our hearts thy dwelling-place,
and worthier thee.

HARRIET AUBER 1773–1862

194

OUR Lord, his Passion ended,
hath gloriously ascended,
yet though from him divided,
he leaves us not unguided;
all his benefits to crown
he hath sent his Spirit down,
burning like a flame of fire
his disciples to inspire.

2 God's Spirit is directing;
no more they sit expecting;
but forth to all the nation
they go with exultation;
that which God in them hath wrought
fills their life and soul and thought;
so their witness now can do
work as great in others too.

3 The centuries go gliding,
but still we have abiding
with us that Spirit holy
to make us brave and lowly,
lowly, for we feel our need:
God alone is strong indeed;
brave, for with the Spirit's aid
we can venture unafraid.

4 O Lord of every nation,
fill us with inspiration;
we know our own unfitness;
yet for thee would bear witness.
By thy Spirit now we raise
to the heavenly Father praise:
Holy Spirit, Father, Son,
make us know thee, ever One.

F. C. BURKITT 1864–1935

195

SPIRIT divine, attend our prayers,
and make this house thy home;
descend with all thy gracious powers;
O come, great Spirit, come!

2 Come as the light: to us reveal
our emptiness and woe;
and lead us in those paths of life
where all the righteous go.

3 Come as the fire, and purge our hearts
like sacrificial flame;
let our whole soul an offering be
to our Redeemer's name.

4 Come as the Dove, and spread thy wings,
the wings of perfect love;
and let thy church on earth become
blest as the church above.

5 Spirit divine, attend our prayers;
make a lost world thy home;
descend with all thy gracious powers;
O come, great Spirit, come!

ANDREW REED 1787–1862

196

SPIRIT of God within me,
possess my human frame;
fan the dull embers of my heart,
stir up the living flame.
Strive till that image Adam lost,
new-minted and restored,
in shining splendour brightly bears
the likeness of the Lord.

2 Spirit of truth within me,
possess my thought and mind;
lighten anew the inward eye
by Satan rendered blind;
shine on the words that wisdom speaks,
and grant me power to see
the truth made known to all in Christ,
and in that truth be free.

3 Spirit of love within me,
possess my hands and heart;
break through the bonds of self-concern
that seeks to stand apart;
grant me the love that suffers long,
that hopes, believes and bears,
the love fulfilled in sacrifice
that cares as Jesus cares.

4 Spirit of life within me,
possess this life of mine;
come as the wind of heaven's breath,
come as the fire divine!
Spirit of Christ, the living Lord,
reign in this house of clay,
till from its dust with Christ I rise
to everlasting day.

TIMOTHY DUDLEY-SMITH *b.* 1926

197

SPIRIT of mercy, truth, and love,
O shed thine influence from above,
and still from age to age convey
the wonders of this sacred day.

2 In every clime, by every tongue,
be God's surpassing glory sung;
let all the listening earth be taught
the acts our great Redeemer wrought.

3 Unfailing comfort, heavenly guide,
still o'er thy holy church preside;
still let us all thy blessings prove,
Spirit of mercy, truth, and love.

Foundling Hospital Collection 1774 *

198

THERE'S a spirit in the air,
telling Christians everywhere:
'praise the love that Christ revealed,
living, working, in our world!'

2 Lose your shyness, find your tongue,
tell the world what God has done:
God in Christ has come to stay.
Live tomorrow's life today!

3 When believers break the bread,
when a hungry child is fed,
praise the love that Christ revealed,
living, working, in our world.

4 Still the Spirit gives us light,
seeing wrong and setting right:
God in Christ has come to stay.
Live tomorrow's life today!

5 When a stranger's not alone,
where the homeless find a home,
praise the love that Christ revealed,
living, working, in our world.

6 May the Spirit fill our praise,
guide our thoughts and change our ways:
God in Christ has come to stay.
Live tomorrow's life today!

7 There's a Spirit in the air,
calling people everywhere:
praise the love that Christ revealed,
living, working, in our world.

BRIAN A. WREN *b.* 1936

199

WHEN God of old came down from heaven,
in power and wrath he came;
before his feet the clouds were riven,
half darkness and half flame.

*2 But when he came the second time,
he came in power and love;
softer than gale at morning prime
hovered his holy Dove.

*3 The fires, that rushed on Sinai down
in sudden torrents dread,
now gently light, a glorious crown,
on every sainted head.

*4 And as on Israel's awestruck ear
the voice exceeding loud,
the trump that angels quake to hear,
thrilled from the deep, dark cloud;

5 So, when the Spirit of our God
came down his flock to find,
a voice from heaven was heard abroad,
a rushing, mighty wind.

6 It fills the Church of God; it fills
the sinful world around:
only in stubborn hearts and wills
no place for it is found.

7 Come, Lord, come Wisdom, Love, and Power,
open our ears to hear;
let us not miss the accepted hour:
save, Lord, by love or fear.

JOHN KEBLE 1792–1866

See also

365 A mighty wind invades the world
383 Be still, for the Spirit of the Lord
399 Christians, lift up your hearts
425 Filled with the Spirit's power
575 Spirit of God descend
576 Spirit of holiness

TRINITY SUNDAY

200

AFFIRM anew the threefold name
of Father, Spirit, Son,
our God whose saving acts proclaim
a world's salvation won.
In him alone we live and move
and breath and being find,
the wayward children of his love
who cares for humankind.

2 Declare in all the earth his grace,
to every heart his call,
the living Lord of time and place
whose love embraces all.
So shall his endless praise be sung,
his teaching truly heard,
and every culture, every tongue,
receive his timeless word.

3 Confirm our faith in this our day
amid earth's shifting sand,
with Christ as life and truth and way,
a rock on which to stand;
the one eternal Son and Lord
by God the Father given,
the true and life-imparting Word,
the way that leads to heaven.

4 Renew once more the ancient fire,
let love our hearts inflame;
renew, restore, unite, inspire
the church that bears your name;
one name exalted over all,
one Father, Spirit, Son,
O grant us grace to heed your call
and in that name be one.

TIMOTHY DUDLEY-SMITH *b.* 1926

201

CAN we by searching find out God
or formulate his ways?
can numbers measure what he is
or words contain his praise?

2 Although his being is too bright
for human eyes to scan,
his meaning lights our shadowed world
through Christ, the Son of Man.

3 Our boastfulness is turned to shame,
our profit counts as loss,
when earthly values stand beside
the manger and the cross.

4 We there may recognise his light,
may kindle in its rays,
find there the source of penitence,
the starting-point for praise.

5 There God breaks in upon our search,
makes birth and death his own:
He speaks to us in human terms
to make his glory known.

Elizabeth Cosnett *b.* 1936

202

HOLY, holy, holy! Lord God Almighty!
early in the morning our song shall rise to thee;
holy, holy, holy! merciful and mighty!
God in three persons, blessèd Trinity!

2 Holy, holy, holy! all the saints adore thee,
casting down their golden crowns around the glassy sea;
cherubim and seraphim falling down before thee,
which wert and art and evermore shalt be.

3 Holy, holy, holy! though the darkness hide thee,
though the eye of sinful man thy glory may not see,
only thou art holy, there is none beside thee
perfect in power, in love, and purity.

4 Holy, holy, holy! Lord God Almighty!
all thy works shall praise thy name in earth and sky and sea;
holy, holy, holy! merciful and mighty!
God in three persons, blessèd Trinity!

Reginald Heber 1783–1826

203

I BIND unto myself today
the strong name of the Trinity,
by invocation of the same,
the Three in One, and One in Three.

2 I bind unto myself today
the virtues of the star-lit heaven,
the glorious sun's life-giving ray,
the whiteness of the moon at even,
the flashing of the lightning free,
the whirling wind's tempestuous shocks,
the stable earth, the deep salt sea
around the old eternal rocks.

3 I bind unto myself today
the power of God to hold and lead,
his eye to watch, his might to stay,
his ear to hearken to my need;
the wisdom of my God to teach,
his hand to guide, his shield to ward,
the word of God to give me speech,
his heavenly host to be my guard.

4 Christ be with me, Christ within me,
Christ behind me, Christ before me,
Christ beside me, Christ to win me,
Christ to comfort and restore me;
Christ beneath me, Christ above me,
Christ in quiet, Christ in danger,
Christ in hearts of all that love me,
Christ in mouth of friend and stranger.

5 I bind unto myself the name,
the strong name of the Trinity,
by invocation of the same,
the Three in One, and One in Three,
of whom all nature hath creation,
eternal Father, Spirit, Word.
Praise to the Lord of my salvation:
Salvation is of Christ the Lord.

attributed to St Patrick 372–466
tr. Cecil Frances Alexander 1818–1895

204

O GOD, by whose almighty plan
first order out of chaos stirred,
and life, progressive at your word,
matured through nature up to man;
grant us in light and love to grow,
your sovereign truth to seek and know.

2 O Christ, whose touch unveiled the blind,
whose presence warmed the lonely soul;
your love made broken sinners whole,
your faith cast devils from the mind.
Grant us your faith, your love, your care
to bring to sufferers everywhere.

3 O Holy Spirit, by whose grace
our skills abide, our wisdom grows,
in every healing work disclose
new paths to probe, new thoughts to trace.
Grant us your wisest way to go
in all we think, or speak, or do.

H. C. A. Gaunt 1902–1983

205

THIS day God gives me
strength of high heaven,
sun and moon shining,
   flame in my hearth;
flashing of lightning,
wind in its swiftness,
deeps of the ocean,
   firmness of earth.

2 This day God sends me
strength as my steersman,
might to uphold me,
   wisdom as guide.
Your eyes are watchful,
your ears are listening,
your lips are speaking,
   friend at my side.

3 God's way is my way,
God's shield is round me,
God's host defends me,
   saving from ill;
angels of heaven,
drive from me always
all that would harm me,
   stand by me still.

4 Rising, I thank you,
mighty and strong one,
King of creation,
   giver of rest,
firmly confessing
threeness of Persons,
oneness of Godhead,
   Trinity blest.

JAMES QUINN *b.* 1919
from 8th-century Irish

206

WE give immortal praise
to God the Father's love
for all our comforts here,
and better hopes above:
he sent his own
eternal Son,
to die for sins
that man had done.

2 To God the Son belongs
immortal glory too,
who bought us with his blood
from everlasting woe:
and now he lives,
and now he reigns,
and sees the fruit
of all his pains.

3 To God the Spirit's name
immortal worship give,
whose new-creating power
makes the dead sinner live:
his work completes
the great design,
and fills the soul
with joy divine.

4 Almighty God, to thee
be endless honours done,
the undivided Three,
and the mysterious One:
where reason fails
with all her powers,
there faith prevails,
and love adores.

Isaac Watts * 1674–1748

See also

DEDICATION

207

BLESSÈD city, heavenly Salem,
vision dear of peace and love,
who of living stones art builded
in the height of heaven above,
and with angel hosts encircled
as a bride dost earthward move.

2 Christ is made the sure foundation,
Christ the Head and corner-stone,
chosen of the Lord, and precious,
binding all the church in one,
Holy Sion's help for ever,
and her confidence alone.

3 To this temple, where we call thee,
come, O Lord of Hosts, to-day;
with thy wonted loving-kindness
hear thy servants as they pray;
and thy fullest benediction
shed within its walls alway.

4 Here vouchsafe to all thy servants
what they ask of thee to gain,
what they gain from thee for ever
with the blessèd to retain,
and hereafter in thy glory
evermore with thee to reign.

Latin, before 9th century
tr. J. M. Neale 1818–1866

208

PART ONE

BLESSÈD city, heavenly Salem,
vision dear of peace and love,
who of living stones art builded
in the height of heaven above,
and with angel hosts encircled,
as a bride dost earthward move.

2 From celestial realms descending,
bridal glory round thee shed,
meet for him whose love espoused thee,
to thy Lord shalt thou be led;
all thy streets and all thy bulwarks
of pure gold are fashionèd.

3 Bright thy gates of pearl are shining,
they are open evermore;
and by virtue of his merits
thither faithful souls do soar,
who for Christ's dear name in this world
pain and tribulation bore.

4 Many a blow and biting sculpture
polished well those stones elect,
in their places now compacted
by the heavenly Architect,
who therewith hath willed for ever
that his palace should be decked.

PART TWO

5 CHRIST is made the sure foundation,
Christ the Head and corner-stone,
chosen of the Lord, and precious,
binding all the church in one,
Holy Sion's help for ever,
and her confidence alone.

6 All that dedicated city,
dearly loved of God on high,
in exultant jubilation
pours perpetual melody,
God the One in Three adoring
in glad hymns eternally.

PART THREE

7 TO this temple, where we call thee,
come, O Lord of Hosts, to-day;
with thy wonted loving-kindness
hear thy servants as they pray,
and thy fullest benediction
shed within its walls alway.

8 Here vouchsafe to all thy servants
what they ask of thee to gain,
what they gain from thee for ever
with the blessèd to retain,
and hereafter in thy glory
evermore with thee to reign.

DOXOLOGY

*To be sung at the end of any part,
or of the whole hymn*

Laud and honour to the Father,
laud and honour to the Son,
laud and honour to the Spirit,
ever Three, and ever One,
consubstantial, co-eternal,
while unending ages run.

Latin, before 9th century
tr. J. M. NEALE * 1818–1866

209

LORD, be thy word my rule,
in it may I rejoice;
thy glory be my aim,
thy holy will my choice;

2 Thy promises my hope,
thy providence my guard,
thine arm my strong support,
thyself my great reward.

CHRISTOPHER WORDSWORTH 1807–1885

210

LORD of the boundless curves of space
and time's deep mystery,
to your creative might we trace
all nature's energy.

2 Your mind conceived the galaxy,
each atom's secret planned,
and every age of history
your purpose, Lord, has spanned.

3 Your Spirit gave the living cell
its hidden, vital force:
the instincts which all life impel
derive from you, their source.

4 Science explores your reason's ways,
and faith can this impart
that in the face of Christ our gaze
looks deep within your heart.

5 Christ is your wisdom's perfect word,
your mercy's crowning deed:
and in his love our hearts have heard
your strong compassion plead.

6 Give us to know your truth; but more,
the strength to do your will;
until the love our souls adore
shall all our being fill.

ALBERT F. BAYLY * 1901–1984

211

WE love the place, O God,
wherein thine honour dwells;
the joy of thine abode
all earthly joy excels.

2 We love the house of prayer,
wherein thy servants meet;
and thou, O Lord, art there
thy chosen flock to greet.

*3 We love the sacred font;
for there the holy Dove
to pour is ever wont
his blessing from above.

*4 We love thine altar, Lord;
O what on earth so dear?
for there, in faith adored,
we find thy presence near.

5 We love the word of life,
the word that tells of peace,
of comfort in the strife,
and joys that never cease.

6 We love to sing below
for mercies freely given;
but O we long to know
the triumph-song of heaven.

7 Lord Jesus, give us grace
on earth to love thee more,
in heaven to see thy face,
and with thy saints adore.

WILLIAM BULLOCK 1798–1874
H. W. BAKER 1821–1877

See also

383 Be still, for the presence of the Lord
395 Christ is our corner-stone
351 In our day of thanksgiving
550 Our Father, by whose servants

SAINTS

212

CAPTAINS of the saintly band,
lights who lighten every land,
princes who with Jesus dwell,
judges of his Israel;

2 On the nations sunk in night
ye have shed the Gospel light;
sin and error flee away,
truth reveals the promised day.

3 Not by warrior's spear and sword,
not by art of human word,
preaching but the cross of shame,
rebel hearts for Christ ye tame.

4 Earth, that long in sin and pain
groaned in Satan's deadly chain,
now to serve its God is free
in the law of liberty.

5 Distant lands with one acclaim
tell the honour of your name,
who, wherever man has trod,
teach the mysteries of God.

6 Glory to the Three in One
while eternal ages run,
who from deepest shades of night
called us to his glorious light.

JEAN DE SANTEUL 1630–1697
tr. H. W. BAKER 1821–1877

213

CHRIST is the world's light, he and none other:
born in our darkness, he became our brother;
if we have seen him, we have seen the Father:
Glory to God on high.

2 Christ is the world's peace, he and none other:
no one can serve him and despise a brother;
who else unites us, one in God the Father?
Glory to God on high.

3 Christ is the world's life, he and none other;
sold once for silver, murdered here, our brother.
He who redeems us, reigns with God the Father:
Glory to God on high.

4 Give God the glory, God and none other;
give God the glory, Spirit, Son and Father;
give God the glory, God in man my brother;
Glory to God on high.

F. PRATT GREEN 1903–2000

214

DISPOSER supreme, and Judge of the earth,
who choosest for thine the meek and the poor;
to frail earthen vessels, and things of no worth,
entrusting thy riches which ay shall endure;

2 Those vessels soon fail, though full of thy light,
and at thy decree are broken and gone;
thence brightly appeareth thy truth in its might,
as through the clouds riven the lightnings have shone.

3 Like clouds are they borne to do thy great will,
and swift as the winds about the world go:
the Word with his wisdom their spirits doth fill;
they thunder, they lighten, the waters o'erflow.

4 Their sound goeth forth, 'Christ Jesus the Lord!'
then Satan doth fear, his citadels fall;
as when the dread trumpets went forth at thy word,
and one long blast shattered the Canaanite's wall.

5 O loud be their trump, and stirring their sound,
to rouse us, O Lord, from slumber of sin:
the lights thou hast kindled in darkness around,
O may they awaken our spirits within.

6 All honour and praise, dominion and might,
to God, Three in One, eternally be,
who round us hath shed his own marvellous light,
and called us from darkness his glory to see.

JEAN DE SANTEUL 1630–1697
tr. ISAAC WILLIAMS 1802–1865

215

FOR all thy saints, O Lord,
who strove in thee to live,
who followed thee, obeyed, adored,
our grateful hymn receive.

2 For all thy saints, O Lord,
who strove in thee to die,
and found in thee a full reward,
accept our thankful cry.

3 Thine earthly members fit
to join thy saints above,
in one communion ever knit,
one fellowship of love.

4 Jesu, thy name we bless,
and humbly pray that we
may follow them in holiness,
who lived and died for thee.

5 All might, all praise, be thine,
Father, co-equal Son,
and Spirit, bond of love divine,
while endless ages run.

RICHARD MANT 1776–1848

216

GIVE us the wings of faith to rise
within the veil, and see
the saints above, how great their joys,
how bright their glories be.

2 Once they were mourning here below,
their couch was wet with tears;
they wrestled hard, as we do now,
with sins and doubts and fears.

3 We ask them whence their victory came:
they, with united breath,
ascribe their conquest to the Lamb,
their triumph to his death.

4 They marked the footsteps that he trod,
his zeal inspired their breast,
and, following their incarnate God,
possess the promised rest.

5 Our glorious Leader claims our praise
for his own pattern given;
while the long cloud of witnesses
show the same path to heaven.

ISAAC WATTS * 1674–1748

217

GLORY to thee, O God,
for all thy saints in light,
who nobly strove and conquered in the well-fought fight.
Their praises sing,
who life outpoured
by fire and sword for Christ their King.

2 Thanks be to thee, O Lord,
for saints thy Spirit stirred
in humble paths to live thy life and speak thy word.
Unnumbered they
whose candles shine
to lead our footsteps after thine.

3 Lord God of truth and love,
'thy kingdom come', we pray;
give us thy grace to know thy truth and walk thy way:
that here on earth
thy will be done,
till saints in earth and heaven are one.

H. C. A. GAUNT 1902–1983

218

GOD is the refuge of his saints,
when storms of sharp distress invade;
ere we can offer our complaints,
behold him present with his aid!

2 Let mountains from their seats be hurled
down to the deep, and buried there,
convulsions shake the solid world,
our faith shall never yield to fear.

3 Loud may the troubled ocean roar;
in sacred peace our souls abide;
while every nation, every shore,
trembles, and dreads the swelling tide.

4 There is a stream, whose gentle flow
makes glad the city of our God,
life, love, and joy still gliding through,
and watering our divine abode:

5 That sacred stream, thine holy word,
that all our raging fear controls;
sweet peace thy promises afford,
and give new strength to fainting souls.

6 Sion enjoys her Monarch's love,
secure against a threatening hour;
nor can her firm foundation move,
built on his truth, and armed with power.

Isaac Watts 1674–1748
Psalm 46

219

GOD, whose city's sure foundation
stands upon his holy hill,
by his mighty inspiration
chose of old and chooseth still
men and women from each nation
his good pleasure to fulfil.

2 Here before us through the ages,
while the Christian years went by,
saints, confessors, martyrs, sages,
strong to live and strong to die,
wrote their names upon the pages
of God's blessèd company.

3 Some there were like lamps of learning
shining in a faithless night,
some on fire with love, and burning
with a flaming zeal for right,
some by simple goodness turning
souls from darkness unto light.

4 As we now with high thanksgiving
their triumphant names record,
grant that we, like them, believing
in the promise of thy word,
may, like them, in all good living
praise and magnify the Lord!

C. A. ALINGTON * 1872–1955

220

HOW beauteous are their feet,
who stand on Sion's hill,
who bring salvation on their tongues
and words of peace reveal!

2 How happy are our ears
that hear this happy sound,
which kings and prophets waited for,
and sought, but never found!

3 How blessèd are our eyes
that see this heavenly light,
prophets and kings desired it long,
but died without the sight!

4 The Lord makes bare his arm
through all the earth abroad:
Let every nation now behold
their Saviour and their God.

ISAAC WATTS 1674–1748
Isaiah 52. 7–10; Matthew 13. 16–17

221

HOW bright these glorious spirits shine!
Whence all their white array?
How came they to the blissful seats
of everlasting day?

2 Lo! these are they from sufferings great
who came to realms of light,
and in the blood of Christ have washed
those robes that shine so bright.

3 Now with triumphal palms they stand
before the throne on high,
and serve the God they love amidst
the glories of the sky.

4 Hunger and thirst are felt no more,
nor sun with scorching ray:
God is their sun, whose cheering beams
diffuse eternal day.

5 The Lamb, who dwells amid the throne,
shall o'er them still preside,
feed them with nourishment divine,
and all their footsteps guide.

6 In pastures green he'll lead his flock
where living streams appear;
and God the Lord from every eye
shall wipe off every tear.

Isaac Watts 1674–1748
and others

222

LET saints on earth in concert sing
with those whose work is done;
for all the servants of our King
in heaven and earth are one.

2 One family, we dwell in him,
one church, above, beneath;
though now divided by the stream,
the narrow stream of death.

3 One army of the living God,
to his command we bow:
part of the host have crossed the flood,
and part are crossing now.

4 E'en now to their eternal home
there pass some spirits blest;
while others to the margin come,
waiting their call to rest.

5 Jesu, be thou our constant guide;
then, when the word is given,
bid Jordan's narrow stream divide,
and bring us safe to heaven.

CHARLES WESLEY 1707–1788
and others

223

LO, round the throne, a glorious band,
the saints in countless myriads stand,
of every tongue redeemed to God,
arrayed in garments washed in blood.

2 Through tribulation great they came;
they bore the cross, despised the shame;
from all their labours now they rest,
in God's eternal glory blest.

3 They see their Saviour face to face,
and sing the triumphs of his grace;
him day and night they ceaseless praise,
to him the loud thanksgiving raise:

4 'Worthy the Lamb, for sinners slain,
through endless years to live and reign;
thou hast redeemed us by thy blood,
and made us kings and priests to God.'

5 O may we tread the sacred road
that saints and holy martyrs trod;
wage to the end the glorious strife,
and win, like them, a crown of life.

ROWLAND HILL 1744–1833
and others

224

LORD, it belongs not to my care
whether I die or live:
to love and serve thee is my share,
and this thy grace must give.

2 Christ leads me through no darker rooms
than he went through before;
he that into God's kingdom comes
must enter by this door.

3 Come, Lord, when grace hath made me meet
thy blessèd face to see;
for if thy work on earth be sweet,
what will thy glory be!

4 Then shall I end my sad complaints
and weary, sinful days,
and join with the triumphant saints
that sing my Saviour's praise.

5 My knowledge of that life is small,
the eye of faith is dim;
but 'tis enough that Christ knows all,
and I shall be with him.

RICHARD BAXTER * 1615–1691

225

O WHAT their joy and their glory must be,
those endless sabbaths the blessèd ones see;
crown for the valiant, to weary ones rest;
God shall be all, and in all ever blest.

*2 What are the Monarch, his court, and his throne?
What are the peace and the joy that they own?
Tell us, ye blest ones, who in it have share,
if what ye feel ye can fully declare.

3 Truly Jerusalem name we that shore,
'Vision of peace,' that brings joy evermore.
Wish and fulfilment can severed be ne'er,
nor the thing prayed for come short of the prayer.

*4 There, where no trouble distraction can bring,
we the sweet anthems of Sion shall sing,
while for thy grace, Lord, their voices of praise
thy blessèd people shall evermore raise.

5 There dawns no sabbath, no sabbath is o'er,
those sabbath-keepers have one and no more;
one and unending is that triumph-song
which to the angels and us shall belong.

6 Now in the meanwhile, with hearts raised on high,
we for that country must yearn and must sigh;
seeking Jerusalem, dear native land,
through our long exile on Babylon's strand.

7 Low before him with our praises we fall,
of whom, and in whom, and through whom are all:
of whom, the Father; and in whom, the Son;
through whom, the Spirit, with these ever One.

PETER ABELARD 1079–1142
tr. J. M. NEALE 1818–1866

226

PALMS of glory, raiment bright,
crowns that never fade away,
gird and deck the saints in light:
priests and kings and conquerors they.

2 Yet the conquerors bring their palms
to the Lamb amidst the throne,
and proclaim in joyful psalms
victory through his cross alone.

3 Kings for harps their crowns resign,
crying, as they strike the chords,
'Take the kingdom, it is thine,
King of kings and Lord of lords.'

4 Round the altar priests confess,
if their robes are white as snow,
'twas the Saviour's righteousness,
and his blood, that made them so.

5 They were mortal too like us:
O, when we like them must die,
may our souls translated thus
triumph, reign, and shine on high.

JAMES MONTGOMERY 1771–1854

227

REJOICE in God's saints, today and all days!
A world without saints forgets how to praise.
Their faith in acquiring the habit of prayer,
their depth of adoring, Lord, help us to share.

2 Some march with events to turn them God's way;
some need to withdraw, the better to pray;
some carry the gospel through fire and through flood:
our world is their parish: their purpose is God.

3 Rejoice in those saints, unpraised and unknown,
who bear someone's cross or shoulder their own:
they shame our complaining, our comforts, our cares:
what patience in caring, what courage, is theirs!

4 Rejoice in God's saints, today and all days!
A world without saints forgets how to praise.
In loving, in living, they prove it is true:
the way of self-giving, Lord, leads us to you.

F. PRATT GREEN 1903–2000

228

SOLDIERS, who are Christ's below,
strong in faith resist the foe:
boundless is the pledged reward
unto them who serve the Lord.
Alleluia.

2 For the souls that overcome
waits the beauteous heavenly home,
where the blessèd evermore
tread on high the starry floor.
Alleluia.

3 'Tis no palm of fading leaves
that the conqueror's hand receives;
joys are there, serene and pure,
light that ever shall endure.
Alleluia.

4 Passing soon and little worth
are the things that tempt on earth;
heavenward lift thy soul's regard:
God himself is thy reward.
Alleluia.

5 Father, who the crown dost give,
Saviour, by whose death we live,
Spirit, who our hearts dost raise,
Three in One, thy name we praise.
Alleluia.

Latin, 18th century
tr. JOHN CLARK 1839–1888

229

WHO are these like stars appearing,
these, before God's throne who stand?
Each a golden crown is wearing:
who are all this glorious band?
Alleluia, hark, they sing,
praising loud their heavenly King.

2 Who are these in dazzling brightness,
clothed in God's own righteousness,
these, whose robes of purest whiteness
shall their lustre still possess,
still untouched by time's rude hand?
Whence came all this glorious band?

3 These are they who have contended
for their Saviour's honour long,
wrestling on till life was ended,
following not the sinful throng;
these, who well the fight sustained,
triumph by the Lamb have gained.

4 These are they whose hearts were riven,
sore with woe and anguish tried,
who in prayer full oft have striven
with the God they glorified;
now, their painful conflict o'er,
God has bid them weep no more.

5 These, th' Almighty contemplating,
did as priests before him stand,
soul and body always waiting
day and night at his command:
now in God's most holy place
blest they stand before his face.

HEINRICH SCHENCK 1656–1727
tr. FRANCES ELIZABETH COX 1812–1897

230

YE watchers and ye holy ones,
bright Seraphs, Cherubim and Thrones,
raise the glad strain, Alleluia.
Cry out, Dominions, Princedoms, Powers,
Virtues, Archangels, Angels' choirs,
Alleluia.

2 O higher than the Cherubim,
more glorious than the Seraphim,
lead their praises, Alleluia.
Thou Bearer of the eternal Word,
most gracious, magnify the Lord.
Alleluia.

3 Respond, ye souls in endless rest,
ye Patriarchs and Prophets blest,
Alleluia, alleluia.
Ye holy Twelve, ye Martyrs strong,
all Saints triumphant, raise the song
Alleluia.

4 O friends, in gladness let us sing,
supernal anthems echoing,
Alleluia, alleluia.
To God the Father, God the Son,
and God the Spirit, Three in One,
Alleluia.

ATHELSTAN RILEY 1858–1945

231

YE who own the faith of Jesus
sing the wonders that were done,
when the love of God the Father
o'er our sin the victory won,
when he made the Virgin Mary
Mother of his only Son.
Hail Mary, full of grace.

2 Blessèd were the chosen people
out of whom the Lord did come,
blessèd was the land of promise
fashioned for his earthly home;
but more blessèd far the Mother
she who bare him in her womb.
Hail Mary, full of grace.

3 Wherefore let all faithful people
tell the honour of her name,
let the church in her foreshadowed
part in her thanksgiving claim;
what Christ's Mother sang in gladness
let Christ's people sing the same.
Hail Mary, full of grace.

*4 Let us weave our supplications,
she with us and we with her,
for the advancement of the faithful,
for each faithful worshipper,
for the doubting, for the sinful,
for each heedless wanderer.
Hail Mary, full of grace.

*5 May the Mother's intercessions
on our homes a blessing win,
that the children all be prospered,
strong and fair and pure within,
following our Lord's own footsteps,
firm in faith and free from sin.
Hail Mary, full of grace.

*6 For the sick and for the aged,
for our dear ones far away,
for the hearts that mourn in secret,
all who need our prayers today,
for the faithful gone before us,
may the holy Virgin pray.
Hail Mary, full of grace.

7 Praise, O Mary, praise the Father,
praise thy Saviour and thy Son,
praise the everlasting Spirit,
who hath made thee ark and throne;
o'er all creatures high exalted,
lowly praise the Three in One.
Hail Mary, full of grace.

V. Stuckey S. Coles 1845–1929

SAINTS: ALL SAINTS' DAY

232

FOR all the saints who from their labours rest,
who thee by faith before the world confessed,
thy name, O Jesu, be for ever blest.
Alleluia.

2 Thou wast their rock, their fortress, and their might;
thou, Lord, their Captain in the well-fought fight;
thou, in the darkness, still their one true light.
Alleluia.

3 O may thy soldiers, faithful, true, and bold,
fight as the saints who nobly fought of old,
and win, with them, the victor's crown of gold.
Alleluia.

4 O blest communion, fellowship divine!
we feebly struggle, they in glory shine;
yet all are one in thee, for all are thine.
Alleluia.

5 And when the strife is fierce, the warfare long,
steals on the ear the distant triumph-song,
and hearts are brave again, and arms are strong.
Alleluia.

6 The golden evening brightens in the west;
soon, soon to faithful warriors comes their rest:
sweet is the calm of paradise the blest.
Alleluia.

7 But lo, there breaks a yet more glorious day;
the saints triumphant rise in bright array:
the King of glory passes on his way.
Alleluia.

8 From earth's wide bounds, from ocean's farthest coast,
through gates of pearl streams in the countless host,
singing to Father, Son, and Holy Ghost
Alleluia.

W. Walsham How 1823–1897

SAINTS: ST ANDREW

233

JESUS calls us: o'er the tumult
Of our life's wild restless sea,
day by day his sweet voice soundeth,
saying, 'Christian, follow me':

2 As of old Saint Andrew heard it
by the Galilean lake,
turned from home and toil and kindred
leaving all for his dear sake.

3 Jesus calls us from the worship
of the vain world's golden store,
from each idol that would keep us,
saying, 'Christian, love me more.'

4 In our joys and in our sorrows,
days of toil and hours of ease,
still he calls, in cares and pleasures,
that we love him more than these.

5 Jesus calls us: by thy mercies,
Saviour, make us hear thy call,
give our hearts to thine obedience,
serve and love thee best of all.

Cecil Frances Alexander 1818–1895

234

SING we the praises of the great forerunner,
tell forth the mighty wonders of his story:
so may his Master cleanse our lips and make them
fit to extol him.

2 Lo, God's high herald, swift from heaven descending,
gives to thy father tidings of thy coming,
telling thy name and all the tale of marvels
that shall befall thee.

3 Oft had the prophets in the time before thee
spoken in vision of the Daystar's coming;
but when he came, 'twas thou that didst proclaim him
Saviour of all men.

PAUL THE DEACON 730–799
tr. C. S. PHILLIPS 1883–1949

235

THE great forerunner of the morn,
the herald of the Word, is born;
and faithful hearts shall never fail
with thanks and praise his light to hail.

2 With heavenly message Gabriel came,
that John should be that herald's name,
and with prophetic utterance told
his actions great and manifold.

3 His mighty deeds exalt his fame
to greater than a prophet's name.
Of woman-born shall never be
a greater prophet than was he.

4 To God the Father, God the Son,
and God the Spirit, Three in One,
praise, honour, might, and glory be
from age to age eternally.

THE VENERABLE BEDE 673–735
tr. J. M. NEALE * 1818–1866

SAINTS: ST PETER

236

THOU art the Christ, O Lord,
the Son of God most high:
for ever be adored
that name in earth and sky,
in which, though mortal strength may fail,
the saints of God at last prevail.

2 O surely he was blest
with blessedness unpriced,
who, taught of God, confessed
the Godhead in the Christ;
for of thy church, Lord, thou didst own
thy saint a true foundation-stone.

3 Thrice fallen, thrice restored,
the bitter lesson learnt,
that heart for thee, O Lord,
with triple ardour burnt.
The cross he took he laid not down
until he grasped the martyr's crown.

4 O bright triumphant faith,
O courage void of fears,
O love most strong in death,
O penitential tears!
By these, Lord, keep us lest we fall,
and make us go where thou shalt call.

W. WALSHAM HOW 1823–1897

SAINTS: ST PAUL

237

WE sing the glorious conquest
  before Damascus' gate,
when Saul, the church's spoiler,
  came breathing threats and hate;
the ravening wolf rushed forward
  full early to the prey;
but lo, the Shepherd met him,
  and bound him fast to-day.

*2 O glory most excelling
  that smote across his path,
O light that pierced and blinded
  the zealot in his wrath,
O voice that spake within him
  the calm reproving word,
O love that sought and held him
  the bondman of his Lord!

3 O wisdom, ordering all things
  in order strong and sweet,
what nobler spoil was ever
  cast at the Victor's feet?
What wiser master-builder
  e'er wrought at thine employ
than he, till now so furious
  thy building to destroy?

4 Lord, teach thy church the lesson,
  still in her darkest hour
of weakness and of danger
  to trust thy hidden power:
thy grace by ways mysterious
  the wrath of man can bind,
and in thy boldest foeman
  thy chosen saint can find.

JOHN ELLERTON 1826–1893

See also

364 A city radiant as a bride
568 Sing alleluia forth ye saints on high
614 We sing for all the unsung saints

BLESSED VIRGIN MARY

238

FOR Mary, Mother of our Lord,
God's holy name be praised,
who first the Son of God adored,
as on her child she gazed.

2 Brave, holy Virgin, she believed,
though hard the task assigned,
and by the Holy Ghost conceived
the Saviour of mankind.

*3 The busy world had got no space
or time for God on earth;
a cattle manger was the place
where Mary gave him birth.

4 She gave her body as God's shrine,
her heart to piercing pain;
she knew the cost of love divine,
when Jesus Christ was slain.

5 Dear Mary, from your lowliness
and home in Galilee
there comes a joy and holiness
to every family.

6 Hail, Mary, you are full of grace,
above all women blest;
and blest your Son, whom your embrace
in birth and death confessed.

J. R. Peacey 1896–1971

239

HER Virgin eyes saw God incarnate born,
when she to Bethlem came that happy morn:
how high her raptures then began to swell,
none but her own omniscient Son can tell.

2 As Eve, when she her fontal sin reviewed,
wept for herself and all she should include,
blest Mary, with man's Saviour in embrace,
joyed for herself and for all human race.

3 All saints are by her Son's dear influence blest;
she kept the very fountain at her breast:
the Son adored and nursed by the sweet Maid
a thousandfold of love for love repaid.

4 Heaven with transcendent joys her entrance graced,
near to his throne her Son his Mother placed;
and here below, now she's of heaven possest,
all generations are to call her blest.

THOMAS KEN 1637–1711

240

PRAISE we the Lord this day,
this day so long foretold,
whose promise shone with cheering ray
on waiting saints of old.

2 The prophet gave the sign
for faithful hearts to read:
a Virgin, born of David's line,
shall bear the promised Seed.

3 Ask not how this should be,
but worship and adore;
like her, whom heaven's majesty
came down to shadow o'er.

4 Meekly she bowed her head
to hear the gracious word,
Mary, the pure and lowly maid,
the favoured of the Lord.

5 Blessèd shall be her name
in all the church on earth,
through whom that wondrous mercy came,
the Incarnate Saviour's birth.

A Selection of Hymns
for Public and Private Use 1847
compiled by T. M. Fallow
AUTHOR UNKNOWN *

241

SING we of the blessèd Mother
who received the angel's word,
and obedient to his summons
bore in love the infant Lord;
sing we of the joys of Mary
at whose breast that child was fed
who is Son of God eternal
and the everlasting Bread.

2 Sing we, too, of Mary's sorrows,
of the sword that pierced her through,
when beneath the cross of Jesus
she his weight of suffering knew,
looked upon her Son and Saviour
reigning high on Calvary's tree,
saw the price of man's redemption
paid to set the sinner free.

3 Sing again the joys of Mary
when she saw the risen Lord,
and in prayer with Christ's apostles,
waited on his promised word:
from on high the blazing glory
of the Spirit's presence came,
heavenly breath of God's own being,
manifest through wind and flame.

4 Sing the chiefest joy of Mary
when on earth her work was done,
and the Lord of all creation
brought her to his heavenly home:
Virgin Mother, Mary blessèd,
raised on high and crowned with grace,
may your Son, the world's redeemer,
grant us all to see his face.

G. B. TIMMS 1910–1997

242

THE Angel Gabriel from heaven came,
his wings as drifted snow, his eyes as flame;
'All hail,' said he, 'thou lowly maiden Mary,
most highly favoured lady.'
Gloria!

2 'For known a blessèd Mother thou shalt be,
all generations laud and honour thee,
thy son shall be Emmanuel, by seers foretold;
most highly favoured lady.'
Gloria!

3 Then gentle Mary meekly bowed her head,
'To me be as it pleaseth God,' she said,
'My soul shall laud and magnify his holy name':
most highly favoured lady.
Gloria!

4 Of her, Emmanuel, the Christ was born
in Bethlehem, all on a Christmas morn,
and Christian folk throughout the world will ever say
'Most highly favoured lady.'
Gloria!

Basque Carol
paraphrased by SABINE BARING-GOULD 1834–1924

243

THE God whom earth and sea and sky
adore and laud and magnify,
whose might they own, whose praise they tell,
in Mary's body deigned to dwell.

2 O Mother blest, the chosen shrine
wherein the Architect divine,
whose hand contains the earth and sky,
vouchsafed in hidden guise to lie:

3 Blest in the message Gabriel brought;
blest in the work the Spirit wrought;
most blest, to bring to human birth
the long-desired of all the earth.

4 O Lord, the Virgin-born, to thee
eternal praise and glory be,
whom with the Father we adore
and Holy Ghost for evermore.

VENANTIUS FORTUNATUS 530–600
tr. J. M. NEALE * 1818–1866

244

VIRGIN-BORN, we bow before thee:
blessèd was the womb that bore thee;
  Mary, mother meek and mild,
  blessèd was she in her child.

2 Blessèd was the breast that fed thee;
blessèd was the hand that led thee;
  blessèd was the parent's eye
  that watched thy slumbering infancy.

3 Blessèd she by all creation,
who brought forth the world's Salvation
  blessèd they, for ever blest,
  who love thee most and serve thee best.

4 Virgin-born, we bow before thee:
blessèd was the womb that bore thee;
Mary, mother meek and mild,
blessèd was she in her child.

REGINALD HEBER 1783–1826

See also

487 Jesus, good above all other
505 Lord Jesus Christ
510 Lord of the home, your only Son
240 Praise we the Lord this day
231 Ye who own the faith of Jesus

SAINT MICHAEL AND ALL ANGELS

245

AROUND the throne of God a band
of glorious angels ever stand;
bright things they see, sweet harps they hold,
and on their heads are crowns of gold.

2 Some wait around him, ready still
to sing his praise and do his will;
and some, when he commands them, go
to guard his servants here below.

3 Lord, give thy angels every day
command to guide us on our way,
and bid them every evening keep
their watch around us while we sleep.

4 So shall no wicked thing draw near,
to do us harm or cause us fear;
and we shall dwell, when life is past,
with angels round thy throne at last.

J. M. NEALE 1818–1866

246

CHRIST, the fair glory of the holy angels,
ruler of all, and author of creation,
grant us in mercy grace to win by patience
joys everlasting.

2 Send thine archangel Michael from thy presence:
peacemaker blessèd, may he hover o'er us,
hallow our dwellings, that for us thy children
all things may prosper.

3 Send thine archangel, Gabriel the mighty:
on strong wings flying, may he come from heaven,
drive from thy temple Satan the old foeman,
succour our weakness.

4 Send thine archangel, Raphael the healer:
through him with wholesome med'cines of salvation
heal our backsliding, and in paths of goodness
guide our steps daily.

5 Father almighty, Son, and Holy Spirit,
Godhead eternal, grant us our petition;
thine be the glory through the whole creation
now and for ever. Amen.

ascribed to RABANUS MAURUS 776–856
tr. C. S. PHILLIPS * 1883–1949

247

STARS of the morning, so gloriously bright,
filled with celestial resplendence and light,
these that, where night never followeth day,
raise the Trisagion ever and ay:

2 These are thy counsellors, these dost thou own,
Lord God of Sabaoth, nearest thy throne;
these are thy ministers, these dost thou send,
help of the helpless ones, us to defend.

*3 These keep the guard amid Salem's dear bowers;
Thrones, Principalities, Virtues, and Powers;
where, with the Living Ones, mystical Four,
Cherubim, Seraphim bow and adore.

4 'Who like the Lord?' thunders Michael the Chief;
Raphael,'the Cure of God', comforteth grief;
and, as at Nazareth, prophet of peace,
Gabriel, 'the Light of God', bringeth release.

5 Then, when the earth was first poised in mid-space,
then, when the planets first sped on their race,
then, when were ended the six days' employ,
then all the Sons of God shouted for joy.

6 Still let them succour us; still let them fight,
Lord of angelic hosts, battling for right;
till, where their anthems they ceaselessly pour,
we with the angels may bow and adore.

St Joseph the Hymnographer [?] *d.* 883
tr. from the Greek hymn J. M. Neale 1818–1866

See also

377 Angel-voices, ever singing
378 As Jacob with travel was weary
401 Come, let us join our cheerful songs
466 How shall I sing that majesty
56 It came upon the midnight clear
574 Songs of praise the angels sang
626 Ye holy angels bright

TRANSFIGURATION

248

'TIS good, Lord, to be here,
thy glory fills the night;
thy face and garments, like the sun,
shine with unborrowed light.

2 'Tis good, Lord, to be here,
thy beauty to behold,
where Moses and Elijah stand,
thy messengers of old.

3 Fulfiller of the past,
promise of things to be,
we hail thy body glorified,
and our redemption see.

4 Before we taste of death,
we see thy kingdom come;
we fain would hold the vision bright,
and make this hill our home.

5 'Tis good, Lord, to be here,
yet we may not remain;
but since thou bidst us leave the mount,
come with us to the plain.

J. Armitage Robinson 1858–1933

See also

513 Lord, the light of your love is shining
566 Shepherd divine, our wants relieve

CREATION

249

ABOVE the moon earth rises,
a sunlit, mossy stone,
a garden that God prizes
where life has richly grown,
an emerald selected
for us to guard with care,
an isle in space protected
by one thin reef of air.

2 The mossy stone is grieving,
its tears are bitter rain,
the garden is unleaving
and all its harvests wane,
the emerald is clouded,
its lustre dims and fades,
the isle of life is shrouded
in thick and stagnant haze.

3 O listen to the sighing
of water, sky and land,
and hear the Spirit crying,
the future is at hand:
the moss and garden thinning
portend a death or birth,
the end or new beginning
for all that lives on earth.

4 A death if hearts now harden,
a birth if we repent
and tend and keep the garden
as God has always meant:
to sow without abusing
the soil where life is grown,
to reap without our bruising
the sunlit mossy stone.

THOMAS H. TROEGER *b.* 1945

250

ALL creatures of our God and King,
lift up your voice and with us sing,
Alleluia, alleluia!
Thou burning sun with golden beam,
thou silver moon with softer gleam:
O praise him, O praise him,
Alleluia, alleluia, allelluia!

2 Thou rushing wind that art so strong,
ye clouds that sail in heaven along,
O praise him, alleluia!
Thou rising morn, in praise rejoice;
ye lights of evening, find a voice:

3 Thou flowing water, pure and clear,
make music for thy Lord to hear,
Alleluia, alleluia!
Thou fire, so masterful and bright,
that givest us both warmth and light:

4 Dear mother earth, who day by day
unfoldest blessings on our way,
O praise him, alleluia!
The flowers and fruits that in thee grow,
let them his glory also show:

5 All ye that are of tender heart,
forgiving others, take your part,
O sing ye, alleluia!
Ye who long pain and sorrow bear,
praise God, and on him cast your care:

6 And thou, most kind and gentle death,
waiting to hush our latest breath,
O praise him, alleluia!
Thou leadest home the child of God,
and Christ our Lord the way has trod:

7 Let all things their creator bless,
and worship him in humbleness;
O praise him, alleluia!
Praise, praise the Father, praise the Son,
and praise the Spirit, Three in One:

WILLIAM HENRY DRAPER * 1855–1933
based on ST FRANCIS OF ASSISI 1182–1226

251

ALL things bright and beautiful,
all creatures great and small,
all things wise and wonderful,
the Lord God made them all.

2 Each little flower that opens,
each little bird that sings,
he made their glowing colours,
he made their tiny wings:

3 The purple-headed mountain,
the river running by,
the sunset, and the morning
that brightens up the sky:

4 The cold wind in the winter,
the pleasant summer sun,
the ripe fruits in the garden,
he made them every one:

*5 The tall trees in the greenwood,
the meadows where we play,
the rushes by the water
we gather every day:

6 He gave us eyes to see them,
and lips that we might tell
how great is God almighty,
who has made all things well:

All things bright and beautiful,
all creatures great and small,
all things wise and wonderful,
the Lord God made them all.

CECIL FRANCES ALEXANDER 1818–1895

252

AS water to the thirsty,
as beauty to the eyes,
as strength that follows weakness,
as truth instead of lies,
as songtime and springtime
and summertime to be,
so is my Lord,
my living Lord,
so is my Lord to me.

2 Like calm in place of clamour,
like peace that follows pain,
like meeting after parting,
like sunshine after rain,
like moonlight and starlight
and sunlight on the sea,
so is my Lord,
my living Lord,
so is my Lord to me.

3 As sleep that follows fever,
as gold instead of grey,
as freedom after bondage,
as sunrise to the day,
as home to the traveller
and all we long to see,
so is my Lord,
my living Lord,
so is my Lord to me.

TIMOTHY DUDLEY-SMITH *b.* 1926

253

FOR the beauty of the earth,
for the beauty of the skies,
for the love which from our birth
over and around us lies,
Lord of all, to thee we raise
this our sacrifice of praise.

2 For the beauty of each hour
of the day and of the night,
hill and vale and tree and flower,
sun and moon and stars of light:

3 For the joy of human love,
brother, sister, parent, child,
friends on earth, and friends above,
pleasures pure and undefiled:

4 For each perfect gift of thine,
to our race so freely given,
graces human and divine,
flowers of earth and buds of heaven:

5 For thy church which evermore
lifteth holy hands above,
offering up on every shore
her pure sacrifice of love,
Lord of all, to thee we raise
this our sacrifice of praise.

F. S. PIERPOINT * 1835–1917

254

FOR the fruits of his creation,
thanks be to God;
for his gifts to every nation,
thanks be to God;
for the ploughing, sowing, reaping,
silent growth while we are sleeping,
future needs in earth's safe keeping,
thanks be to God.

2 In the just reward of labour,
God's will is done;
in the help we give our neighbour,
God's will is done;
in our world-wide task of caring
for the hungry and despairing,
in the harvests we are sharing,
God's will is done.

3 For the harvests of his Spirit,
thanks be to God;
for the good we all inherit,
thanks be to God;
for the wonders that astound us,
for the truths that still confound us,
most of all, that love has found us,
thanks be to God.

F. PRATT GREEN 1903–2000

255

GOD is a name my soul adores,
the almighty Three, the eternal One;
nature and grace with all their powers
confess the infinite unknown.

2 Thy voice produced the sea and spheres,
bade the waves roar, the planets shine;
but nothing like thyself appears
through all these spacious works of thine.

3 Still restless nature dies and grows;
from change to change the creatures run:
thy being no succession knows,
and all thy vast designs are one.

4 A glance of thine runs through the globe,
rules the bright worlds and moves their frame;
of light thou form'st thy dazzling robe,
thy ministers are living flame.

5 How shall polluted mortals dare
to sing thy glory or thy grace?
Beneath thy feet we lie afar,
and see but shadows of thy face.

6 Who can behold the blazing light?
Who can approach consuming flame?
None but thy wisdom knows thy might,
none but thy word can speak thy name.

Isaac Watts * 1674–1748

256

GOD, you have giv'n us power to sound
depths hitherto unknown:
to probe earth's hidden mysteries,
and make their might our own.

2 Great are your gifts: yet greater far
this gift, O God, bestow,
that as to knowledge we attain
we may in wisdom grow.

3 Let wisdom's godly fear dispel
all fears that hate impart;
give understanding to the mind,
and, with new mind, new heart.

4 So for your glory and our good
may we your gifts employ,
lest, maddened by the lust of power,
we shall ourselves destroy.

G. W. Briggs * 1875–1959

257

LORD, bring the day to pass
when forest, rock and hill,
the beasts, the birds, the grass,
will know your finished will:
when we attain our destiny
and nature lives in harmony.

2 Forgive our careless use
of water, ore and soil —
the plenty we abuse
supplied by others' toil:
save us from making self our creed,
turn us towards each other's need.

3 Give us, when we release
creation's secret powers,
to harness them for peace —
our children's peace and ours:
teach us the art of mastering
in servant form, which draws death's sting.

4 Creation groans, travails,
futile its present plight,
bound — till the hour it hails
God's children born of light,
who enter on their true estate.
Come, Lord: new heavens and earth create.

IAN FRASER *b.* 1917

258

LORD of beauty, thine the splendour
shown in earth and sky and sea,
burning sun and moonlight tender,
hill and river, flower and tree:
lest we fail our praise to render
touch our eyes that they may see.

2 Lord of wisdom, whom obeying
mighty waters ebb and flow,
while unhasting, undelaying,
planets on their courses go:
in thy laws thyself displaying,
teach our minds thyself to know.

3 Lord of life, alone sustaining
all below and all above,
Lord of love, by whose ordaining
sun and stars sublimely move:
in our earthly spirits reigning,
lift our hearts that we may love.

4 Lord of beauty, bid us own thee,
Lord of truth, our footsteps guide,
till as Love our hearts enthrone thee,
and, with vision purified,
Lord of all, when all have known thee,
thou in all art glorified.

C. A. ALINGTON 1872–1955

259

MORNING glory, starlit sky,
soaring music, scholars' truth,
flight of swallows, autumn leaves,
memory's treasure, grace of youth:

2 Open are the gifts of God,
gifts of love to mind and sense;
hidden is love's agony,
love's endeavour, love's expense.

3 Love that gives, gives ever more,
gives with zeal, with eager hands,
spares not, keeps not, all outpours,
ventures all, its all expends.

4 Drained is love in making full,
bound in setting others free,
poor in making many rich,
weak in giving power to be.

5 Therefore he who shows us God
helpless hangs upon the tree;
and the nails and crown of thorns
tell of what God's love must be.

6 Here is God: no monarch he,
throned in easy state to reign;
here is God, whose arms of love
aching, spent, the world sustain.

W. H. VANSTONE 1923–1999

260

MORNING has broken, like the first morning;
blackbird has spoken, like the first bird.
Praise for the singing! Praise for the morning!
Praise for them, springing fresh from the Word!

2 Sweet the rain's new fall sunlit from heaven,
like the first dewfall on the first grass.
Praise for the sweetness of the wet garden,
sprung in completeness where his feet pass.

3 Mine is the sunlight! Mine is the morning
born of the one light Eden saw play!
Praise with elation, praise every morning,
God's re-creation of the new day!

ELEANOR FARJEON 1881–1965

261

MY soul, there is a country
far beyond the stars,
where stands a wingèd sentry
all skilful in the wars.

2 There, above noise and danger,
sweet peace sits crowned with smiles,
and One born in a manger
commands the beauteous files.

3 He is thy gracious Friend,
and – O my soul, awake! –
did in pure love descend,
to die here for thy sake.

4 If thou canst get but thither,
there grows the flower of peace,
the rose that cannot wither,
thy fortress and thy ease.

5 Leave then thy foolish ranges,
for none can thee secure
but one who never changes,
thy God, thy life, thy cure.

HENRY VAUGHAN 1622–1695

262

O LORD my God, when I in awesome wonder
consider all the works thy hand hath made,
I see the stars, I hear the mighty thunder,
thy power throughout the universe displayed;
Then sings my soul, my Saviour God, to thee,
how great thou art, how great thou art!
Then sings my soul, my Saviour God, to thee,
how great thou art, how great thou art!

2 When through the woods and forest glades I wander,
and hear the birds sing sweetly in the trees;
when I look down from lofty mountain grandeur,
and hear the brook, and feel the gentle breeze;
Then sings my soul, ...

3 And when I think that God, his Son not sparing,
sent him to die — I scarce can take it in:
that on the cross, my burden gladly bearing,
he bled and died to take away my sin;
Then sings my soul, ...

4 When Christ shall come with shout of acclamation
and take me home — what joy shall fill my heart!
Then shall I bow in humble adoration,
and there proclaim, my God, how great thou art!
Then sings my soul, my Saviour God, to thee,
how great thou art, how great thou art!
Then sings my soul, my Saviour God, to thee,
how great thou art, how great thou art!

Russian hymn
tr. STUART K. HINE 1899–1989

263

O LORD of every shining constellation
that wheels in splendour through the midnight sky,
grant us your Spirit's true illumination
to read the secrets of your work on high.

2 You, Lord, have made the atom's hidden forces,
your laws its mighty energies fulfil;
teach us, to whom you give such rich resources,
in all we use, to serve your holy will.

3 O Life, awaking life in cell and tissue,
from flower to bird, from beast to brain of man;
help us to trace, from birth to final issue,
the sure unfolding of your age-long plan.

4 You, Lord, have stamped your image on your creatures,
and, though they mar that image, love them still;
lift up our eyes to Christ, that in his features
we may discern the beauty of your will.

5 Great Lord of nature, shaping and renewing,
you made us more than nature's sons to be;
you help us tread, with grace our souls enduing,
the road to life and immortality.

ALBERT F. BAYLY 1901–1984

264

THE heavens declare thy glory, Lord;
in every star thy wisdom shines;
but when our eyes behold thy word,
we read thy name in fairer lines.

2 The rolling sun, the changing light,
and nights and days, thy power confess;
but the blest volume thou hast writ
reveals thy justice and thy grace.

3 Sun, moon, and stars convey thy praise
round the whole earth, and never stand;
so, when thy truth began its race,
it touched and glanced on every land.

4 Nor shall thy spreading gospel rest
till through the world thy truth has run;
till Christ has all the nations blest
that see the light or feel the sun.

5 Great Sun of Righteousness, arise;
bless the dark world with heavenly light;
thy gospel makes the simple wise,
thy laws are pure, thy judgements right.

6 Thy noblest wonders here we view,
in souls renewed and sins forgiven:
Lord, cleanse my sins, my soul renew,
and make thy word my guide to heaven.

ISAAC WATTS 1674–1748
Psalm 19

265

THE spacious firmament on high,
with all the blue ethereal sky,
and spangled heavens, a shining frame,
their great Original proclaim.
The unwearied sun from day to day
does his Creator's power display,
and publishes to every land
the work of an almighty hand.

2 Soon as the evening shades prevail
the moon takes up the wondrous tale,
and nightly to the listening earth
repeats the story of her birth;
whilst all the stars that round her burn,
and all the planets in their turn,
confirm the tidings, as they roll,
and spread the truth from pole to pole.

3 What though in solemn silence all
move round the dark terrestrial ball;
what though nor real voice nor sound
amid their radiant orbs be found;
in reason's ear they all rejoice,
and utter forth a glorious voice,
for ever singing as they shine,
'The hand that made us is divine.'

JOSEPH ADDISON 1672–1719
Psalm 19. 1–6

266

THE works of the Lord are created in wisdom;
we view the earth's wonders and call him to mind:
we hear what he says in the world we discover
and God shows his glory in all that we find.

2 Not even the angels have ever been granted
to tell the full story of nature and grace;
but open to God is all human perception,
the mysteries of time and the secrets of space.

3 The sun every morning lights up his creation,
the moon marks the rhythm of months in their turn;
the glittering stars are arrayed in his honour,
adorning the years as they ceaselessly burn.

4 The wind is his breath and the clouds are his signal,
the rain and the snow are the robes of his choice;
the storm and the lightning, his watchmen and heralds,
the crash of the thunder, the sound of his voice.

5 The song is unfinished; how shall we complete it,
and where find the skill to perfect all God's praise?
At work in all places, he cares for all peoples:
how great is the Lord to the end of all days!

CHRISTOPHER M. IDLE *b.* 1938
Ecclesiasticus 42–43

267

THOU, whose almighty word
chaos and darkness heard,
and took their flight;
hear us, we humbly pray,
and where the gospel-day
sheds not its glorious ray,
let there be light.

2 Thou, who didst come to bring
on thy redeeming wing
healing and sight,
health to the sick in mind,
sight to the inly blind,
O now to all mankind
let there be light.

3 Spirit of truth and love,
life-giving, holy Dove,
speed forth thy flight;
move on the water's face,
bearing the lamp of grace,
and in earth's darkest place
let there be light.

4 Holy and blessèd Three,
glorious Trinity,
Wisdom, Love, Might;
boundless as ocean's tide
rolling in fullest pride,
through the earth far and wide
let there be light.

JOHN MARRIOTT 1780–1825

268

TIMELESS love! We sing the story,
praise his wonders, tell his worth;
love more fair than heaven's glory,
love more firm than ancient earth!
Tell his faithfulness abroad:
who is like him? Praise the Lord!

2 By his faithfulness surrounded,
north and south his hand proclaim;
earth and heaven formed and founded,
skies and seas, declare his Name!
Wind and storm obey his word:
who is like him? Praise the Lord!

3 Truth and righteousness enthrone him,
just and equal are his ways;
more than happy, those who own him,
more than joy, their songs of praise!
Sun and Shield and great Reward:
who is like him? Praise the Lord!

TIMOTHY DUDLEY-SMITH *b.* 1926
Psalm 89. 1–18

269

WITH wonder, Lord, we see your works,
we see the beauty you have made,
this earth, the skies, all things that are
in beauty made.

2 With wonder, Lord, we see your works,
and childlike in our joy we sing
to praise you, bless you, Maker, Lord
of everything.

3 The stars that fill the skies above,
the sun and moon which give our light,
are your designing for our use
and our delight.

4 We praise your works, yet we ourselves
are works of wonder made by you,
not far from you in all we are
and all we do.

5 All you have made is ours to rule,
the birds and beasts at will to tame,
all things to order for the glory
of your name.

BRIAN FOLEY 1919–2000
Psalm 8

See also

370 All praise to God who reigns above
445 God moves in a mysterious way
453 Great is thy faithfulness
498 Let us with a gladsome mind
540 O Lord of heaven and earth and sea
546 O worship the King

HARVEST

270

COME, ye thankful people, come,
raise the song of harvest-home:
all be safely gathered in,
ere the winter storms begin;
God, our Maker, doth provide
for our wants to be supplied;
come to God's own temple, come;
raise the song of harvest-home!

2 All the world is God's own field,
fruit unto his praise to yield;
wheat and tares together sown,
unto joy or sorrow grown;
first the blade and then the ear,
then the full corn shall appear:
grant, O harvest Lord, that we
wholesome grain and pure may be.

3 For the Lord our God shall come,
and shall take his harvest home;
from his field shall purge away
all that doth offend, that day;
give his angels charge at last
in the fire the tares to cast,
but the fruitful ears to store
in his garner evermore.

4 Then, thou Church Triumphant, come,
raise the song of harvest-home;
all be safely gathered in,
free from sorrow, free from sin,
there for ever purified
in God's garner to abide:
come, ten thousand angels, come,
raise the glorious harvest-home!

HENRY ALFORD * 1810–1871

271

GOD, whose farm is all creation,
take the gratitude we give;
take the finest of our harvest,
crops we grow that we may live.

2 Take our ploughing, seeding, reaping,
hopes and fears of sun and rain,
all our thinking, planning, waiting,
ripened in this fruit and grain.

3 All our labour, all our watching,
all our calendar of care
in these crops of your creation,
take, O God: they are our prayer.

JOHN ARLOTT 1914–1991

272

PRAISE and thanksgiving,
Father, we offer,
for all things living
thou madest good;
harvest of sown fields,
fruits of the orchard,
hay from the mown fields,
blossom and wood.

2 Bless thou the labour
we bring to serve thee,
that with our neighbour
we may be fed.
Sowing or tilling,
we would work with thee;
harvesting, milling
for daily bread.

3 Father, providing
food for thy children,
thy wisdom guiding
teaches us share
one with another,
so that rejoicing
with us, our brother
may know thy care.

4 Then will thy blessing
reach every people;
freely confessing
thy gracious hand.
Where thy will reigneth
no one will hunger:
thy love sustaineth;
fruitful the land.

ALBERT F. BAYLY 1901–1984

273

PRAISE, O praise our God and King;
hymns of adoration sing:
For his mercies still endure
ever faithful, ever sure.

2 Praise him that he made the sun
day by day his course to run:

3 And the silver moon by night,
shining with her gentle light:

4 Praise him that he gave the rain
to mature the swelling grain:

5 And hath bid the fruitful field
crops of precious increase yield:

6 Praise him for our harvest-store;
he hath filled the garner-floor:

7 And for richer food than this,
pledge of everlasting bliss:

8 Glory to our bounteous King;
glory let creation sing:
Glory to the Father, Son,
and blest Spirit, Three in One.

H. W. BAKER 1821–1877

274

TO thee, O Lord, our hearts we raise
in hymns of adoration,
to thee bring sacrifice of praise
with shouts of exultation:
bright robes of gold the fields adorn,
the hills with joy are ringing,
the valleys stand so thick with corn
that even they are singing.

2 And now, on this our festal day,
thy bounteous hand confessing,
upon thine altar, Lord, we lay
the first-fruits of thy blessing:
by thee the hungry soul is fed
with gifts of grace supernal;
thou who dost give us earthly bread,
give us the bread eternal.

3 We bear the burden of the day,
and often toil seems dreary;
but labour ends with sunset ray,
and rest comes for the weary:
may we, the angel-reaping o'er,
stand at the last accepted,
Christ's golden sheaves for evermore
to garners bright elected.

4 O blessèd is that land of God,
where saints abide for ever;
where golden fields spread far and broad,
where flows the crystal river:
the strains of all its holy throng
with ours today are blending;
thrice blessèd is that harvest-song
which never hath an ending.

William Chatterton Dix * 1837–1898

275

WE plough the fields, and scatter
the good seed on the land,
but it is fed and watered
by God's almighty hand:
he sends the snow in winter,
the warmth to swell the grain,
the breezes, and the sunshine,
and soft, refreshing rain.
All good gifts around us
are sent from heaven above;
then thank the Lord, O thank the Lord,
for all his love.

2 He only is the maker
of all things near and far;
he paints the wayside flower,
he lights the evening star;
the winds and waves obey him,
by him the birds are fed;
much more to us, his children,
he gives our daily bread.
All good gifts ...

3 We thank thee then, O Father,
for all things bright and good,
the seed-time and the harvest,
our life, our health, our food.
Accept the gifts we offer
for all thy love imparts,
and, what thou most desirest,
our humble, thankful hearts.
All good gifts around us
are sent from heaven above;
then thank the Lord, O thank the Lord,
for all his love.

MATTHIAS CLAUDIUS 1740–1815
tr. JANE MONTGOMERY CAMPBELL 1817–1878

HOLY COMMUNION

276

ACCORDING to thy gracious word
in meek humility,
this will I do, my dying Lord,
I will remember thee.

2 Thy body, broken for my sake,
my bread from heaven shall be;
thy cup of blessing I will take,
and thus remember thee.

3 Can I Gethsemane forget
or there thy conflict see,
thine agony and bloody sweat,
and not remember thee?

4 When to the cross I turn mine eyes,
and rest on Calvary,
O Lamb of God, my sacrifice,
I must remember thee:

5 Remember thee, and all thy pains,
and all thy love to me;
yea, while a breath, a pulse remains,
will I remember thee.

6 And when these failing lips grow dumb,
and mind and memory flee,
when thou shalt in thy kingdom come,
then, Lord, remember me.

JAMES MONTGOMERY * 1771–1854

277

ALL for Jesus, all for Jesus,
this our song shall ever be;
for we have no hope, nor Saviour,
if we have not hope in thee.

2 All for Jesus, thou wilt give us
strength to serve thee, hour by hour;
none can move us from thy presence
while we trust thy love and power.

3 All for Jesus, at thine altar
thou wilt give us sweet content;
there, dear Lord, we shall receive thee
in the solemn sacrament.

4 All for Jesus, thou hast loved us;
all for Jesus, thou hast died;
all for Jesus, thou art with us;
all for Jesus crucified.

5 All for Jesus, all for Jesus,
this the church's song must be,
till, at last, we all are gathered
one in love and one in thee.

W. J. SPARROW-SIMPSON * 1859–1952

278

ALLELUIA, sing to Jesus!
his the sceptre, his the throne;
alleluia, his the triumph,
his the victory alone:
hark, the songs of peaceful Sion
thunder like a mighty flood;
Jesus out of every nation
hath redeemed us by his blood.

2 Alleluia, not as orphans
are we left in sorrow now;
alleluia, he is near us,
faith believes, nor questions how:
though the cloud from sight received him,
when the forty days were o'er,
shall our hearts forget his promise,
'I am with you evermore'?

3 Alleluia, bread of angels,
thou on earth our food, our stay;
alleluia, here the sinful
flee to thee from day to day:
Intercessor, Friend of sinners,
earth's Redeemer, plead for me,
where the songs of all the sinless
sweep across the crystal sea.

4 Alleluia, King eternal,
thee the Lord of lords we own;
alleluia, born of Mary,
earth thy footstool, heaven thy throne:
thou within the veil hast entered,
robed in flesh, our great High Priest;
thou on earth both Priest and Victim
in the eucharistic feast.

WILLIAM CHATTERTON DIX 1837–1898

279

AND now, O Father, mindful of the love
that bought us, once for all, on Calvary's tree,
and having with us him that pleads above,
we here present, we here spread forth to thee
that only offering perfect in thine eyes,
the one true, pure, immortal sacrifice.

2 Look, Father, look on his anointed face,
and only look on us as found in him;
look not on our misusings of thy grace,
our prayer so languid, and our faith so dim:
for lo, between our sins and their reward
we set the Passion of thy Son our Lord.

*3 And then for those, our dearest and our best,
by this prevailing presence we appeal:
O fold them closer to thy mercy's breast,
O do thine utmost for their souls' true weal;
from tainting mischief keep them white and clear,
and crown thy gifts with strength to persevere.

4 And so we come: O draw us to thy feet,
most patient Saviour, who canst love us still;
and by this food, so aweful and so sweet,
deliver us from every touch of ill:
in thine own service make us glad and free,
and grant us never more to part with thee.

William Bright 1824–1901

280

AS the disciples, when thy Son had left them,
met in a love-feast, joyfully conversing,
all the stored memory of the Lord's last supper
fondly rehearsing;

2 So may we here, who gather now in friendship,
seek for the spirit of those earlier churches,
welcoming him who stands and for an entrance,
patiently searches.

3 As, when their converse closed and supper ended,
taking the bread and wine they made thanksgiving,
breaking and blessing, thus to have communion
with Christ the living;

4 So may we here, a company of faithful,
make this our love-feast and commemoration,
that in his Spirit we may have more worthy
participation.

5 And as they prayed and sang to thee rejoicing,
ere in the night-fall they embraced and parted,
in their hearts singing as they journeyed homeward,
brave and true-hearted;

6 So may we here, like corn that once was scattered
over the hill-side, now one bread united,
led by the Spirit, do thy work rejoicing,
lamps filled and lighted.

PERCY DEARMER * 1867–1936

281

AUTHOR of life divine
who hast a table spread,
furnished with mystic wine
and everlasting bread,
preserve the life thyself hast given,
and feed and train us up for heaven.

2 Our needy souls sustain
with fresh supplies of love,
till all thy life we gain,
and all thy fullness prove,
and, strengthened by thy perfect grace,
behold without a veil thy face.

CHARLES WESLEY 1707–1788

282

BE known to us in breaking bread,
but do not then depart;
Saviour, abide with us, and spread
thy table in our heart.

2 There sup with us in love divine,
thy body and thy blood,
that living bread, that heavenly wine,
be our immortal food.

JAMES MONTGOMERY 1771–1854

283

BEFORE the throne of God above
I have a strong, a perfect plea:
a great High Priest, whose name is Love,
who ever lives and pleads for me.

2 My name is graven on his hands,
my name is written on his heart;
I know that while in heaven he stands
no tongue can bid me thence depart.

3 When Satan tempts me to despair,
and tells me of the guilt within,
upward I look, and see him there
who made an end of all my sin.

4 Because the sinless Saviour died,
my sinful soul is counted free;
for God, the just, is satisfied
to look on him and pardon me.

5 Behold him there! the risen Lamb!
My perfect, spotless righteousness,
the great unchangeable I AM,
the King of glory and of grace!

6 One with himself, I cannot die:
my soul is purchased by his blood;
my life is hid with Christ on high,
with Christ, my Saviour and my God.

CHARITIE DE CHENEZ 1841–1923

284

BREAD of heaven, on thee we feed,
for thy flesh is meat indeed;
ever may our souls be fed
with this true and living bread;
day by day with strength supplied
through the life of him who died.

2 Vine of heaven, thy blood supplies
this blest cup of sacrifice;
Lord, thy wounds our healing give,
to thy cross we look and live:
Jesus, may we ever be
grafted, rooted, built in thee.

JOSIAH CONDER 1789–1855

285

BREAD of the world in mercy broken,
wine of the soul in mercy shed,
by whom the words of life were spoken,
and in whose death our sins are dead:
look on the heart by sorrow broken,
look on the tears by sinners shed,
and be thy feast to us the token
that by thy grace our souls are fed!

REGINALD HEBER 1783–1826

286

BREAK thou the bread of life,
dear Lord, to me,
as thou didst break the loaves
beside the sea:
beyond the sacred page
I seek thee, Lord;
my spirit pants for thee,
O living Word!

2 Thou art the bread of life,
O Lord, to me,
thy holy word the truth
that saveth me.
Give me to eat and live
with thee above;
teach me to love thy truth,
for thou art love.

3 O send thy Spirit, Lord,
now unto me,
that he may touch my eyes,
and make me see:
show me the truth concealed
within thy word,
and in thy book revealed
I see thee, Lord.

4 Bless thou the truth, dear Lord,
to me, to me,
as thou didst bless the bread
by Galilee:
then shall all bondage cease,
all fetters fall,
and I shall find my peace,
my all in all!

vv. 1, 4 MARY LATHBURY 1841–1913
vv. 2, 3 ALEXANDER GROVES 1842–1909

287

BROKEN for me, broken for you,
the body of Jesus broken for you.

1 He offered his body, he poured out his soul,
Jesus was broken that we might be whole:
Broken for me ...

2 Come to my table and with me dine,
eat of my bread and drink of my wine:
Broken for me ...

3 This is my body given for you,
eat it remembering I died for you:
Broken for me ...

4 This is my blood I shed for you,
for your forgiveness, making you new:
Broken for me, broken for you,
the body of Jesus broken for you.

JANET LUNT *b.* 1954

288

CHRIST is the heavenly food that gives
to every famished soul
new life and strength, new joy and hope,
and faith to make them whole.

2 We all are made for God alone,
without him we are dead;
no food suffices for the soul
but Christ, the living bread.

3 Christ is the unity that binds,
in one the near and far;
for we who share his life divine
his living body are.

4 On earth and in the realms beyond
one fellowship are we;
and at his altar we are knit
in mystic unity.

TIMOTHY REES 1874–1939

289

CHRISTIAN people, raise your song,
chase away all grieving;
sing your joy and be made strong,
our Lord's life receiving;
nature's gifts of wheat and vine
now are set before us:
as we offer bread and wine
Christ comes to restore us.

2 Come to welcome Christ today,
God's great revelation;
he has pioneered the way
of the new creation.
Greet him, Christ our risen King
gladly recognizing,
as with joy we greet the spring
out of winter rising.

COLIN P. THOMPSON *b.* 1945

290

CHRISTIANS, lift your hearts and voices,
let your praises be outpoured;
come with joy and exultation
to the table of the Lord;
come believing, come expectant,
in obedience to his word.

2 See, presiding at his table,
Jesus Christ our great High Priest;
where he summons all his people,
none is greatest, none is least;
graciously he bids them welcome
to the eucharistic feast.

3 Lord, we offer in thanksgiving
life and work for you to bless;
yet unworthy is the offering,
marred by pride and carelessness;
so, Lord, pardon our transgressions,
plant in us true holiness.

4 On the evening of his passion
Jesus gave the wine and bread,
so that all who love and serve him
shall for evermore be fed.
Taste and see the Lord is gracious,
feed upon the living bread.

JOHN E. BOWERS *b.* 1923

291

COME, dearest Lord, descend and dwell
by faith and love in every breast;
then shall we know and taste and feel
the joys that cannot be expressed.

2 Come, fill our hearts with inward strength,
make our enlargèd souls possess
and learn the height and breadth and length
of thine immeasurable grace.

3 Now to the God whose power can do
more than our thoughts or wishes know,
be everlasting honours done
by all the church, through Christ his Son.

ISAAC WATTS 1674–1748
Ephesians 3. 16–21

292

COME, Holy Ghost, thine influence shed,
and realize the sign;
thy life infuse into the bread,
thy power into the wine.

2 Effectual let the tokens prove
and made, by heavenly art,
fit channels to convey thy love
to every faithful heart.

CHARLES WESLEY 1707–1788

293

COME, risen Lord, and deign to be our guest;
nay, let us be thy guests; the feast is thine;
thyself at thine own board make manifest,
in thine own sacrament of bread and wine.

2 We meet, as in that upper room they met;
thou at the table, blessing, yet dost stand:
'This is my body': so thou givest yet:
faith still receives the cup as from thy hand.

3 One body we, one body who partake,
one church united in communion blest;
one name we bear, one bread of life we break,
with all thy saints on earth and saints at rest.

4 One with each other, Lord, for one in thee,
who art one Saviour and one living Head;
then open thou our eyes, that we may see;
be known to us in breaking of the bread.

G. W. BRIGGS 1875–1959

294

DEAREST Jesu, we are here,
   at thy call, thy presence owning;
pleading now in holy fear
   that great sacrifice atoning:
Word incarnate, much in wonder
on this mystery deep we ponder.

2 Jesu, strong to save — the same
   yesterday, to-day, for ever —
make us fear and love thy name,
   serving thee with best endeavour:
in this life, O ne'er forsake us,
but to bliss hereafter take us.

G. R. WOODWARD 1848–1934
after TOBIAS CLAUSNITZER 1619–1684

295

PART ONE

DECK thyself, my soul, with gladness,
leave the gloomy haunts of sadness;
come into the daylight's splendour,
there with joy thy praises render
unto him whose grace unbounded
hath this wondrous banquet founded:
high o'er all the heavens he reigneth,
yet to dwell with thee he deigneth.

2 Now I sink before thee lowly,
filled with joy most deep and holy,
as with trembling awe and wonder
on thy mighty works I ponder:
how, by mystery surrounded,
depth no mortal ever sounded,
none may dare to pierce unbidden
secrets that with thee are hidden.

3 SUN, who all my life dost brighten,
light, who dost my soul enlighten,
joy, the sweetest heart e'er knoweth,
fount, whence all my being floweth,
at thy feet I cry, my Maker,
let me be a fit partaker
of this blessèd food from heaven,
for our good, thy glory, given.

4 Jesus, Bread of Life, I pray thee,
let me gladly here obey thee;
never to my hurt invited,
be thy love with love requited:
from this banquet let me measure,
Lord, how vast and deep its treasure;
through the gifts thou here dost give me,
as thy guest in heaven receive me.

JOHANN FRANCK 1618–1677
tr. CATHERINE WINKWORTH * 1827–1878

296

DRAW nigh and take the body of the Lord,
and drink the holy blood for you outpoured.

2 Saved by that body and that holy blood,
with souls refreshed, we render thanks to God.

3 Salvation's giver, Christ, the only Son,
by his dear cross and blood the victory won.

4 Offered was he for greatest and for least,
himself the victim, and himself the priest.

5 Approach ye then with faithful hearts sincere,
and take the pledges of salvation here.

Bangor Antiphoner c. 690
tr. J. M. NEALE * 1818–1866

297

FATHER, we adore you,
lay our lives before you:
how we love you!

2 Jesus, we adore you,
lay our lives before you:
how we love you!

3 Spirit, we adore you,
lay our lives before you:
how we love you!

TERRYE COELHO *b.* 1952

298

FATHER, we thank thee who hast planted
thy holy name within our hearts.
Knowledge and faith and life immortal
Jesus thy Son to us imparts.

2 Thou, Lord, didst make all for thy pleasure,
didst give us food for all our days,
giving in Christ the bread eternal;
thine is the power, be thine the praise.

3 Watch o'er thy church, O Lord, in mercy,
save it from evil, guard it still,
perfect it in thy love, unite it,
cleansed and conformed unto thy will.

4 As grain, once scattered on the hillsides,
was in this broken bread made one,
so from all lands thy church be gathered
into thy kingdom by thy Son.

From the *Didache,* 1st century
tr. F. BLAND TUCKER 1895–1984

299

FROM glory to glory advancing, we praise thee, O Lord;
thy name with the Father and Spirit be ever adored.
From strength unto strength we go forward
on Sion's highway,
to appear before God in the city of infinite day.

2 Thanksgiving and glory and worship and
blessing and love,
one heart and one song have the saints upon
earth and above.
Evermore, O Lord, to thy servants thy presence be nigh;
ever fit us by service on earth for thy service on high.

Liturgy of St James
tr. CHARLES W. HUMPHREYS 1840–1921

300

GLORY in the highest to the God of heaven!
Peace to all your people through the earth be given:
mighty God and Father, thanks and praise we bring,
singing alleluias to our heavenly King.

2 Jesus Christ is risen, God the Father's Son:
with the Holy Spirit, you are Lord alone!
Lamb once killed for sinners, all our guilt to bear,
show us now your mercy, now receive our prayer.

3 Christ the world's true Saviour, high and holy one,
seated now and reigning from your Father's throne:
Lord and God, we praise you; highest heaven adores:
in the Father's glory, all the praise be yours!

CHRISTOPHER M. IDLE *b.* 1938

301

GOD is here! As we his people
meet to offer praise and prayer,
may we find in fuller measure
what it is in Christ we share.
Here, as in the world around us,
all our varied skills and arts
wait the coming of his Spirit
into open minds and hearts.

2 Here are symbols to remind us
of our lifelong need of grace;
here are table, font and pulpit;
here the cross has central place.
Here in honesty of preaching,
here in silence, as in speech,
here in newness and renewal,
God the Spirit comes to each.

3 Here our children find a welcome
in the Shepherd's flock and fold,
here as bread and wine are taken,
Christ sustains us as of old.
Here the servants of the Servant
seek in worship to explore
what it means in daily living
to believe and to adore.

4 Lord of all, of Church and Kingdom,
in an age of change and doubt,
keep us faithful to the gospel,
help us work your purpose out.
Here, in this day's dedication,
all we have to give, receive:
we, who cannot live without you,
we adore you! We believe.

F. PRATT GREEN 1903–2000

302

HAIL, true Body, born of Mary,
by a wondrous virgin-birth.
Thou who on the cross wast offered
to redeem the sons of earth;

2 Thou whose side became a fountain
pouring forth thy precious blood,
give us now, and at our dying,
thine own self to be our food.

3 O sweetest Jesu,
O gracious Jesu,
O Jesu, blessèd Mary's Son.

Latin, 14th century
tr. H. N. OXENHAM 1829–1888

303

HANDS that have been handling,
holy things and high,
still, Lord, in thy service
bless and fortify.

2 Ears which heard the message
of the words of life,
keep thou closed and guarded
from the noise of strife.

3 Eyes whose contemplation
looked upon thy love,
let them gaze expectant
on the world above.

4 'Holy, Holy, Holy,'
thee our lips confessed:
on those lips for ever
let no falsehood rest.

5 Feet which trod the pavement
round about God's board,
let them walk in glory
where God's light is poured.

6 Bodies that have tasted
of the living bread,
be they re-created
in their living Head.

*7 Be we all one Body,
all our members one,
measured by the stature
of God's full-grown Son.

Adam Fox 1883–1977
based on Liturgy of Malabar

304

HERE, O my Lord, I see thee face to face;
here would I touch and handle things unseen,
here grasp with firmer hand the eternal grace,
and all my weariness upon thee lean.

2 Here would I feed upon the bread of God,
here drink with thee the royal wine of heaven;
here would I lay aside each earthly load,
here taste afresh the calm of sin forgiven.

3 Mine is the sin, but thine the righteousness;
mine is the guilt, but thine the cleansing blood;
here is my robe, my refuge, and my peace —
thy blood, thy righteousness, O Lord, my God.

4 I have no help but thine; nor do I need
another arm save thine to lean upon;
it is enough, my Lord, enough indeed;
my strength is in thy might, thy might alone.

5 Too soon we rise; the symbols disappear;
the feast, though not the love, is past and gone;
the bread and wine remove, but thou art here,
nearer than ever, still our shield and sun.

6 Feast after feast thus comes and passes by,
yet, passing, points to the glad feast above,
giving sweet foretaste of the festal joy,
the Lamb's great bridal feast of bliss and love.

HORATIUS BONAR 1808–1889

305

I COME with joy, a child of God,
forgiven, loved and free,
the life of Jesus to recall,
in love laid down for me.

2 I come with Christians far and near
to find, as all are fed,
the new community of love
in Christ's communion bread.

3 As Christ breaks bread, and bids us share,
each proud division ends.
The love that made us, makes us one,
and strangers now are friends.

4 The Spirit of the risen Christ,
unseen, but ever near,
is in such friendship better known,
alive among us here.

5 Together met, together bound
by all that God has done,
we'll go with joy, to give the world
the love that makes us one.

BRIAN A. WREN *b.* 1936

306

I HUNGER and I thirst:
  Jesu, my manna be;
ye living waters, burst
  out of the rock for me.

2 Thou bruised and broken Bread,
  my life-long wants supply;
as living souls are fed,
  O feed me, or I die.

3 Thou true life-giving Vine,
  let me thy sweetness prove;
renew my life with thine,
  refresh my soul with love.

4 Rough paths my feet have trod
  since first their course began:
feed me, thou Bread of God;
  help me, thou Son of Man.

5 For still the desert lies
  my thirsting soul before:
O living waters, rise
  within me evermore.

J. S. B. MONSELL 1811–1875

307

JESU, we thus obey
  thy last and kindest word;
here in thine own appointed way
  we come to meet thee, Lord.

2 Our hearts we open wide
  to make the Saviour room;
and lo, the Lamb, the Crucified,
  the sinner's friend, is come!

3 Thy presence makes the feast;
now let our spirits feel
the glory not to be expressed,
the joy unspeakable.

4 With high and heavenly bliss
thou dost our spirits cheer;
thy house of banqueting is this
and thou hast brought us here.

5 Now let our souls be fed
with manna from above,
and over us thy banner spread
of everlasting love.

CHARLES WESLEY * 1707–1788

308

JUST as I am, without one plea
but that thy blood was shed for me,
and that thou bidst me come to thee,
O Lamb of God, I come.

2 Just as I am, though tossed about
with many a conflict, many a doubt,
fightings and fears within, without,
O Lamb of God, I come.

3 Just as I am, poor, wretched, blind;
sight, riches, healing of the mind,
yea, all I need, in thee to find,
O Lamb of God, I come.

4 Just as I am, thou wilt receive,
wilt welcome, pardon, cleanse, relieve:
because thy promise I believe,
O Lamb of God, I come.

5 Just as I am, thy love unknown
has broken every barrier down;
now to be thine, yea, thine alone,
O Lamb of God, I come.

6 Just as I am, of that free love
the breadth, length, depth, and height to prove,
here for a season, then above,
O Lamb of God, I come.

CHARLOTTE ELLIOTT 1789–1871

309

LET all mortal flesh keep silence
and with fear and trembling stand;
ponder nothing earthly-minded,
for with blessing in his hand
Christ our God to earth descendeth,
our full homage to demand.

2 King of kings, yet born of Mary,
as of old on earth he stood,
Lord of lords, in human vesture –
in the body and the blood –
he will give to all the faithful
his own self for heavenly food.

3 Rank on rank the host of heaven
spreads its vanguard on the way,
as the Light of light descendeth
from the realms of endless day,
that the powers of hell may vanish
as the darkness clears away.

4 At his feet the six-winged seraph;
cherubim with sleepless eye
veil their faces to the Presence,
as with ceaseless voice they cry,
Alleluia, alleluia,
alleluia, Lord most high.

Liturgy of St James
tr. GERARD MOULTRIE 1829–1885
after J. M. NEALE and R. F. LITTLEDALE

310

LET thy blood in mercy poured,
let thy gracious body broken,
be to me, O gracious Lord,
of thy boundless love the token.
Thou didst give thyself for me,
now I give myself to thee.

2 Thou didst die that I might live;
blessèd Lord, thou cam'st to save me;
all that love of God could give
Jesus by his sorrows gave me.
Thou didst give ...

3 By the thorns that crowned thy brow,
by the spear-wound and the nailing,
by the pain and death, I now
claim, O Christ, thy love unfailing.
Thou didst give ...

4 Wilt thou own the gift I bring?
All my penitence I give thee;
thou art my exalted King,
of thy matchless love forgive me.
Thou didst give thyself for me,
now I give myself to thee.

JOHN BROWNLIE 1859–1925

311

LORD, enthroned in heavenly splendour
first-begotten from the dead,
thou alone, our strong defender,
liftest up thy people's head.
Alleluia, alleluia,
Jesu, true and living bread.

2 Here our humblest homage pay we,
here in loving reverence bow;
here for faith's discernment pray we,
lest we fail to know thee now.
Alleluia, alleluia,
thou art here, we ask not how.

3 Though the lowliest form doth veil thee
as of old in Bethlehem,
here as there thine angels hail thee,
branch and flower of Jesse's stem.
Alleluia, alleluia,
we in worship join with them.

4 Paschal Lamb, thine offering, finished
once for all when thou wast slain,
in its fullness undiminished
shall for evermore remain,
Alleluia, alleluia,
cleansing souls from every stain.

5 Life-imparting heavenly manna,
stricken rock with streaming side,
heaven and earth with loud hosanna
worship thee, the Lamb who died,
Alleluia, alleluia,
risen, ascended, glorified!

George Bourne 1840–1925

312

Lord Jesus Christ, be present now,
and let your Holy Spirit bow
all hearts in love and fear today
to hear the truth and keep your way.

2 Open our lips to sing your praise,
our hearts in true devotion raise,
strengthen our faith, increase our light,
that we may know your name aright.

German, anonymous
tr. Catherine Winkworth * 1827–1878

313

MY God, and is thy table spread,
  and doth thy cup with love o'erflow?
Thither be all thy children led,
  and let them all thy sweetness know.

2 Hail, sacred feast which Jesus makes,
  rich banquet of his flesh and blood!
Thrice happy he who here partakes
  that sacred stream, that heavenly food.

*3 Why are its bounties all in vain
  before unwilling hearts displayed?
Was not for them the Victim slain?
  Are they forbid the children's bread?

4 O let thy table honoured be,
  and furnished well with joyful guests;
and may each soul salvation see,
  that here its sacred pledges tastes.

PHILIP DODDRIDGE 1702–1751

314

NOW from the heavens descending
  is seen a glorious light,
the bride of Christ in splendour,
  arrayed in purest white.
She is the holy city,
  whose radiance is the grace
of all the saints in glory,
  from every time and place.

2 This is the hour of gladness
for bridegroom and for bride.
The Lamb's great feast is ready,
his bride is at his side.
How blest are those invited
to share his wedding-feast:
the least become the greatest,
the greatest are the least.

3 He who is throned in heaven
takes up his dwelling-place
among his chosen people,
who see him face to face.
No sound is heard of weeping,
for pain and sorrow cease,
and sin shall reign no longer,
but love and joy and peace.

4 See how a new creation
is brought at last to birth,
a new and glorious heaven,
a new and glorious earth.
Death's power for ever broken,
its empire swept away,
the promised dawn of glory
begins its endless day.

JAMES QUINN *b.* 1919

315

NOW let us from this table rise
renewed in body, mind and soul;
with Christ we die and rise again,
his selfless love has made us whole.

2 With minds alert, upheld by grace,
to spread the word in speech and deed,
we follow in the steps of Christ,
at one with all in hope and need.

3 To fill each human house with love,
it is the sacrament of care;
the work that Christ began to do
we humbly pledge ourselves to share.

4 Then grant us grace, Companion-God,
to choose again the pilgrim way,
and help us to accept with joy
the challenge of tomorrow's day.

FRED KAAN *b.* 1929

316

PART ONE

NOW, my tongue, the mystery telling
 of the glorious body sing,
and the blood, all price excelling,
 which the Gentiles' Lord and King,
in a Virgin's womb once dwelling,
 shed for this world's ransoming.

2 Given for us, and condescending
 to be born for us below,
he, with us in converse blending,
 dwelt the seed of truth to sow,
till he closed with wondrous ending
 his most patient life of woe.

3 That last night, at supper lying,
 'mid the Twelve, his chosen band,
Jesus, with the law complying,
 keeps the feast its rites demand;
then, more precious food supplying,
 gives himself with his own hand.

4 Word-made-flesh, true bread he maketh
by his word his flesh to be,
wine his blood; which whoso taketh
must from carnal thoughts be free:
faith alone, though sight forsaketh,
shows true hearts the mystery.

PART TWO

5 THEREFORE we, before him bending,
this great sacrament revere:
types and shadows have their ending,
for the newer rite is here;
faith, our outward sense befriending,
makes our inward vision clear.

6 Glory let us give and blessing
to the Father and the Son,
honour, might, and praise addressing,
while eternal ages run;
ever too his love confessing,
who, from both, with both is One. Amen.

ST THOMAS AQUINAS 1227–1274
tr. J. M. NEALE, EDWARD CASWALL and others

317

O FOOD to pilgrims given,
O bread of life from heaven,
O manna from on high!
We hunger; Lord, supply us,
nor thy delights deny us,
whose hearts to thee draw nigh.

2 O stream of love past telling,
O purest fountain, welling
from out the Saviour's side!
We faint with thirst; revive us,
of thine abundance give us,
and all we need provide.

3 O Jesus, by thee bidden,
we here adore thee, hidden
in forms of bread and wine.
Grant, when the veil is riven,
we may behold, in heaven,
thy countenance divine.

Latin, 17th century
tr. ATHELSTAN RILEY * 1858–1945

318

O THOU, who at thy Eucharist didst pray
that all thy church might be for ever one,
grant us at every Eucharist to say
with longing heart and soul, 'Thy will be done':
O may we all one bread, one body be,
through this blest sacrament of unity.

2 For all thy church, O Lord, we intercede;
make thou our sad divisions soon to cease;
draw us the nearer each to each, we plead,
by drawing all to thee, O Prince of Peace:
thus may we all one bread, one body be,
through this blest sacrament of unity.

3 We pray thee too for wanderers from thy fold;
O bring them back, good Shepherd of the sheep,
back to the faith which saints believed of old,
back to the church which still that faith doth keep:
soon may we all one bread, one body be,
through this blest sacrament of unity.

4 So, Lord, at length when sacraments shall cease,
may we be one with all thy church above,
one with thy saints in one unbroken peace,
one with thy saints in one unbounded love:
more blessèd still, in peace and love to be
one with the Trinity in Unity.

WILLIAM TURTON 1856–1938

319

PRAISE the Lord, rise up rejoicing,
worship, thanks, devotion voicing:
   Glory be to God on high!
Christ, your cross and passion sharing,
by this Eucharist declaring
   yours the eternal victory.

2 Scattered flock, one Shepherd sharing,
lost and lonely, one voice hearing,
   ears are open to your word;
by your blood new life receiving,
in your body firm believing,
   we are yours, and you the Lord.

3 Send us forth alert and living,
sins forgiven, wrongs forgiving,
   in your Spirit strong and free.
Finding love in all creation,
bringing peace in every nation,
   may we faithful followers be.

H. C. A. GAUNT 1902–1983

320

PRAISE we now the word of grace;
may our hearts its truth embrace:
from its pages may we hear
Christ our teacher, speaking clear.

2 May the gospel of the Lord
everywhere be spread abroad,
that the world around may own
Christ as King, and Christ alone.

S. N. SEDGWICK * 1872–1941

321

RISE and hear! The Lord is speaking,
as the gospel words unfold;
we, in all our agelong seeking,
find no firmer truth to hold.

2 Word of goodness, truth, and beauty,
heard by simple folk and wise,
word of freedom, word of duty,
word of life beyond our eyes.

3 Word of God's forgiveness granted
to the wild or guilty soul,
word of love that works undaunted,
changes, heals, and makes us whole.

4 Speak to us, O Lord, believing,
as we hear, the sower sows;
may our hearts, your word receiving,
be the good ground where it grows.

H. C. A. GAUNT * 1902–1983

322

SOUL of my Saviour, sanctify my breast,
body of Christ, be thou my saving guest,
blood of my Saviour, bathe me in thy tide,
wash me with water flowing from thy side.

2 Strength and protection may thy Passion be,
O blessèd Jesu, hear and answer me;
deep in thy wounds, Lord, hide and shelter me,
so shall I never, never part from thee.

3 Guard and defend me from the foe malign,
in death's dread moments make me only thine;
call me and bid me come to thee on high
where I may praise thee with thy saints for ay.

Latin, 14th century
tr. AUTHOR UNKNOWN

323

STRENGTHEN for service, Lord, the hands
that holy things have taken;
let ears that now have heard thy songs
to clamour never waken.

2 Lord, may the tongues which 'Holy' sang
keep free from all deceiving;
the eyes which saw thy love be bright,
thy blessèd hope perceiving.

3 The feet that tread thy holy courts
from light do thou not banish;
the bodies by thy Body fed
with thy new life replenish.

ascribed to EPHRAIM THE SYRIAN *c.* 306–373
tr. CHARLES W. HUMPHREYS 1841–1921
and PERCY DEARMER 1867–1936

324

SWEET Sacrament divine,
hid in thine earthly home,
lo, round thy lowly shrine,
with suppliant hearts we come;
Jesus, to thee our voice we raise
in songs of love and heartfelt praise:
sweet Sacrament divine.

2 Sweet Sacrament of peace,
dear home for every heart,
where restless yearnings cease
and sorrows all depart;
there in thine ear all trustfully
we tell our tale of misery:
sweet Sacrament of peace.

3 Sweet Sacrament of rest,
ark from the ocean's roar,
within thy shelter blest
soon may we reach the shore;
save us, for still the tempest raves,
save, lest we sink beneath the waves:
sweet Sacrament of rest.

4 Sweet Sacrament divine,
earth's light and jubilee,
in thy far depths doth shine
thy Godhead's majesty;
sweet light, so shine on us, we pray,
that earthly joys may fade away:
sweet Sacrament divine.

FRANCIS STANFIELD 1835–1914

325

THE church of God a kingdom is,
where Christ in power doth reign;
where spirits yearn till, seen in bliss,
their Lord shall come again.

2 Glad companies of saints possess
this church below, above;
and God's perpetual calm doth bless
their paradise of love.

3 An altar stands within the shrine
whereon, once sacrificed,
is set, immaculate, divine,
the Lamb of God, the Christ.

4 There rich and poor, from countless lands,
praise Christ on mystic rood;
there nations reach forth holy hands
to take God's holy food.

5 There pure life-giving streams o'erflow
the sower's garden-ground;
and faith and hope fair blossoms show,
and fruits of love abound.

6 O King, O Christ, this endless grace
to all thy people bring,
to see the vision of thy face
in joy, O Christ, our King.

L. B. C. L. MUIRHEAD * 1845–1925

326

PART ONE

THE heavenly Word, proceeding forth
yet leaving not the Father's side,
accomplishing his work on earth
had reached at length life's eventide.

2 By false disciple to be given
to foemen for his life athirst,
himself, the very bread of heaven,
he gave to his disciples first.

*3 He gave himself in either kind,
his precious flesh, his precious blood;
in love's own fullness thus designed
of the whole man to be the food.

*4 By birth their fellow-man was he,
their meat, when sitting at the board;
he died, their ransomer to be;
he ever reigns, their great reward.

PART TWO

5 O SAVING Victim, opening wide
the gate of heaven to man below,
our foes press on from every side:
thine aid supply, thy strength bestow.

6 All praise and thanks to thee ascend
for evermore, blest One in Three;
O grant us life that shall not end
in our true native land with thee. Amen.

St Thomas Aquinas 1227–1274
tr. J. M. Neale, Edward Caswall and others

327

THE prophets spoke in days of old
to those of stubborn will.
Their message lives and is retold
where hearts are stubborn still.

2 And Jesus told his hearers then
of love, of joy, of peace.
His message lives, he speaks again,
and sinners find release.

3 Shall we not hear that message, Lord,
to lead us on the way?
Come, Christ, make plain your saving word,
and speak to us today.

John E. Bowers *b.* 1923

328

THE Son of God proclaim,
the Lord of time and space;
the God who bade the light break forth
now shines in Jesus' face.

2 He, God's creative Word,
the church's Lord and Head,
here bids us gather as his friends
and share his wine and bread.

3 The Lord of life and death
with wond'ring praise we sing;
we break the bread at his command
and name him God and King.

4 We take this cup in hope;
for he, who gladly bore
the shameful cross, is risen again
and reigns for evermore.

BASIL E. BRIDGE *b.* 1927

329

THEE we adore, O hidden Saviour, thee
who in thy sacrament art pleased to be;
both flesh and spirit in thy presence fail,
yet here thy presence we devoutly hail.

2 O blest memorial of our dying Lord,
who living bread to us doth here afford;
O may our souls for ever feed on thee,
and thou, O Christ, for ever precious be.

3 Fountain of goodness, Jesu, Lord and God,
cleanse us, unclean, with thy most cleansing blood;
increase our faith and love, that we may know
the hope and peace which from thy presence flow.

4 O Christ, whom now beneath a veil we see,
may what we thirst for soon our portion be:
to gaze on thee unveiled, and see thy face,
the vision of thy glory and thy grace.

ST THOMAS AQUINAS 1227–1274
tr. J. R. WOODFORD 1820–1885

330

WE come to this your table, Lord,
unburdened of our sin;
and as we kneel we see again
our free salvation bought with pain
and our new birth begin.

2 We come to this your table, Lord,
unworthy of your care;
yet love unbounded floods our souls,
confirms our faith, defines our goals,
and speaks of joys to share.

3 We come to this your table, Lord,
to take the bread and wine;
we go away with thankful hearts
for all the joy this feast imparts,
for this most precious sign.

4 And far from this your table, Lord,
when anxious cares invade,
help us remember this dear place,
your mighty power, your saving grace,
your table richly laid.

PAUL WIGMORE *b.* 1925

331

WE pray thee, heavenly Father,
to hear us in thy love,
and pour upon thy children
the unction from above;
that so in love abiding,
from all defilement free,
we may in pureness offer
our Eucharist to thee.

2 Be thou our guide and helper,
O Jesus Christ, we pray;
so may we well approach thee,
if thou wilt be the Way:
thou, very Truth, hast promised
to help us in our strife,
food of the weary pilgrim,
eternal source of Life.

3 And thou, creator Spirit,
look on us, we are thine;
renew in us thy graces,
upon our darkness shine;
that, with thy benediction
upon our souls outpoured,
we may receive in gladness
the body of the Lord.

4 O Trinity of Persons,
O Unity most high,
on thee alone relying
thy servants would draw nigh:
unworthy in our weakness,
on thee our hope is stayed,
and blessed by thy forgiveness
we will not be afraid.

V. Stuckey S. Coles 1845–1929

332

WHEREFORE, O Father, we thy humble servants
here bring before thee Christ thy well-belovèd,
all-perfect offering, sacrifice immortal,
spotless oblation.

2 See now thy children, making intercession
through him our Saviour, Son of God incarnate,
for all thy people, living and departed,
pleading before thee.

William Jervois 1852–1905

333

YOU, living Christ, our eyes behold,
  amid your Church appearing,
all girt about your breast with gold
  and bright apparel wearing;
your countenance is burning bright,
a sun resplendent in its might:
  Lord Christ, we see your glory.

2 Your glorious feet have sought and found
  your own of every nation;
with everlasting voice you sound
  the call of our salvation;
your eyes of flame still search and know
the whole outspreading realm below:
  Lord Christ, we see your glory.

3 O risen Christ, today alive,
  amid your Church abiding,
who now your blood and body give,
  new life and strength providing,
we join in heavenly company
to sing your praise triumphantly,
  for we have seen your glory.

EDMUND R. MORGAN * 1888–1979
Revelation 1. 12–16

See also

408 Come to me, says Jesus
436 Glory, love, and praise, and honour
330 We come to this your table, Lord

334

AWAKE, awake: fling off the night!
For God has sent his glorious light;
and we who live in Christ's new day
must works of darkness put away.

2 Awake and rise, with love renewed,
and with the Spirit's power endued.
The light of life in us must glow,
and fruits of truth and goodness show.

3 Let in the light; all sin expose
to Christ, whose life no darkness knows.
Before his cross for guidance kneel;
his light will judge and, judging, heal.

4 Awake, and rise up from the dead,
and Christ his light on you will shed.
Its power will wrong desires destroy,
and your whole nature fill with joy.

5 Then sing for joy, and use each day;
give thanks for everything alway.
Lift up your hearts; with one accord
praise God through Jesus Christ our Lord.

J. R. Peacey 1896–1971
based on Ephesians 5. 6–20

335

COME, Lord, to our souls come down,
through the gospel speaking;
let your words, your cross and crown,
lighten all our seeking.

2 Drive out darkness from the heart,
banish pride and blindness;
plant in every inward part
truthfulness and kindness.

3 Eyes be open, spirits stirred,
minds new truth receiving;
make us, Lord, by your own word,
more and more believing.

H. C. A. GAUNT 1902–1983

336

ETERNAL God, we consecrate
these children to your care,
to you their talents dedicate,
for they your image bear.

2 To them our solemn pledge we give
their lives by prayer to shield.
May they in truth and honour live,
and to your guidance yield.

3 Your Spirit's power on them bestow,
from sin their hearts preserve;
in Christ their master may they grow,
and him for ever serve.

4 So may the waters of this rite
become a means of grace,
and these your children show the light
that shone in Jesus' face.

ROBERT DOBBIE 1901–1995

337

GOD the Father, name we treasure,
each new generation draws
from the past that you have given
for the future that is yours;
may these children, in your keeping,
love your ways, obey your laws.

2 Christ, the name that Christians carry,
Christ, who from the Father came,
calling us to share your sonship,
for these children grace we claim;
may they be your true disciples,
yours in deed as well as name.

3 Holy Spirit, from the Father
on the friends of Jesus poured,
may our children share those graces
promised to them in the word,
and their gifts find rich fulfilment,
dedicated to our Lord.

BASIL E. BRIDGE *b.* 1927

338

MY God, accept my heart this day,
and make it always thine,
that I from thee no more may stray,
no more from thee decline.

2 Before the cross of him who died,
behold, I prostrate fall;
let every sin be crucified,
and Christ be all in all.

3 Anoint me with thy heavenly grace,
and seal me for thine own;
that I may see thy glorious face,
and worship near thy throne.

4 Let every thought and work and word
to thee be ever given:
Then life shall be thy service, Lord,
and death the gate of heaven.

*5 All glory to the Father be,
all glory to the Son,
all glory, Holy Ghost, to thee,
while endless ages run.

MATTHEW BRIDGES 1800–1894

339

WE bring our children, Lord, today
as once they did in Galilee,
embrace them with your love, we pray,
and bless each home and family.

2 On their behalf and in their name
our own commitment we renew,
with them we die to sin and shame,
with them we live again in you.

3 Help us in all our ways to show
these growing souls your truth and grace,
till they shall come themselves to know
the beauty of our Father's face.

ELIZABETH COSNETT *b.* 1936

340

WE praise you, Lord, for Jesus Christ
who died and rose again;
he lives to break the power of sin,
and over death to reign.

2 We praise you that this child now shares
the freedom Christ can give,
has died to sin with Christ, and now
with Christ is raised to live.

3 We praise you, Lord, that now this child
is grafted to the vine,
is made a member of your house
and bears the cross as sign.

4 We praise you, Lord, for Jesus Christ;
he loves this child we bring:
he frees, forgives, and heals us all,
he lives and reigns as King.

JUDITH BEATRICE O'NEILL *b.* 1930

See also

365 A mighty wind invades the world
383 Be still, for the presence of the Lord
397 Christ the Way of life possess me
424 Fill thou my life, O Lord my God
470 I, the Lord of sea and sky
538 O Jesus, I have promised
575 Spirit of God, descend upon my heart
576 Spirit of holiness, wisdom and faithfulness
581 Take my life, and let it be

MARRIAGE

341

AT Cana's wedding, long ago,
they knew his presence by this sign,
a virtue none but Christ could show,
to turn their water into wine:
and still on us his blessing be
as in the days of Galilee.

2 What if the way be far to go
and life at times a weary load?
yet may our hearts within us glow
as theirs on that Emmaus road:
the risen Christ become our guest,
with him to walk, in him to rest.

3 O Lord of all our life below,
O risen Lord of realms above,
eternal joy be theirs to know,
united in the bond of love:
one in the faith, with one accord,
one with each other and the Lord.

TIMOTHY DUDLEY-SMITH *b.* 1926

342

JESUS, Lord, we pray,
be our guest today;
gospel story has recorded
how your glory was afforded
to a wedding day;
be our guest, we pray.

2 Lord of love and life,
blessing man and wife,
as they stand, their need confessing,
may your hand take theirs in blessing;
you will share their life;
bless this man and wife.

3 Lord of hope and faith,
faithful unto death,
let the ring serve as a token
of a love sincere, unbroken,
love more strong than death,
Lord of hope and faith.

BASIL E. BRIDGE *b.* 1927

343

O PERFECT Love, all human thought transcending,
lowly we kneel in prayer before thy throne,
that theirs may be the love which knows no ending,
whom thou for evermore dost join in one.

2 O perfect Life, be thou their full assurance
of tender charity and steadfast faith,
of patient hope, and quiet brave endurance,
with childlike trust that fears nor pain nor death.

3 Grant them the joy which brightens earthly sorrow,
grant them the peace which calms all earthly strife;
and to life's day the glorious unknown morrow
that dawns upon eternal love and life.

DOROTHY F. GURNEY 1858–1932

344

THE grace of life is theirs
who, on this wedding-day,
delight to make their vows,
and for each other pray.
May they, O Lord, together prove
the lasting joy of Christian love.

2 Where love is, God abides;
and God shall surely bless
a home where trust and care
give birth to happiness.
May they, O Lord, together prove
the lasting joy of such a love.

3 How slow to take offence
love is! How quick to heal!
How ready in distress
to know how others feel!
May they, O Lord, together prove
the lasting joys of such a love.

4 And when time lays its hand
on all we hold most dear,
and life, by life consumed,
fulfills its purpose here,
may we, O Lord, together prove
the lasting joy of Christian love.

F. PRATT GREEN 1903–2000 based on 1 Peter 3. 7

345

FROM thee all skill and science flow,
all pity, care, and love,
all calm and courage, faith and hope:
O pour them from above.

2 Impart them, Lord, to each and all,
as each and all shall need,
to rise, like incense, each to thee,
in noble thought and deed.

3 And hasten, Lord, that perfect day
when pain and death shall cease,
and thy just rule shall fill the earth
with health and light and peace.

CHARLES KINGSLEY * 1819–1875

346

O CHRIST, the Healer, we have come
to pray for health, to plead for friends.
How can we fail to be restored,
when reached by love that never ends?

2 From every ailment flesh endures
our bodies clamour to be freed;
yet in our hearts we would confess
that wholeness is our deepest need.

3 How strong, O Lord, are our desires,
how weak our knowledge of ourselves!
Release in us those healing truths
unconscious pride resists or shelves.

4 In conflicts that destroy our health
we diagnose the world's disease;
our common life declares our ills:
is there no cure, O Christ, for these?

5 Grant that we all, made one in faith,
in your community may find
the wholeness that, enriching us,
shall reach the whole of humankind.

F. Pratt Green 1903–2000

347

THINE arm, O Lord, in days of old
was strong to heal and save;
it triumphed o'er disease and death,
o'er darkness and the grave:
to thee they went, the deaf, the dumb,
the palsied and the lame,
the beggar with his sightless eyes,
the sick with fevered frame.

2 And lo, thy touch brought life and health,
gave speech and strength and sight;
and youth renewed and frenzy calmed
owned thee, the Lord of light:
and now, O Lord, be near to bless,
almighty as of yore,
in crowded street, by restless couch,
as by Gennesareth's shore.

3 Be thou our great deliverer still,
thou Lord of life and death;
restore and quicken, soothe and bless,
with thine almighty breath:
to hands that work, and eyes that see,
give wisdom's heavenly lore,
that whole and sick, and weak and strong,
may praise thee evermore.

E. H. Plumptre * 1821–1891

348

WE cannot measure how you heal
   or answer every sufferer's prayer,
yet we believe your grace responds
   where faith and doubt unite to care.

2 The pain that will not go away,
   the guilt that clings from things long past,
the fear of what the future holds
   are present as if meant to last.

3 But present too is love which tends
   the hurt we never hoped to find,
the private agonies inside,
   the memories that haunt the mind.

4 Your hands, though bloodied on the cross,
   survive to hold and heal and warn,
to carry all through death to life
   and cradle children yet unborn.

5 So some have come who need your help,
   and some have come to make amends:
your hands which shaped and saved the world
   are present in the touch of friends.

6 Lord, let your Spirit meet us here
   to mend the body, mind and soul,
to disentangle peace from pain
   and make your broken people whole.

JOHN BELL *b.* 1949
and GRAHAM MAULE *b.* 1958

349

WHEN to our world the Saviour came
the sick and helpless heard his name,
and in their weakness longed to see
the healing Christ of Galilee.

2 That good physician! Night and day
the people thronged about his way;
and wonder ran from soul to soul,
'The touch of Christ has made us whole!'

3 His praises then were heard and sung
by opened ears and loosened tongue,
while lightened eyes could see and know
the healing Christ of long ago.

4 Of long ago: yet living still,
who died for us on Calvary's hill;
who triumphed over cross and grave,
his healing hands stretched forth to save.

5 His sovereign purpose still remains
who rose in power, and lives and reigns;
till every tongue confess his praise,
the healing Christ of all our days.

TIMOTHY DUDLEY-SMITH *b.* 1926

See also

12 At even, ere the sun was set
475 Immortal Love for ever full
204 O God, by whose almighty plan

FUNERALS, COMMEMORATION, REMEMBRANCE and ALL SOULS

350

GIVE rest, O Christ,
to thy servant with thy saints,
where sorrow and pain are no more;
neither sighing, but life everlasting.

Thou only art immortal,
the Creator and Maker of man;
and we are mortal, formed of the earth,
and unto earth shall we return;
for so thou didst ordain
when thou createdst me, saying:
'Dust thou art, and unto dust shalt thou return.'
All we go down to the dust,
and, weeping o'er the grave we make our song:
Alleluia, alleluia, alleluia.

Give rest, O Christ,
to thy servant with thy saints,
where sorrow and pain are no more;
neither sighing, but life everlasting.

Russian
tr. W. J. Birkbeck 1869–1916

351

IN our day of thanksgiving one psalm let us offer
for the saints who before us have found their reward;
when the shadow of death fell upon them, we sorrowed,
but now we rejoice that they rest in the Lord.

2 In the morning of life, and at noon, and at even,
he called them away from our worship below;
but not till his love, at the font and the altar,
had girt them with grace for the way they should go.

3 These stones that have echoed their praises are holy,
and dear is the ground where their feet have once trod;
yet here they confessed they were strangers and pilgrims,
and still they were seeking the city of God.

4 Sing praise, then, for all who here sought and here found him,
whose journey is ended, whose perils are past:
they believed in the light; and its glory is round them,
where the clouds of earth's sorrow are lifted at last.

WILLIAM HENRY DRAPER 1855–1933

352

JESU, Son of Mary,
fount of life alone,
here we hail thee present
on thine altar-throne:
humbly we adore thee,
Lord of endless might,
in the mystic symbols
veiled from earthly sight.

2 Think, O Lord, in mercy
on the souls of those
who, in faith gone from us,
now in death repose.
Here 'mid stress and conflict
toils can never cease;
there, the warfare ended,
bid them rest in peace.

3 Often were they wounded
in the deadly strife;
heal them, Good Physician,
with the balm of life.
Every taint of evil,
frailty and decay,
good and gracious Saviour,
cleanse and purge away.

4 Rest eternal grant them,
after weary fight;
shed on them the radiance
of thy heavenly light.
Lead them onward, upward,
to the holy place,
where thy saints made perfect
gaze upon thy face.

from the Swahili
tr. E. S. PALMER 1856–1931

See also

364 A city radiant as a bride
10 Abide with me; fast falls the eventide
384 Be still, my soul
471 I to the hills will lift mine eyes
478 In heavenly love abiding
482 Jerusalem the golden
491 Jesus, these eyes have never seen
529 Nothing distress you
537 O God, our help in ages past
542 O love that wilt not let me go
565 Rock of ages, cleft for me
580 Sweet is the work, my God, my King
22 The day thou gavest, Lord, is ended
587 The God of love my shepherd is
589 The King of love my shepherd is
594 The Lord's my Shepherd

353

AND did those feet in ancient time
walk upon England's mountains green?
And was the holy Lamb of God
on England's pleasant pastures seen?
And did the countenance divine
shine forth upon our clouded hills?
And was Jerusalem builded here
among these dark satanic mills?

2 Bring me my bow of burning gold!
Bring me my arrows of desire!
Bring me my spear! O clouds, unfold!
Bring me my chariot of fire!
I will not cease from mental fight,
nor shall my sword sleep in my hand,
till we have built Jerusalem
in England's green and pleasant land.

William Blake 1757–1827

354

GOD save our gracious Queen,
long live our noble Queen,
God save the Queen.
Send her victorious,
happy and glorious,
long to reign over us:
God save the Queen.

2 Thy choicest gifts in store
on her be pleased to pour,
long may she reign.
May she defend our laws,
and ever give us cause
to sing with heart and voice,
God save the Queen.

Author Unknown *c.* 1745

355

I VOW to thee, my country, all earthly things above,
entire and whole and perfect, the service of my love:
the love that asks no question, the love that
stands the test,
that lays upon the altar the dearest and the best;
the love that never falters, the love that pays the price,
the love that makes undaunted the final sacrifice.

2 And there's another country I've heard of long ago,
most dear to them that love her, most great to
them that know;
we may not count her armies, we may not see her King;
her fortress is a faithful heart, her pride is suffering;
and soul by soul and silently her shining
bounds increase,
and her ways are ways of gentleness and all her
paths are peace.

CECIL SPRING-RICE 1859–1918

356

JUDGE eternal, throned in splendour,
Lord of lords and King of kings,
with thy living fire of judgment
purge this realm of bitter things:
solace all its wide dominion
with the healing of thy wings.

2 Still the weary folk are pining
for the hour that brings release:
and the city's crowded clangour
cries aloud for sin to cease;
and the homesteads and the woodlands
plead in silence for their peace.

3 Crown, O Lord, thine own endeavour;
cleave our darkness with thy sword;
cheer the faint and feed the hungry
with the richness of thy word;
cleanse the body of this nation
through the glory of the Lord.

HENRY SCOTT HOLLAND * 1847–1918

357

LORD of lords and King eternal,
down the years in wondrous ways
you have blessed our land and guided,
leading us through darkest days.
For your rich and faithful mercies,
Lord, accept our thankful praise.

2 Speak to us and every nation,
bid our jarring discords cease;
to the starving and the homeless
bid us bring a full release;
and on all this earth's sore turmoil
breathe the healing of your peace.

3 Love that binds us all together
be upon the church outpoured;
shame our pride and quell our factions,
smite them with your Spirit's sword;
till the world, our love beholding,
claims your power and calls you Lord.

*4 Brace the wills of all your people
who in every land and race
know the secrets of your kingdom,
share the treasures of your grace;
till the summons of your Spirit
wakes new life in every place.

5 Saviour, by your mighty Passion
once you turned sheer loss to gain,
wresting in your risen glory
victory from your cross and pain;
now O Saviour, dead and risen,
in us triumph, live, and reign.

JACK C. WINSLOW * 1882–1974

358

O GOD of earth and altar,
bow down and hear our cry,
our earthly rulers falter,
our people drift and die;
the walls of gold entomb us,
the swords of scorn divide,
take not thy thunder from us,
but take away our pride.

2 From all that terror teaches,
from lies of tongue and pen,
from all the easy speeches
that comfort cruel men,
from sale and profanation
of honour and the sword,
from sleep and from damnation,
deliver us, good Lord!

3 Tie in a living tether
the prince and priest and thrall,
bind all our lives together,
smite us and save us all;
in ire and exultation
aflame with faith, and free,
lift up a living nation,
a single sword to thee.

G. K. CHESTERTON 1874–1936

359

REJOICE, O land, in God thy might;
his will obey, him serve aright;
for thee the saints uplift their voice:
fear not, O land, in God rejoice.

2 Glad shalt thou be, with blessing crowned,
with joy and peace thou shalt abound;
yea, love with thee shall make his home
until thou see God's kingdom come.

3 He shall forgive thy sins untold:
remember thou his love of old;
walk in his way, his word adore,
and keep his truth for evermore.

ROBERT BRIDGES 1844–1930

See also

537 O God, our help in ages past

GENERAL LITURGICAL SECTION

360

FAITHFUL vigil ended,
  watching, waiting cease;
Master, grant your servant
  his discharge in peace.

2 All the Spirit promised,
  all the Father willed,
now these eyes behold it
  perfectly fulfilled.

3 This your great deliverance
sets your people free;
Christ their light uplifted
all the nations see.

4 Christ, your people's glory!
Watching, doubting cease:
grant to us your servants
our discharge in peace.

TIMOTHY DUDLEY-SMITH *b.* 1926
Luke 2. 29–32

361

GLORY be to God on high,
and peace on earth descend;
God comes down, he bows the sky,
and shows himself our friend!
God the invisible appears,
God the blest, the great I AM,
sojourns in this vale of tears,
and Jesus is his name.

2 Him the angels all adored,
their maker and their king:
tidings of their humbled Lord
they now to mortals bring:
emptied of his majesty,
of his dazzling glories shorn,
being's source begins to be,
and God himself is born!

3 See the eternal Son of God
a mortal son of man,
dwelling in an earthy clod
whom heaven cannot contain!
Stand amazed ye heavens at this!
See the Lord of earth and skies
humbled to the dust he is,
and in a manger lies!

4 We earth's children now rejoice,
the Prince of peace proclaim,
with heaven's host lift up our voice,
and shout Emmanuel's name;
knees and hearts to him we bow;
of our flesh, and of our bone,
Jesus is our brother now,
and God is all our own!

CHARLES WESLEY * 1707–1788

362

Magnificat

TELL out, my soul, the greatness of the Lord!
Unnumbered blessings, give my spirit voice;
tender to me the promise of his word;
in God my Saviour shall my heart rejoice.

2 Tell out, my soul, the greatness of his name!
Make known his might, the deeds his
arm has done;
his mercy sure, from age to age the same;
his holy name, the Lord, the mighty one.

3 Tell out, my soul, the greatness of his might!
Powers and dominions lay their glory by.
Proud hearts and stubborn wills are put to flight,
the hungry fed, the humble lifted high.

4 Tell out, my soul, the glories of his word!
Firm is his promise, and his mercy sure.
Tell out, my soul, the greatness of the Lord
to children's children and for evermore!

TIMOTHY DUDLEY-SMITH *b.* 1926
Luke 1. 46–55

363

WE believe in God the Father,
  God almighty, by whose plan
earth and heaven sprang to being,
  all created things began.
We believe in Christ the Saviour,
  Son of God in human frame,
virgin-born, the child of Mary
  upon whom the Spirit came.

2 Christ, who on the cross forsaken,
  like a lamb to slaughter led,
suffered under Pontius Pilate,
  he descended to the dead.
We believe in Jesus risen,
  heaven's king to rule and reign,
to the Father's side ascended
  till as judge he comes again.

3 We believe in God the Spirit;
  in one church, below, above:
saints of God in one communion,
  one in holiness and love.
So by faith, our sins forgiven,
  Christ our Saviour, Lord and friend,
we shall rise with him in glory
  to the life that knows no end.

TIMOTHY DUDLEY-SMITH *b.* 1926
from the Apostles' Creed

See also

450 God, we praise you, God, we bless you *Te Deum*

364

A CITY radiant as a bride
   and bright with gold and gem,
a crystal river clear and wide,
   the new Jerusalem;
a city wrought of wealth untold,
   her jewelled walls aflame
with green and amethyst and gold
   and colours none can name.

2 A holy city, clear as glass,
   where saints in glory dwell;
through gates of pearl her people pass
   to fields of asphodel.
In robes of splendour, pure and white,
   they walk the golden floor,
where God himself shall be their light
   and night shall be no more.

3 A city ever new and fair,
   the Lamb's eternal bride;
no suffering or grief is there
   and every tear is dried.
There Christ prepares for us a place,
   from sin and death restored,
and we shall stand before his face,
   the ransomed of the Lord.

TIMOTHY DUDLEY-SMITH *b.* 1926
Revelation 21

365

A MIGHTY wind invades the world,
   so strong and free on beating wing:
it is the spirit of the Lord
   from whom all truth and freedom spring.

2 The Spirit is a fountain clear
for ever leaping to the sky,
whose waters give unending life,
whose timeless source is never dry.

3 The Spirit comes in tongues of flame,
with love and wisdom burning bright:
the wind, the fountain and the fire
combine in this great feast of light.

4 O tranquil Spirit, bring us peace,
with God the Father and the Son:
we praise you, blessèd Trinity,
unchanging, and for ever One.

from Stanbrook Abbey

366

A SAFE stronghold our God is still,
a trusty shield and weapon;
he'll keep us clear from all the ill
that hath us now o'ertaken.
The ancient prince of hell
hath risen with purpose fell;
strong mail of craft and power
he weareth in this hour;
on earth is not his fellow.

2 With force of arms we nothing can,
full soon were we down-ridden;
but for us fights the proper man,
whom God himself hath bidden.
Ask ye, 'Who is this same?'
Christ Jesus is his name,
the Lord Sabaoth's Son;
he, and no other one,
shall conquer in the battle.

*3 And were this world all devils o'er,
and watching to devour us,
we lay it not to heart so sore;
not they can overpower us.
And let the prince of ill
look grim as e'er he will,
he harms us not a whit;
for why? His doom is writ;
a word shall quickly slay him.

4 God's word, for all their craft and force,
one moment will not linger,
but, spite of hell, shall have its course;
'tis written by his finger.
And though they take our life,
goods, honour, children, wife,
yet is their profit small;
these things shall vanish all:
The City of God remaineth.

MARTIN LUTHER 1483–1546
tr. THOMAS CARLYLE 1795–1881

367

ALL glory be to God on high,
his peace on earth proclaim;
to all his people tell abroad
the grace and glory of the Lord,
and bless his holy name.

2 In songs of thankfulness and praise
our hearts their homage bring
to worship him who reigns above
almighty Father, Lord of love,
our God and heavenly King.

3 O Christ, the Father's only Son,
O Lamb enthroned on high,
O Jesus, who for sinners died
and reigns at God the Father's side,
in mercy hear our cry.

4 Most high and holy is the Lord,
most high his heavenly throne;
where God the Father, God the Son,
and God the Spirit, ever One,
in glory reigns alone.

TIMOTHY DUDLEY-SMITH *b.* 1926
from *Gloria in Excelsis*

368

ALL my hope on God is founded;
he doth still my trust renew.
Me through change and chance he guideth,
only good and only true.
God unknown,
he alone
calls my heart to be his own.

2 Pride of man and earthly glory,
sword and crown betray his trust;
what with care and toil he buildeth,
tower and temple, fall to dust.
But God's power,
hour by hour,
is my temple and my tower.

3 God's great goodness aye endureth,
deep his wisdom, passing thought:
splendour, light, and life attend him,
beauty springeth out of naught.
Evermore
from his store
new-born worlds rise and adore.

4 Daily doth th' Almighty giver
bounteous gifts on us bestow;
his desire our soul delighteth,
pleasure leads us where we go.
Love doth stand
at his hand;
joy doth wait on his command.

5 Still from man to God eternal
sacrifice of praise be done,
high above all praises praising
for the gift of Christ his Son.
Christ doth call
one and all:
ye who follow shall not fall.

ROBERT BRIDGES 1844–1930
based on the German of JOACHIM NEANDER 1650–1680

369

ALL people that on earth do dwell,
sing to the Lord with cheerful voice;
him serve with fear, his praise forth tell,
come ye before him, and rejoice.

2 The Lord, ye know, is God indeed;
without our aid he did us make;
we are his folk, he doth us feed,
and for his sheep he doth us take.

3 O enter then his gates with praise,
approach with joy his courts unto;
praise, laud, and bless his name always,
for it is seemly so to do.

4 For why? The Lord our God is good;
his mercy is for ever sure;
his truth at all times firmly stood,
and shall from age to age endure.

5 To Father, Son, and Holy Ghost,
the God whom heaven and earth adore,
from men and from the angel-host
be praise and glory evermore.

WILLIAM KETHE *d.* 1594
Psalm 100 in *Anglo-Genevan Psalter* 1560

370

ALL praise to God who reigns above,
  the God of all creation,
the God of power, the God of love,
  the God of our salvation;
with healing balm my soul he fills,
and every faithless murmur stills:
  to God be praise and glory!

2 What God's almighty power hath made
  his gracious mercy keepeth;
by morning glow or evening shade
  his watchful eye ne'er sleepeth:
within the kingdom of his might
lo, all is just, and all is right:
  to God be praise and glory!

3 Then all my gladsome way along
  I sing aloud thy praises,
that all may hear the grateful song
  my voice unwearied raises:
be joyful in the Lord, my heart;
both soul and body bear your part:
  to God be praise and glory!

4 O ye who name Christ's holy name,
  give God all praise and glory:
all ye who own his power, proclaim
  aloud the wondrous story.
Cast each false idol from his throne,
the Lord is God, and he alone:
  to God be praise and glory!

JOHANN JAKOB SCHÜTZ 1640–1690
tr. FRANCES ELIZABETH COX * 1812–1897

371

ALL praise to our redeeming Lord,
who joins us by his grace,
and bids us, each to each restored,
together seek his face.

2 He bids us build each other up;
and, gathered into one,
to our high calling's glorious hope
we hand in hand go on.

3 The gift which he on one bestows,
we all delight to prove;
the grace through every vessel flows,
in purest streams of love.

4 Ev'n now we think and speak the same,
and cordially agree;
concentred all, through Jesus' name,
in perfect harmony.

5 We all partake the joy of one,
the common peace we feel,
a peace to sensual minds unknown,
a joy unspeakable.

6 And if our fellowship below
in Jesus be so sweet,
what heights of rapture shall we know
when round his throne we meet!

CHARLES WESLEY 1707–1788

372

ALL praise to thee, for thou, O King divine,
didst yield the glory that of right was thine,
that in our darkened hearts thy grace might shine:
Alleluia!

2 Thou cam'st to us in lowliness of thought;
by thee the outcast and the poor were sought,
and by thy death was God's salvation wrought:
Alleluia!

3 Let this mind be in us which was in thee,
who wast a servant that we might be free,
humbling thyself to death on Calvary:
Alleluia!

4 Wherefore, by God's eternal purpose, thou
art high exalted o'er all creatures now,
and given the name to which all knees shall bow:
Alleluia!

5 Let every tongue confess with one accord
in heaven and earth that Jesus Christ is Lord;
and God the Father be by all adored:
Alleluia!

F. Bland Tucker 1895–1984
based on Philippians 2. 5–11

373

ALL who love and serve your city,
all who bear its daily stress,
all who cry for peace and justice,
all who curse and all who bless,

*2 In your day of loss and sorrow,
in your day of helpless strife,
honour, love and peace retreating,
seek the Lord who is your life.

3 In your day of wealth and plenty,
wasted work and wasted play,
call to mind the word of Jesus,
'I must work while it is day.'

4 For all days are days of judgement,
and the Lord is waiting still
drawing near to those who spurn him,
offering peace from Calvary's hill.

5 Risen Lord! Shall still the city
be the city of despair?
Come to-day, our judge, our glory,
be its name, 'The Lord is there.'

ERIK ROUTLEY * 1917–1982

374

ALMIGHTY Father, who for us thy Son didst give,
that all the nations through his precious death might live,
in mercy guard us, lest by sloth and selfish pride
we cause to stumble those for whom the Saviour died.

2 We are thy stewards; thine our talents, wisdom, skill;
our only glory that we may thy trust fulfil;
that we thy pleasure in our neighbours' good pursue,
if thou but workest in us both to will and do.

3 On just and unjust thou thy care dost freely shower;
make us, thy children, free from greed and lust for power,
lest human justice, yoked with our unequal laws,
oppress the needy and neglect the humble cause.

4 Let not our worship blind us to the claims of love,
but let thy manna lead us to the feast above,
to seek the country which by faith we now possess,
where Christ, our treasure, reigns in peace
and righteousness.

GEORGE B. CAIRD * 1917–1984

375

AMAZING grace (how sweet the sound)
 that saved a wretch like me!
I once was lost, but now am found,
 was blind, but now I see.

2 'Twas grace that taught my heart to fear,
 and grace my fears relieved;
how precious did that grace appear
 the hour I first believed!

3 Through many dangers, toils and snares
 I have already come:
'tis grace has brought me safe thus far,
 and grace will lead me home.

4 The Lord has promised good to me,
 his word my hope secures;
he will my shield and portion be
 as long as life endures.

5 Yes, when this flesh and heart shall fail,
 and mortal life shall cease:
I shall possess, within the veil,
 a life of joy and peace.

6 The earth shall soon dissolve like snow,
 the sun forbear to shine;
but God, who called me here below,
 will be forever mine.

JOHN NEWTON 1725–1807

376

AND can it be that I should gain
 an interest in the Saviour's blood?
Died he for me, who caused his pain?
 For me, who him to death pursued?
Amazing love! How can it be
that thou, my God, shouldst die for me?

2 'Tis mystery all: the Immortal dies!
Who can explore his strange design?
In vain the first-born seraph tries
to sound the depths of love divine.
'Tis mercy all! Let earth adore,
let angel minds enquire no more.

3 He left his Father's throne above —
so free, so infinite his grace —
emptied himself of all but love,
and bled for Adam's helpless race.
'Tis mercy all, immense and free;
for, O my God, it found out me!

4 Long my imprisoned spirit lay
fast bound in sin and nature's night;
thine eye diffused a quickening ray;
I woke, the dungeon flamed with light;
my chains fell off, my heart was free,
I rose, went forth, and followed thee.

5 No condemnation now I dread;
Jesus, and all in him, is mine!
Alive in him, my living Head,
and clothed in righteousness divine,
bold I approach the eternal throne,
and claim the crown, through Christ, my own.

CHARLES WESLEY 1707–1788

377

ANGEL-VOICES ever singing
round thy throne of light,
angel-harps for ever ringing,
rest not day nor night;
thousands only live to bless thee
and confess thee
Lord of might.

2 Thou who art beyond the farthest
mortal eye can scan,
can it be that thou regardest
songs of sinful man?
Can we know that thou art near us,
and wilt hear us?
Yea, we can.

3 Yea, we know that thou rejoicest
o'er each work of thine;
thou didst ears and hands and voices
for thy praise design;
craftsman's art and music's measure
for thy pleasure
all combine.

4 In thy house, great God, we offer
of thine own to thee;
and for thine acceptance proffer
all unworthily
hearts and minds and hands and voices
in our choicest
psalmody.

5 Honour, glory, might, and merit
thine shall ever be,
Father, Son, and Holy Spirit,
blessèd Trinity.
Of the best that thou hast given
earth and heaven
render thee.

FRANCIS POTT 1832–1909

378

AS Jacob with travel was weary one day,
at night on a stone for a pillow he lay;
he saw in a vision a ladder so high
that its foot was on earth and its top in the sky:
Alleluia to Jesus who died on the tree,
and has raised up a ladder of mercy for me!

2 This ladder is long, it is strong and well-made,
has stood hundreds of years and is not yet decayed;
many millions have climbed it and reached Sion's hill;
by faith many millions are climbing it still:

3 Come let us ascend! All may climb it who will;
for the angels of Jacob are guarding it still:
and remember, each step that by faith we pass o'er,
some prophet or martyr has trod it before:

4 And when we arrive at the haven of rest
we shall hear the glad words, 'Come up hither, ye blest,
here are regions of light, here are mansions of bliss'.
O who would not climb such a ladder as this?
Alleluia to Jesus who died on the tree,
and has raised up a ladder of mercy for me!

18th century

379

AS pants the hart for cooling streams
when heated in the chase,
so longs my soul, O God, for thee,
and thy refreshing grace.

2 For thee, my God, the living God,
my thirsty soul doth pine:
O when shall I behold thy face,
thou majesty divine?

3 Why restless, why cast down, my soul?
Hope still, and thou shalt sing
the praise of him who is thy God,
thy health's eternal spring.

4 To Father, Son, and Holy Ghost,
the God whom we adore,
be glory, as it was, is now,
and shall be evermore.

NAHUM TATE 1652–1715
and NICHOLAS BRADY 1659–1726
Psalm 42 in *A New Version of the Psalms of David* 1696

380

AT the name of Jesus
every knee shall bow,
every tongue confess him
King of glory now:
'tis the Father's pleasure
we should call him Lord,
who from the beginning
was the mighty Word.

*2 At his voice creation
sprang at once to sight,
all the angel faces,
all the hosts of light,
thrones and dominations,
stars upon their way,
all the heavenly orders,
in their great array.

3 Humbled for a season,
to receive a name
from the lips of sinners
unto whom he came,
faithfully he bore it
spotless to the last,
brought it back victorious,
when from death he passed:

*4 Bore it up triumphant
with its human light,
through all ranks of creatures,
to the central height,
to the throne of Godhead,
to the Father's breast;
filled it with the glory,
of that perfect rest.

5 Name him, Christians, name him,
with love strong as death,
but with awe and wonder
and with bated breath:
he is God the Saviour,
he is Christ the Lord,
ever to be worshipped,
trusted, and adored.

*6 In your hearts enthrone him;
there let him subdue
all that is not holy,
all that is not true:
crown him as your Captain
in temptation's hour;
let his will enfold you
in its light and power.

7 Surely, this Lord Jesus
shall return again,
with his Father's glory,
with his angel train;
for all wreaths of empire
meet upon his brow,
and our hearts confess him
King of glory now.

CAROLINE M. NOEL * 1817–1877

381

AUTHOR of faith, eternal Word,
whose Spirit breathes the active flame;
faith, like its finisher and Lord,
today as yesterday the same:

2 To thee our humble hearts aspire,
and ask the gift unspeakable;
increase in us the kindled fire,
in us the work of faith fulfil.

3 By faith we know thee strong to save —
save us, a present Saviour thou!
Whate'er we hope, by faith we have,
future and past subsisting now.

4 The things unknown to feeble sense,
unseen by reason's glimmering ray,
with strong, commanding evidence
their heav'nly origin display.

5 Faith lends its realizing light,
the clouds disperse, the shadows fly;
the Invisible appears in sight,
and God is seen by mortal eye.

CHARLES WESLEY 1707–1788

382

AWAKE, our souls; away, our fears;
let every trembling thought be gone;
awake and run the heavenly race,
and put a cheerful courage on.

2 True, 'tis a strait and thorny road,
and mortal spirits tire and faint;
but they forget the mighty God
that feeds the strength of every saint:

3 The mighty God, whose matchless power
is ever new and ever young,
and firm endures, while endless years
their everlasting circles run.

4 From thee, the overflowing spring,
our souls shall drink a fresh supply,
while such as trust their native strength
shall melt away, and droop, and die.

5 Swift as an eagle cuts the air,
we'll mount aloft to thine abode;
on wings of love our souls shall fly,
nor tire amidst the heavenly road.

ISAAC WATTS 1674–1748
Isaiah 40. 28–31

383

BE still, for the presence of the Lord, the Holy One, is here.
Come, bow before him now, with reverence and fear.
In him no sin is found, we stand on holy ground.
Be still, for the presence of the Lord, the Holy One, is here.

2 Be still, for the glory of the Lord is shining all around;
he burns with holy fire, with splendour he is crowned.
How awesome is the sight, our radiant King of light!
Be still, for the glory of the Lord is shining all around.

3 Be still, for the power of the Lord is moving in this place,
he comes to cleanse and heal, to minister his grace.
No work too hard for him, in faith receive from him;
be still, for the power of the Lord is moving in this place.

DAVID J. EVANS *b.* 1957

384

BE still, my soul: the Lord is on your side;
bear patiently the cross of grief and pain;
leave to your God to order and provide;
in every change he faithful will remain.
Be still, my soul: your best, your heavenly friend
through thorny ways leads to a joyful end.

2 Be still, my soul: your God will undertake
to guide the future as he has the past.
Your hope, your confidence let nothing shake,
all now mysterious shall be clear at last.
Be still, my soul: the waves and winds still know
his voice, who ruled them while he dwelt below.

3 Be still, my soul: when dearest friends depart
and all is darkened in the vale of tears,
then you shall better know his love, his heart,
who comes to soothe your sorrow, calm your fears.
Be still, my soul: for Jesus can repay
from his own fullness all he takes away.

4 Be still, my soul: the hour is hastening on
when we shall be for ever with the Lord,
when disappointment, grief and fear are gone,
sorrow forgotten, love's pure joy restored.
Be still, my soul: when change and tears are past,
all safe and blessèd we shall meet at last.

KATHARINA VON SCHLEGEL *b.* 1697
tr. JANE LAURIE BORTHWICK * 1813–1897

385

BE thou my guardian and my guide,
and hear me when I call;
let not my slippery footsteps slide,
and hold me lest I fall.

2 The world, the flesh, and Satan dwell
around the path I tread;
O save me from the snares of hell,
thou quickener of the dead.

3 And if I tempted am to sin,
and outward things are strong,
do thou, O Lord, keep watch within,
and save my soul from wrong.

4 Still let me ever watch and pray,
and feel that I am frail;
that if the tempter cross my way,
yet he may not prevail.

ISAAC WILLIAMS 1802–1865

386

BE thou my vision, O Lord of my heart,
be all else but naught to me, save that thou art;
be thou my best thought in the day and the night,
both waking and sleeping, thy presence my light.

2 Be thou my wisdom, be thou my true word,
be thou ever with me, and I with thee, Lord;
be thou my great Father, and I thy true son;
be thou in me dwelling, and I with thee one.

3 Be thou my breastplate, my sword for the fight;
be thou my whole armour, be thou my true might;
be thou my soul's shelter, be thou my strong tower:
O raise thou me heavenward, great Power of my power.

4 Riches I heed not, nor man's empty praise:
be thou mine inheritance now and always;
be thou and thou only the first in my heart;
O Sovereign of heaven, my treasure thou art.

5 High King of heaven, thou heaven's bright Sun,
O grant me its joys after vict'ry is won;
great Heart of my own heart, whatever befall,
still be thou my vision, O Ruler of all.

Irish, 8th century, *tr.* MARY BYRNE 1880–1931
versified ELEANOR HULL 1860–1935

387

BEFORE Jehovah's aweful throne,
ye nations, bow with sacred joy;
know that the Lord is God alone:
he can create, and he destroy.

2 His sovereign power, without our aid,
made us of clay, and formed us then;
and, when like wandering sheep we strayed,
he brought us to his fold again.

3 We'll crowd thy gates with thankful songs,
high as the heavens our voices raise;
and earth, with her ten thousand tongues,
shall fill thy courts with sounding praise.

4 Wide as the world is thy command,
vast as eternity thy love;
firm as a rock thy truth must stand,
when rolling years shall cease to move.

ISAAC WATTS * 1674–1748
Psalm 100

388

BEGIN, my tongue, some heavenly theme;
awake, my voice, and sing
the mighty works, or mightier name,
of our eternal King.

2 Tell of his wondrous faithfulness,
and sound his power abroad;
sing the sweet promise of his grace,
the quickening word of God.

3 Engraved as in eternal brass,
the mighty promise shines;
nor can the powers of darkness rase
those everlasting lines.

4 His every word of grace is strong
as that which built the skies;
the voice that rolls the stars along
speaks all the promises.

5 Now shall my leaping heart rejoice
to know thy favour sure:
I trust the all-creating voice,
and faith desires no more.

Isaac Watts * 1674–1748

389

BEHOLD the amazing gift of love
the Father has bestowed
on us, the sinful sons of men,
to call us sons of God!

2 Concealed as yet this honour lies,
by this dark world unknown,
a world that knew not when he came,
ev'n God's eternal Son.

3 High is the rank we now possess;
but higher we shall rise,
though what we shall hereafter be
is hid from mortal eyes.

4 Our lives, we know, when he appears,
shall bear his image bright;
for all his glory, full disclosed,
shall open to our sight.

5 A hope so great and so divine
may trials well endure;
and purify us all from sin,
as Christ himself is pure.

Scottish Paraphrases 1781 *
based on 1 John 3. 1–3

390

BLESSÈD assurance, Jesus is mine:
O what a foretaste of glory divine!
Heir of salvation, purchase of God;
born of his Spirit, washed in his blood:
This is my story, this is my song,
praising my Saviour all the day long.

2 Perfect submission, perfect delight,
visions of rapture burst on my sight;
angels descending bring from above
echoes of mercy, whispers of love:
This is my story ...

3 Perfect submission, all is at rest,
I in my Saviour am happy and blest —
watching and waiting, looking above,
filled with his goodness, lost in his love:
This is my story, this is my song,
praising my Saviour all the day long.

FANNY CROSBY
(FRANCES JANE VAN ALSTYNE) 1820–1915

391

BLEST are the pure in heart,
for they shall see our God;
the secret of the Lord is theirs,
their soul is Christ's abode.

2 The Lord, who left the heavens
our life and peace to bring,
to dwell in lowliness with men,
their pattern and their King;

3 Still to the lowly soul
he doth himself impart,
and for his dwelling and his throne
chooseth the pure in heart.

4 Lord, we thy presence seek;
may ours this blessing be;
give us a pure and lowly heart,
a temple meet for thee.

JOHN KEBLE 1792–1866 and others

392

BRIGHT the vision that delighted
once the sight of Judah's seer;
sweet the countless tongues united
to entrance the prophet's ear.

2 Round the Lord in glory seated
cherubim and seraphim
filled his temple, and repeated
each to each the alternate hymn:

3 'Lord, thy glory fills the heaven;
earth is with its fullness stored;
unto thee be glory given,
holy, holy, holy, Lord.'

4 Heaven is still with glory ringing,
earth takes up the angels' cry,
'Holy, holy, holy,' singing,
'Lord of hosts, the Lord most high.'

5 With his seraph train before him,
with his holy church below,
thus unite we to adore him,
bid we thus our anthem flow:

6 'Lord, thy glory fills the heaven;
earth is with its fullness stored;
unto thee be glory given,
holy, holy, holy, Lord.'

RICHARD MANT 1776–1848
based on Isaiah 6

393

BROTHER, sister, let me serve you,
let me be as Christ to you;
pray that I may have the grace to
let you be my servant too.

2 We are pilgrims on a journey
and companions on the road;
we are here to help each other
walk the mile and bear the load.

3 I will hold the Christ-light for you
in the night-time of your fear;
I will hold my hand out to you,
speak the peace you long to hear.

4 I will weep when you are weeping;
when you laugh I'll laugh with you;
I will share your joy and sorrow
till we've seen this journey through.

5 When we sing to God in heaven
we shall find such harmony,
born of all we've known together
of Christ's love and agony.

6 Brother, sister, let me serve you,
let me be as Christ to you;
pray that I may have the grace to
let you be my servant too.

RICHARD GILLARD *b.* 1953

394

CHRIST for the world we sing!
The world to Christ we bring
with fervent prayer;
the wayward and the lost,
by restless passions tossed,
redeemed at countless cost
from dark despair.

2 Christ for the world we sing!
The world to Christ we bring
with one accord;
with us the work to share,
with us reproach to dare,
with us the cross to bear,
for Christ our Lord.

3 Christ for the world we sing!
The world to Christ we bring
with joyful song;
the new-born souls, whose days,
reclaimed from error's ways,
inspired with hope and praise,
to Christ belong.

SAMUEL WOLCOTT 1813–1886

395

CHRIST is our corner-stone,
on him alone we build;
with his true saints alone
the courts of heaven are filled:
on his great love
our hopes we place
of present grace
and joys above.

2 O then with hymns of praise
these hallowed courts shall ring;
our voices we will raise
the Three in One to sing;
and thus proclaim
in joyful song,
both loud and long,
that glorious name.

3 Here, gracious God, do thou
for evermore draw nigh;
accept each faithful vow,
and mark each suppliant sigh;
in copious shower
on all who pray
each holy day
thy blessings pour.

4 Here may we gain from heaven
the grace which we implore;
and may that grace, once given,
be with us evermore,
until that day
when all the blest
to endless rest
are called away.

Latin, before 9th century
tr. JOHN CHANDLER 1806–1876

396

CHRIST is the world's true light,
its captain of salvation,
the daystar clear and bright
of every land and nation;
new life, new hope awakes,
where peoples own his sway:
freedom her bondage breaks,
and night is turned to day.

2 In Christ all races meet,
their ancient feuds forgetting,
the whole round world complete,
from sunrise to its setting:
when Christ is throned as Lord,
lands shall forsake their fear,
to ploughshare beat the sword,
to pruning-hook the spear.

3 One Lord, in one great name
unite us all who own thee;
cast out our pride and shame
that hinder to enthrone thee;
the world has waited long,
has travailed long in pain;
to heal its ancient wrong,
come, Prince of peace, and reign!

G. W. Briggs 1875–1959

397

CHRIST the Way of life possess me,
lift my heart to love and praise;
guide and keep, sustain and bless me,
all my days.

2 Well of life, for ever flowing,
make my barren soul and bare
like a watered garden growing
fresh and fair.

3 May the Tree of life in splendour
from its leafy boughs impart
grace divine and healing tender,
strength of heart.

4 Path of life before me shining,
let me come when earth is past,
sorrow, self and sin resigning,
home at last.

Timothy Dudley-Smith *b.* 1926

398

CHRIST triumphant, ever reigning,
Saviour, Master, King!
Lord of heaven, our lives sustaining,
hear us as we sing:
Yours the glory and the crown,
the high renown, the eternal name!

2 Word incarnate, truth revealing,
Son of Man on earth!
power and majesty concealing
by your humble birth:
Yours the glory ...

3 Suffering servant, scorned, ill-treated,
victim crucified!
death is through the cross defeated,
sinners justified:
Yours the glory ...

4 Priestly king, enthroned for ever
high in heaven above!
sin and death and hell shall never
stifle hymns of love:
Yours the glory ...

5 So, our hearts and voices raising
through the ages long,
ceaselessly upon you gazing,
this shall be our song:
Yours the glory and the crown,
the high renown, the eternal name!

MICHAEL SAWARD *b.* 1932

399

CHRISTIANS, lift up your hearts,
and make this a day of rejoicing;
God is our strength and song;
glory and praise to his name!

2 Praise for the Spirit of God,
who came to the waiting disciples;
there in the wind and the fire
God gave new life to his own:

3 God's mighty power was revealed
when those who once were so fearful
now could be seen by the world
witnessing bravely for Christ:

*4 Praise that his love overflowed
in the hearts of all who received him,
joining together in peace
those once divided by sin:

*5 Strengthened by God's mighty power
the disciples went out to all nations,
preaching the gospel of Christ,
laughing at danger and death:

6 Come, Holy Spirit, to us,
who live by your presence within us,
come to direct our course,
give us your life and your power:

7 Spirit of God, send us out
to live to your praise and your glory;
yours is the power and the might,
ours be the courage and faith:

Christians, lift up your hearts,
and make this a day of rejoicing;
God is our strength and song;
glory and praise to his name!

JOHN E. BOWERS *b.* 1923

400

CITY of God, how broad and far
  outspread thy walls sublime!
The true thy chartered freemen are
  of every age and clime:

2 One holy church, one army strong,
  one steadfast, high intent;
one working band, one harvest-song,
  one King omnipotent.

3 How purely hath thy speech come down
  from man's primaeval youth!
How grandly hath thine empire grown
  of freedom, love, and truth!

4 How gleam thy watch-fires through the night
  with never-fainting ray!
How rise thy towers, serene and bright,
  to meet the dawning day!

5 In vain the surge's angry shock,
  in vain the drifting sands:
unharmed upon the eternal Rock
  the eternal city stands.

SAMUEL JOHNSON 1822–1882

401

COME, let us join our cheerful songs
  with angels round the throne;
ten thousand thousand are their tongues,
  but all their joys are one.

2 'Worthy the Lamb that died,' they cry,
  'to be exalted thus';
'Worthy the Lamb,' our lips reply,
  'for he was slain for us.'

3 Jesus is worthy to receive
honour and power divine;
and blessings, more than we can give,
be, Lord, for ever thine.

4 Let all that dwell above the sky,
and air, and earth, and seas,
conspire to lift thy glories high,
and speak thine endless praise.

5 The whole creation joins in one
to bless the sacred name
of him that sits upon the throne,
and to adore the Lamb.

Isaac Watts * 1674–1748
Revelation 5. 11–13

402

COME, let us to the Lord our God
with contrite hearts return;
our God is gracious, nor will leave
the desolate to mourn.

2 His voice commands the tempest forth,
and stills the stormy wave;
and though his arm be strong to smite,
'tis also strong to save.

3 Long has the night of sorrow reigned;
the dawn shall bring us light;
God shall appear, and we shall rise
with gladness in his sight.

4 Our hearts, if God we seek to know,
shall know him and rejoice;
his coming like the morn shall be,
like morning songs his voice.

5 As dew upon the tender herb,
diffusing fragrance round;
as showers that usher in the spring,
and cheer the thirsty ground:

6 So shall his presence bless our souls,
and shed a joyful light;
that hallowed morn shall chase away
the sorrows of the night.

JOHN MORISON 1750–1798
based on Hosea 6. 1–4

403

COME, living God, when least expected,
when minds are dull and hearts are cold,
through sharpening word and warm affection
revealing truth as yet untold.

2 Break from the tomb in which we hide you
to speak again in startling ways;
break through the words in which we bind you
to resurrect our lifeless praise.

3 Come now, as once you came to Moses
within the bush alive with flame;
or to Elijah on the mountain,
by silence pressing home your claim.

4 So, let our minds be sharp to read you
in sight or sound or printed page,
and let us greet you in our neighbours,
in ardent youth or mellow age.

5 Then, through our gloom, your Son will meet us
as vivid truth and living Lord,
exploding doubt and disillusion
to scatter hope and joy abroad.

6 Then we will share his radiant brightness,
and, blazing through the dread of night,
illuminate by love and reason,
for those in darkness, faith's delight.

ALAN GAUNT *b.* 1935

404

COME, my soul, thy suit prepare:
Jesus loves to answer prayer;
he himself has bid thee pray,
therefore will not say thee nay.

2 Thou art coming to a King:
large petitions with thee bring;
for his grace and power are such,
none can ever ask too much.

3 With my burden I begin:
Lord, remove this load of sin;
let thy blood, for sinners spilt,
set my conscience free from guilt.

4 Lord, I come to thee for rest;
take possession of my breast;
there thy blood-bought right maintain,
and without a rival reign.

5 While I am a pilgrim here,
let thy love my spirit cheer;
be my guide, my guard, my friend,
lead me to my journey's end.

JOHN NEWTON 1725–1807

405

COME my way, my truth, my life:
such a way, as gives us breath;
such a truth, as ends all strife;
such a life, as killeth death.

2 Come, my light, my feast, my strength:
such a light, as shows a feast;
such a feast, as mends in length;
such a strength, as makes his guest.

3 Come, my joy, my love, my heart:
such a joy, as none can move;
such a love, as none can part;
such a heart, as joys in love.

George Herbert 1593–1633

406

COME, thou fount of every blessing,
tune my heart to sing thy grace;
streams of mercy never ceasing
call for songs of loudest praise.
Teach me some melodious measure
sung by flaming tongues above;
O the vast, the boundless treasure
of my Lord's unchanging love!

2 Here I find my greatest treasure:
hither by thy help I've come,
and I hope, by thy good pleasure,
safely to arrive at home.
Jesus sought me when a stranger,
wandering from the fold of God;
he, to rescue me from danger,
interposed his precious blood.

3 O to grace how great a debtor
daily I'm constrained to be!
Let that grace, Lord, like a fetter,
bind my wandering heart to thee.
Prone to wander, Lord, I feel it,
prone to leave the God I love;
take my heart, O take and seal it,
seal it from thy courts above!

Robert Robinson * 1735–1790

407

COME, O thou Traveller unknown,
  whom still I hold, but cannot see;
my company before is gone,
  and I am left alone with thee;
with thee all night I mean to stay,
and wrestle till the break of day.

2 I need not tell thee who I am,
  my misery or sin declare;
thyself hast called me by my name;
  look on thy hands, and read it there!
But who, I ask thee, who art thou?
Tell me thy name, and tell me now.

3 In vain thou strugglest to get free;
  I never will unloose my hold.
Art thou the man that died for me?
  The secret of thy love unfold:
wrestling, I will not let thee go,
till I thy name, thy nature know.

4 Yield to me now, for I am weak,
  but confident in self-despair;
speak to my heart, in blessings speak,
  be conquered by my instant prayer.
Speak, or thou never hence shalt move,
and tell me if thy name is Love!

5 'Tis Love! 'tis Love! Thou diedst for me!
  I hear thy whisper in my heart!
The morning breaks, the shadows flee;
  pure universal Love thou art:
to me, to all, thy mercies move;
thy nature and thy name is Love.

Charles Wesley 1707–1788
Genesis 32. 24-30

408

'COME to me,' says Jesus,
   'all who are distressed;
take my yoke upon you,
   I will give you rest.

2 I am meek and humble,
   find, with me, release
from false airs and graces;
   come, and be at peace.'

3 Hear the call of Jesus,
   come, be deeply blessed;
his the invitation,
   you the honoured guest.

4 Here, where bread is broken,
   here, where wine is poured,
thankfully receive him,
   find your faith restored.

5 Pardon, feed and heal us,
   humble, courteous Lord,
gracious host, for ever
   honoured and adored.

ALAN GAUNT *b.* 1935

409

COME, ye faithful, raise the anthem,
   cleave the skies with shouts of praise;
sing to him who found the ransom,
   Ancient of eternal Days,
God of God, the Word incarnate,
   whom the heaven of heaven obeys.

2 Ere he raised the lofty mountains,
formed the seas, or built the sky,
love eternal, free, and boundless,
moved the Lord of life to die,
fore-ordained the Prince of princes
for the throne of Calvary.

3 There, for us and our redemption,
see him all his life-blood pour!
There he wins our full salvation,
dies that we may die no more;
then, arising, lives for ever,
reigning where he was before.

4 High on yon celestial mountains
stands his sapphire throne, all bright,
midst unending alleluias
bursting from the sons of light;
Zion's people tell his praises,
victor after hard-won fight.

*5 Bring your harps, and bring your incense,
sweep the string and pour the lay;
let the earth proclaim his wonders,
King of that celestial day;
he the Lamb once slain is worthy,
who was dead, and lives for ay.

*6 Laud and honour to the Father,
laud and honour to the Son,
laud and honour to the Spirit,
ever Three and ever One,
consubstantial, co-eternal,
while unending ages run.

J. Hupton 1762–1849
and J. M. Neale * 1818–1866

410

CREATOR of the earth and skies,
to whom the words of life belong,
grant us thy truth to make us wise;
grant us thy power to make us strong.

2 Like theirs of old, our life is death,
our light is darkness, till we see
the eternal Word made flesh and breath,
the God who walked by Galilee.

3 We have not known thee: to the skies
our monuments of folly soar,
and all our self-wrought miseries
have made us trust ourselves the more.

4 We have not loved thee: far and wide
the wreckage of our hatred spreads,
and evils wrought by human pride
recoil on unrepentant heads.

5 For this, our foolish confidence,
our pride of knowledge and our sin,
we come to thee in penitence;
in us the work of grace begin.

6 Teach us to know and love thee, Lord,
and humbly follow in thy way.
Speak to our souls the quickening word
and turn our darkness into day.

DONALD WYNN HUGHES 1911–1967

411

DEAR Lord and Father of mankind,
forgive our foolish ways;
re-clothe us in our rightful mind,
in purer lives thy service find,
in deeper reverence praise.

2 In simple trust like theirs who heard,
beside the Syrian sea,
the gracious calling of the Lord,
let us, like them, without a word
rise up and follow thee.

*3 O Sabbath rest by Galilee!
O calm of hills above,
where Jesus knelt to share with thee
the silence of eternity,
interpreted by love!

4 Drop thy still dews of quietness,
till all our strivings cease;
take from our souls the strain and stress,
and let our ordered lives confess
the beauty of thy peace.

5 Breathe through the heats of our desire
thy coolness and thy balm;
let sense be dumb, let flesh retire;
speak through the earthquake, wind, and fire,
O still small voice of calm.

JOHN GREENLEAF WHITTIER 1807–1892

412

DEAR Lord, we long to see your face,
to know you risen from the grave,
but we have missed the joy and grace
of seeing you, as others have;
yet in your company we'll wait,
and we shall see you, soon or late.

2 Dear Friend, we do not know the way,
nor clearly see the path ahead,
so often, therefore, we delay
and doubt your power to raise the dead;
yet with you we will firmly stay —
you are the Truth, the Life, the Way.

3 We find it hard, Lord, to believe.
Long habit makes us want to prove:
to see, to touch, and thus perceive
the truth and person whom we love;
yet, as in fellowship we meet,
you come yourself, each one to greet.

4 You come to us, our God, our Lord.
You do not show your hands and side,
but give, instead, your best reward
as in your promise we abide.
By faith we know, and grow, and wait
to see and praise you, soon or late.

J. R. PEACEY 1896–1971

413

ETERNAL Father, strong to save,
whose arm hath bound the restless wave,
who bidd'st the mighty ocean deep
its own appointed limits keep:
O hear us when we cry to thee
for those in peril on the sea.

2 O Christ, whose voice the waters heard
and hushed their raging at thy word,
who walkedst on the foaming deep,
and calm amid the storm didst sleep:
O hear us when we cry to thee
for those in peril on the sea.

3 O Holy Spirit, who didst brood
upon the waters dark and rude,
and bid their angry tumult cease,
and give, for wild confusion, peace:
O hear us when we cry to thee
for those in peril on the sea.

4 O Trinity of love and power,
our brethren shield in danger's hour;
from rock and tempest, fire and foe,
protect them wheresoe'er they go:
thus evermore shall rise to thee
glad hymns of praise from land and sea.

William Whiting 1825–1878

414

ETERNAL Light! Eternal Light!
How pure the soul must be,
when, placed within thy searching sight,
it shrinks not, but with calm delight
can live and look on thee.

2 The spirits that surround thy throne
may bear the burning bliss;
but that is surely theirs alone,
since they have never, never known
a fallen world like this.

3 O how shall I, whose native sphere
is dark, whose mind is dim,
before the Ineffable appear,
and on my naked spirit bear
the uncreated beam?

4 There is a way for us to rise
to that sublime abode:
an offering and a sacrifice,
a Holy Spirit's energies,
an Advocate with God:

5 These, these prepare us for the sight
of holiness above;
the sons of ignorance and night
may dwell in the eternal light
through the eternal Love!

Thomas Binney 1798–1874

415

ETERNAL light, shine in my heart;
eternal hope, lift up my eyes;
eternal power, be my support;
eternal wisdom, make me wise.

2 Eternal life, raise me from death;
eternal brightness, make me see;
eternal Spirit, give me breath;
eternal Saviour, come to me:

3 Until by your most costly grace,
invited by your holy word,
at last I come before your face
to know you, my eternal God.

CHRISTOPHER M. IDLE *b.* 1938

416

FATHER, hear the prayer we offer:
not for ease that prayer shall be,
but for strength that we may ever
live our lives courageously.

2 Not for ever in green pastures
do we ask our way to be;
but the steep and rugged pathway
may we tread rejoicingly.

3 Not for ever by still waters
would we idly rest and stay;
but would smite the living fountains
from the rocks along our way.

4 Be our strength in hours of weakness,
in our wanderings be our guide;
through endeavour, failure, danger,
Father, be thou at our side.

LOVE MARIA WILLIS 1824–1908

417

FATHER in whom we live,
in whom we are and move,
the glory, power, and praise receive
of thy creating love.
Let all the angel throng
give thanks to God on high,
while earth repeats the joyful song,
and echoes to the sky.

2 Incarnate Deity,
let all the ransomed race
render in thanks their lives to thee
for thy redeeming grace.
The grace to sinners showed
ye heavenly choirs proclaim,
and cry: 'Salvation to our God,
salvation to the Lamb!'

3 Spirit of holiness,
let all thy saints adore
thy sacred energy, and bless
thine heart-renewing power.
Not angel tongues can tell
thy love's ecstatic height,
the glorious joy unspeakable,
the beatific sight.

4 Eternal triune Lord!
Let all the hosts above,
let all the sons of men, record
and dwell upon thy love.
When heaven and earth are fled
before thy glorious face,
sing all the saints thy love hath made
thine everlasting praise.

CHARLES WESLEY 1707–1788

418

FATHER, Lord of all creation,
ground of being, life and love;
height and depth beyond description
only life in you can prove:
you are mortal life's dependence:
thought, speech, sight are ours by grace;
yours is every hour's existence,
sovereign Lord of time and space.

2 Jesus Christ, the Man for others,
we, your people, make our prayer:
help us love — as sisters, brothers —
all whose burdens we can share.
Where your name binds us together
you, Lord Christ, will surely be;
where no selfishness can sever
there your love the world may see.

3 Holy Spirit, rushing, burning
wind and flame of Pentecost,
fire our hearts afresh with yearning
to regain what we have lost.
May your love unite our action,
never more to speak alone:
God, in us abolish faction,
God, through us your love make known.

STEWART CROSS 1928–1989

419

FATHER most holy, merciful and loving,
Jesu, Redeemer, ever to be worshipped,
life-giving Spirit, Comforter most gracious,
God everlasting;

2 Three in a wondrous Unity unbroken,
one perfect Godhead, love that never faileth,
light of the angels, succour of the needy,
hope of all living;

3 All thy creation serveth its Creator,
thee every creature praiseth without ceasing;
we too would sing thee psalms of true devotion:
hear, we beseech thee.

4 Lord God Almighty, unto thee be glory,
One in Three Persons, over all exalted.
Thine, as is meet, be honour, praise and blessing,
now and for ever.

Latin, before 10th century
tr. A. E. ALSTON 1862–1927

420

FATHER of everlasting grace,
thy goodness and thy truth we praise,
thy goodness and thy truth we prove;
thou hast, in honour of thy Son,
the gift unspeakable sent down,
the Spirit of life, and power, and love.

2 Send us the Spirit of thy Son,
to make the depths of Godhead known,
to make us share the life divine;
send him the sprinkled blood to apply,
send him our souls to sanctify,
and show and seal us ever thine.

3 So shall we pray, and never cease,
so shall we thankfully confess
thy wisdom, truth, and power, and love;
with joy unspeakable adore,
and bless and praise thee evermore,
and serve thee as thy hosts above:

4 Till, added to that heavenly choir,
we raise our songs of triumph higher,
and praise thee in a bolder strain,
out-soar the first-born seraph's flight,
and sing, with all our friends in light,
thy everlasting love to man.

CHARLES WESLEY 1707–1788

421

FATHER of heaven, whose love profound
a ransom for our souls hath found,
before thy throne we sinners bend,
to us thy pardoning love extend.

2 Almighty Son, incarnate Word,
our Prophet, Priest, Redeemer, Lord,
before thy throne we sinners bend,
to us thy saving grace extend.

3 Eternal Spirit, by whose breath
the soul is raised from sin and death,
before thy throne we sinners bend,
to us thy quickening power extend.

4 Thrice Holy! Father, Spirit, Son;
mysterious Godhead, Three in One,
before thy throne we sinners bend,
grace, pardon, life to us extend.

EDWARD COOPER 1770–1833

422

FATHER of peace, and God of love,
we own thy power to save,
that power by which our Shepherd rose
victorious o'er the grave.

2 Him from the dead thou brought'st again,
when, by his sacred blood,
confirmed and sealed for evermore
the eternal covenant stood.

3 O may thy Spirit seal our souls,
and mould them to thy will,
that our weak hearts no more may stray,
but keep thy precepts still;

4 That to perfection's sacred height
we nearer still may rise,
and all we think, and all we do,
be pleasing in thine eyes.

PHILIP DODDRIDGE 1702–1751
Hebrews 13. 20–21
as in *Scottish Paraphrases* 1781

423

FIGHT the good fight with all thy might;
Christ is thy strength, and Christ thy right;
lay hold on life, and it shall be
thy joy and crown eternally.

2 Run the straight race through God's good grace,
lift up thine eyes, and seek his face;
life with its way before us lies;
Christ is the path, and Christ the prize.

3 Cast care aside, lean on thy guide;
his boundless mercy will provide;
trust, and thy trusting soul shall prove
Christ is its life, and Christ its love.

4 Faint not nor fear, his arms are near;
he changeth not, and thou art dear;
only believe, and thou shalt see
that Christ is all in all to thee.

J. S. B. MONSELL * 1811–1875

424

FILL thou my life, O Lord my God,
in every part with praise,
that my whole being may proclaim
thy being and thy ways.

2 Not for the lip of praise alone,
nor e'en the praising heart
I ask, but for a life made up
of praise in every part:

3 Praise in the common things of life,
its goings out and in;
praise in each duty and each deed,
however small and mean.

4 Fill every part of me with praise:
let all my being speak
of thee and of thy love, O Lord,
poor though I be and weak.

*5 So shalt thou, Lord, receive from me
the praise and glory due;
and so shall I begin on earth
the song for ever new.

*6 So shall each fear, each fret, each care,
be turnèd into song;
and every winding of the way
the echo shall prolong.

7 So shall no part of day or night
unblest or common be,
but all my life, in every step,
be fellowship with thee.

HORATIUS BONAR * 1808–1889

425

FILLED with the Spirit's power, with one accord
the infant church confessed its risen Lord.
O Holy Spirit, in the church to-day
no less your power of fellowship display.

2 Now with the mind of Christ set us on fire,
that unity may be our great desire.
Give joy and peace; give faith to hear your call,
and readiness in each to work for all.

3 Widen our love, good Spirit, to embrace
in your strong care all those of every race.
Like wind and fire with life among us move,
till we are known as Christ's, and Christians prove.

J. R. PEACEY 1896–1971

426

FIRMLY I believe and truly
God is Three and God is One;
and I next acknowledge duly
manhood taken by the Son.

2 And I trust and hope most fully
in that manhood crucified;
and each thought and deed unruly
do to death, as he has died.

3 Simply to his grace and wholly
light and life and strength belong,
and I love supremely, solely,
him the holy, him the strong.

4 And I hold in veneration,
for the love of him alone,
Holy Church as his creation,
and her teachings as his own.

5 Adoration ay be given,
with and through the angelic host,
to the God of earth and heaven,
Father, Son, and Holy Ghost.

JOHN HENRY NEWMAN 1801–1890

427

FOR the healing of the nations,
Lord, we pray with one accord,
for a just and equal sharing
of the things that earth affords.
To a life of love in action
help us rise and pledge our word.

2 Lead us forward into freedom,
from despair your world release,
that, redeemed from war and hatred,
all may come and go in peace.
Show us how through care and goodness
fear will die and hope increase.

3 All that kills abundant living,
let it from the earth be banned:
pride of status, race or schooling,
dogmas that obscure your plan.
In our common quest for justice
may we hallow life's brief span.

4 You, Creator-God, have written
your great name on humankind;
for our growing in your likeness
bring the life of Christ to mind;
that by our response and service
earth its destiny may find.

FRED KAAN *b.* 1929

428

'FORGIVE our sins as we forgive'
you taught us, Lord, to pray;
but you alone can grant us grace
to live the words we say.

2 How can your pardon reach and bless
the unforgiving heart
that broods on wrongs, and will not let
old bitterness depart?

3 In blazing light your cross reveals
the truth we dimly knew,
how small the debts men owe to us,
how great our debt to you.

4 Lord, cleanse the depths within our souls,
and bid resentment cease;
then, reconciled to God and man,
our lives will spread your peace.

ROSAMOND HERKLOTS 1905–1987

429

FORTH in the peace of Christ we go;
Christ to the world with joy we bring;
Christ in our minds, Christ on our lips,
Christ in our hearts, the world's true King.

2 King of our hearts, Christ makes us kings;
kingship with him his servants gain;
with Christ, the Servant-Lord of all,
Christ's world we serve to share Christ's reign.

3 Priests of the world, Christ sends us forth
this world of time to consecrate,
this world of sin by grace to heal,
Christ's world in Christ to re-create.

4 Christ's are our lips, his word we speak;
prophets are we whose deeds proclaim
Christ's truth in love, that we may be
Christ in the world, to spread Christ's name.

5 We are the church; Christ bids us show
that in his church all nations find
their hearth and home, where Christ restores
true peace, true love, to humankind.

JAMES QUINN *b.* 1919

430

FORTH in thy name, O Lord, I go,
my daily labour to pursue;
thee, only thee, resolved to know,
in all I think or speak or do.

2 The task thy wisdom hath assigned
O let me cheerfully fulfil;
in all my works thy presence find,
and prove thy good and perfect will.

3 Preserve me from my calling's snare,
and hide my simple heart above,
above the thorns of choking care,
the gilded baits of worldly love.

4 Thee may I set at my right hand,
whose eyes my inmost substance see,
and labour on at thy command,
and offer all my works to thee.

5 Give me to bear thy easy yoke,
and every moment watch and pray,
and still to things eternal look,
and hasten to thy glorious day;

6 For thee delightfully employ
whate'er thy bounteous grace hath given,
and run my course with even joy,
and closely walk with thee to heaven.

CHARLES WESLEY * 1707–1788

431

FROM all that dwell below the skies
let the Creator's praise arise:
let the Redeemer's name be sung
through every land by every tongue.

2 Eternal are thy mercies, Lord;
eternal truth attends thy word:
thy praise shall sound from shore to shore,
till suns shall rise and set no more.

Isaac Watts 1674–1748
Psalm 117

432

FROM heaven you came, helpless babe,
entered our world, your glory veiled;
not to be served, but to serve,
and give your life that we might live.
This is our God, the Servant King,
he calls us now to follow him,
to bring our lives as a daily offering
of worship to the Servant King.

2 There in the garden of tears,
my heavy load he chose to bear;
his heart with sorrow was torn,
'Yet not my will but yours,' he said.
This is our God ...

3 Come see his hands and his feet,
the scars that speak of sacrifice,
hands that flung stars into space
to cruel nails surrendered.
This is our God ...

4 So let us learn how to serve,
and in our lives enthrone him;
each other's needs to prefer,
for it is Christ we're serving.
This is our God, the Servant King,
he calls us now to follow him,
to bring our lives as a daily offering
of worship to the Servant King.

GRAHAM KENDRICK *b.* 1950

433

GIVE me joy in my heart, keep me praising,
give me joy in my heart, I pray;
give me joy in my heart, keep me praising,
keep me praising till the break of day:
Sing hosanna, sing hosanna,
sing hosanna to the King of kings!
Sing hosanna, sing hosanna,
sing hosanna to the King!

2 Give me peace in my heart, keep me loving,
give me peace in my heart, I pray;
give me peace in my heart, keep me loving,
keep me loving till the break of day:
Sing hosanna ...

3 Give me love in my heart, keep me serving,
give me love in my heart, I pray;
give me love in my heart, keep me serving,
keep me serving till the break of day:
Sing hosanna, sing hosanna,
sing hosanna to the King of kings!
Sing hosanna, sing hosanna,
sing hosanna to the King!

AUTHOR UNKNOWN

434

GIVE to our God immortal praise;
mercy and truth are all his ways:
wonders of grace to God belong,
repeat his mercies in your song.

2 Give to the Lord of lords renown,
the King of kings with glory crown:
his mercies ever shall endure
when lords and kings are known no more.

3 He sent his Son with power to save
from guilt and darkness and the grave:
wonders of grace to God belong,
repeat his mercies in your song.

4 Through this vain world he guides our feet,
and leads us to his heavenly seat:
his mercies ever shall endure
when this vain world shall be no more.

ISAAC WATTS 1674–1748
Psalm 136

435

GLORIOUS things of thee are spoken,
  Zion, city of our God;
he whose word cannot be broken
  formed thee for his own abode.
On the Rock of ages founded,
  what can shake thy sure repose?
With salvation's walls surrounded,
  thou may'st smile at all thy foes.

2 See, the streams of living waters,
springing from eternal love,
well supply thy sons and daughters,
and all fear of want remove.
Who can faint while such a river
ever flows their thirst to assuage:
grace which, like the Lord the giver,
never fails from age to age?

*3 Round each habitation hovering,
see the cloud and fire appear
for a glory and a covering,
showing that the Lord is near.
Thus they march, the pillar leading,
light by night and shade by day;
daily on the manna feeding
which he gives them when they pray.

4 Saviour, if of Zion's city
I through grace a member am,
let the world deride or pity,
I will glory in thy name.
Fading is the worldling's pleasure,
all his boasted pomp and show;
solid joys and lasting treasure,
none but Zion's children know.

JOHN NEWTON * 1725–1807
Isaiah 33. 20–21

436

GLORY, love, and praise, and honour
for our food
now bestowed
render we the Donor.
Bounteous God, we now confess thee;
God, who thus
blessest us,
meet it is to bless thee.

2 Thankful for our every blessing,
let us sing
Christ the spring,
never, never ceasing.
Source of all our gifts and graces
Christ we own;
Christ alone
calls for all our praises.

3 He dispels our sin and sadness,
life imparts,
cheers our hearts,
fills with food and gladness.
Who himself for all hath given,
us he feeds,
us he leads
to a feast in heaven.

CHARLES WESLEY 1707–1788

437

GO forth and tell! O Church of God, awake!
God's saving news to all the nations take:
proclaim Christ Jesus, Saviour, Lord and King,
that all the world his glorious praise may sing.

2 Go forth and tell! God's love embraces all,
he will in grace respond to all who call:
how shall they call if they have never heard
the gracious invitation of his word?

3 Go forth and tell! The doors are open wide:
share God's good gifts — let no one be denied;
live out your life as Christ your Lord shall choose,
your ransomed powers for his sole glory use.

4 Go forth and tell! O Church of God, arise!
Go in the strength which Christ your Lord supplies;
go till all nations his great name adore
and serve him, Lord and King for evermore.

JAMES E. SEDDON 1915–1983

438

GO forth for God; go forth to the world in peace;
be of good courage, armed with heavenly grace,
in God's good Spirit daily to increase,
till in his kingdom we behold his face.

2 Go forth for God; go forth to the world in strength;
hold fast the good, be urgent for the right,
render to no one evil; Christ at length
shall overcome all darkness with his light.

3 Go forth for God; go forth to the world in love;
strengthen the faint, give courage to the weak,
help the afflicted; richly from above
his love supplies the grace and power we seek.

4 Go forth for God; go forth to the world in joy,
to serve God's people every day and hour,
and serving Christ, his every gift employ,
rejoicing in the Holy Spirit's power.

5 Sing praise to him who brought us on our way,
sing praise to him who bought us with his blood,
sing praise to him who sanctifies each day,
sing praise to him who reigns one Lord and God.

J. R. Peacey * 1896–1971
and Editors of *New English Hymnal* 1986

439

GOD be in my head,
and in my understanding;

2 God be in mine eyes,
and in my looking;

3 God be in my mouth,
and in my speaking;

4 God be in my heart,
and in my thinking;

5 God be at mine end,
and at my departing.

Horae beatae Mariae Virginis London 1514
possibly of French origin

440

GOD be with you till we meet again;
by his counsels guide, uphold you,
with his sheep securely fold you:
God be with you till we meet again.

2 God be with you till we meet again;
'neath his wings protecting hide you,
daily manna still provide you:
God be with you till we meet again.

3 God be with you till we meet again;
when life's perils thick confound you,
put his arm unfailing round you:
God be with you till we meet again.

4 God be with you till we meet again;
keep love's banner floating o'er you,
smite death's threatening wave before you:
God be with you till we meet again.

JEREMIAH RANKIN 1828–1904

441

GOD is love, and where true love is, God himself is there.

2 Here in Christ we gather, love of Christ our calling.
Christ, our love, is with us, gladness be his greeting.
Let us all revere and love him, God eternal.
Let each love Christ in sisters and in brothers all.

God is love, and where true love is, God himself is there.

3 When we Christians gather, members of one Body,
let there be in us no discord, but one spirit.
Banished now be anger, strife and every quarrel.
Christ, our God, be present always here among us.

God is love, and where true love is, God himself is there.

4 Grant us love's fulfilment, joy with all the blessèd,
when we see your face, O Saviour, in its glory.
Shine on us, O purest Light of all creation,
be our bliss while endless ages sing your praises.

God is love, and where true love is, God himself is there.

Liturgy of Maundy Thursday
tr. JAMES QUINN *b.* 1919

442

GOD is Love: let heav'n adore him;
God is Love: let earth rejoice;
let creation sing before him,
and exalt him with one voice.
He who laid the earth's foundation,
he who spread the heav'ns above,
he who breathes through all creation,
he is Love, eternal Love.

2 God is Love: and he enfoldeth
all the world in one embrace;
with unfailing grasp he holdeth
every child of every race.
And when human hearts are breaking
under sorrow's iron rod,
then they find that selfsame aching
deep within the heart of God.

3 God is Love: and though with blindness
sin afflicts the souls of all,
God's eternal loving-kindness
holds and guides us when we fall.
Sin and death and hell shall never
o'er us final triumph gain;
God is Love, so Love for ever
o'er the universe must reign.

TIMOTHY REES * 1874–1939

443

GOD is our strength and refuge,
our present help in trouble;
and we therefore will not fear,
though the earth should change!
Though mountains shake and tremble,
though swirling floods are raging,
God the Lord of hosts
is with us evermore!

2 There is a flowing river,
within God's holy city;
God is in the midst of her –
she shall not be moved!
God's help is swiftly given,
thrones vanish at his presence –
God the Lord of hosts
is with us evermore!

3 Come, see the works of our maker,
learn of his deeds all-powerful:
wars will cease across the world
when he shatters the spear!
Be still and know your creator,
uplift him in the nations –
God the Lord of hosts
is with us evermore!

RICHARD BEWES *b.* 1934
Psalm 46

444

GOD is working his purpose out,
as year succeeds to year,
God is working his purpose out,
and the time is drawing near;
nearer and nearer draws the time,
the time that shall surely be,
when the earth shall be filled with the glory of God
as the waters cover the sea.

2 From utmost east to utmost west,
wherever feet have trod,
by the mouth of many messengers
goes forth the voice of God,
'Give ear to me, ye continents,
ye isles, give ear to me,
that the earth may be filled with the glory of God
as the waters cover the sea.'

3 What can we do to work God's work,
to prosper and increase
the love of God in all mankind,
the reign of the Prince of peace?
What can we do to hasten the time,
the time that shall surely be,
when the earth shall be filled with the glory of God
as the waters cover the sea?

4 March we forth in the strength of God,
with the banner of Christ unfurled,
that the light of the glorious gospel of truth
may shine throughout the world;
fight we the fight with sorrow and sin,
to set their captives free,
that the earth may be filled with the glory of God
as the waters cover the sea.

5 All we can do is nothing worth
unless God blesses the deed;
vainly we hope for the harvest-tide
till God gives life to the seed;
yet nearer and nearer draws the time,
the time that shall surely be,
when the earth shall be filled with the glory of God
as the waters cover the sea.

ARTHUR C. AINGER * 1841–1919

445

GOD moves in a mysterious way
his wonders to perform;
he plants his footsteps in the sea,
and rides upon the storm.

2 Deep in unfathomable mines
of never-failing skill
he treasures up his bright designs,
and works his sovereign will.

3 Ye fearful saints, fresh courage take;
the clouds ye so much dread
are big with mercy, and shall break
in blessings on your head.

4 Judge not the Lord by feeble sense,
but trust him for his grace;
behind a frowning providence
he hides a smiling face.

5 His purposes will ripen fast,
unfolding every hour;
the bud may have a bitter taste,
but sweet will be the flower.

6 Blind unbelief is sure to err,
and scan his work in vain;
God is his own interpreter,
and he will make it plain.

WILLIAM COWPER 1731–1800

446

GOD of all power, and truth, and grace,
which shall from age to age endure,
whose word, when heaven and earth shall pass,
remains and stands for ever sure;

2 That I thy mercy may proclaim,
that all mankind thy truth may see,
hallow thy great and glorious name,
and perfect holiness in me.

3 Thy sanctifying Spirit pour
to quench my thirst and make me clean;
now, Father, let the gracious shower
descend, and make me pure from sin.

4 Give me a new, a perfect heart,
from doubt, and fear, and sorrow free;
the mind which was in Christ impart,
and let my spirit cleave to thee.

5 O that I now, from sin released,
thy word may to the utmost prove,
enter into the promised rest,
the Canaan of thy perfect love!

CHARLES WESLEY 1707–1788

447

GOD of freedom, God of justice,
God whose love is strong as death,
God who saw the dark of prison,
God who knew the price of faith:
touch our world of sad oppression
with your Spirit's healing breath.

2 Rid the earth of torture's terror,
God whose hands were nailed to wood;
hear the cries of pain and protest,
God who shed the tears and blood;
move in us the power of pity,
restless for the common good.

3 Make in us a captive conscience
quick to hear, to act, to plead;
make us truly sisters, brothers,
of whatever race or creed:
teach us to be fully human,
open to each other's need.

SHIRLEY ERENA MURRAY * *b.* 1931

448

GOD of grace and God of glory,
on thy people pour thy power;
now fulfil thy church's story;
bring her bud to glorious flower.
Grant us wisdom, grant us courage,
for the facing of this hour.

2 Lo, the hosts of evil round us
scorn thy Christ, assail his ways;
from the fears that long have bound us
free our hearts to faith and praise.
Grant us wisdom, grant us courage,
for the living of these days.

3 Cure thy children's warring madness,
bend our pride to thy control;
shame our wanton selfish gladness,
rich in goods and poor in soul.
Grant us wisdom, grant us courage,
lest we miss thy kingdom's goal.

4 Set our feet on lofty places,
gird our lives that they may be
armoured with all Christlike graces
in the fight till all be free.
Grant us wisdom, grant us courage,
that we fail not earth nor thee.

HARRY E. FOSDICK * 1878–1969

449

GOD of mercy, God of grace,
show the brightness of thy face;
shine upon us, Saviour, shine,
fill thy church with light divine;
and thy saving health extend
unto earth's remotest end.

2 Let the people praise thee, Lord;
be by all that live adored;
let the nations shout and sing
glory to their Saviour King;
at thy feet their tribute pay,
and thy holy will obey.

3 Let the people praise thee, Lord;
earth shall then her fruits afford;
God to man his blessing give,
man to God devoted live;
all below, and all above,
one in joy and light and love.

HENRY FRANCIS LYTE 1793–1847
Psalm 67

450

GOD, we praise you, God, we bless you!
God, we name you sovereign Lord!
Mighty King whom angels worship,
Father, by your church adored:
all creation shows your glory,
heaven and earth draw near your throne,
singing, 'Holy, holy, holy,
Lord of hosts, and God alone!'

2 True apostles, faithful prophets,
saints who set their world ablaze,
martyrs, once unknown, unheeded,
join one growing song of praise,
while your church on earth confesses
one majestic Trinity:
Father, Son, and Holy Spirit,
God, our hope eternally.

3 Jesus Christ, the King of glory,
everlasting Son of God,
humble was your virgin mother,
hard the lonely path you trod.
By your cross is sin defeated,
hell confronted face to face,
heaven opened to believers,
sinners justified by grace.

4 Christ, at God's right hand victorious,
you will judge the world you made;
Lord, in mercy help your servants
for whose freedom you have paid.
Raise us up from dust to glory,
guard us from all sin today;
King enthroned above all praises,
save your people, God, we pray!

CHRISTOPHER M. IDLE *b.* 1938
from *Te Deum Laudamus*

451

GOD with humanity made one
is seen in Christ, God's only Son:
in you, Lord Christ, the Son of Man,
we see God's reconciling plan.

2 To save a broken world you came,
and from chaotic depths reclaim
your whole creation; so we share
your reconciling work and care.

3 In you all humankind can see
the people God would have us be.
In you we find how God forgives,
through you, the Spirit in us lives.

4 Where race or creed or hate divide,
the church, like God, must stand beside,
with arms outstretched, to heal and bless
the refugees of emptiness.

5 Then give us strength, great Lord of life,
to work until all human strife
is reconciled, and all shall praise
your endless love, your glorious ways.

DAVID FOX * *b.* 1956

452

GREAT God of wonders, all thy ways
are matchless, God-like and divine;
but the fair glories of thy grace
more God-like and unrivalled shine:
Who is a pardoning God like thee,
or who has grace so rich and free?

2 Such dire offences to forgive,
such guilty rebel souls to spare;
this is thy grand prerogative,
and none shall in the honour share:
Who is a pardoning God ...

3 In wonder lost, with trembling joy,
we take the pardon of our God,
pardon for sins of deepest dye,
a pardon sealed with Jesus' blood:
Who is a pardoning God ...

4 O may this glorious matchless love,
this God-like miracle of grace,
teach mortal tongues, like those above,
to raise this song of lofty praise:
Who is a pardoning God like thee,
or who has grace so rich and free?

SAMUEL DAVIES * 1723–1761

453

GREAT is thy faithfulness, O God my Father,
there is no shadow of turning with thee;
thou changest not, thy compassions they fail not;
as thou hast been thou for ever wilt be:
Great is thy faithfulness! Great is thy faithfulness!
Morning by morning new mercies I see;
all I have needed thy hand has provided,
great is thy faithfulness, Lord, unto me.

2 Summer and winter, and springtime and harvest,
sun, moon and stars in their courses above,
join with all nature in manifold witness
to thy great faithfulness, mercy and love:

3 Pardon for sin and a peace that endureth,
thy own dear presence to cheer and to guide;
strength for today and bright hope for tomorrow,
blessings all mine, with ten thousand beside!

THOMAS CHISHOLM 1866–1960

454

GREAT Shepherd of thy people, hear,
  thy presence now display;
as thou hast given a place for prayer,
  so give us hearts to pray.

2 Within these walls let holy peace
  and love and concord dwell;
here give the troubled conscience ease,
  the wounded spirit heal.

3 May we in faith receive thy word,
  in faith present our prayers,
and in the presence of our Lord
  unbosom all our cares.

4 The hearing ear, the seeing eye,
  the contrite heart, bestow;
and shine upon us from on high,
  that we in grace may grow.

JOHN NEWTON * 1725–1807

455

GUIDE me, O thou great Redeemer,
  pilgrim through this barren land;
I am weak, but thou art mighty;
  hold me with thy powerful hand:
    Bread of heaven,
  feed me now and evermore.

2 Open now the crystal fountain
  whence the healing stream doth flow;
let the fiery cloudy pillar
  lead me all my journey through:
    strong deliverer,
  be thou still my strength and shield.

3 When I tread the verge of Jordan,
bid my anxious fears subside;
death of death, and hell's destruction,
land me safe on Canaan's side:
songs and praises
I will ever give to thee.

Welsh, WILLIAM WILLIAMS 1717–1791
tr. PETER and WILLIAM WILLIAMS *

456

HAPPY are they, they that love God,
whose hearts have Christ confest,
who by his cross have found their life,
and 'neath his yoke their rest.

2 Glad is the praise, sweet are the songs,
when they together sing;
and strong the prayers that bow the ear
of heaven's eternal King.

3 Christ to their homes giveth his peace,
and makes their loves his own:
but ah, what tares the evil one
hath in his garden sown!

4 Sad were our lot, evil this earth,
did not its sorrows prove
the path whereby the sheep may find
the fold of Jesus' love.

5 Then shall they know, they that love him,
how all their pain is good;
and death itself cannot unbind
their happy brotherhood.

ROBERT BRIDGES 1844–1930
based on *O quam juvat* CHARLES COFFIN 1676–1749

457

HARK, my soul, it is the Lord;
'tis thy Saviour, hear his word;
Jesus speaks, and speaks to thee,
'Say, poor sinner, lov'st thou me?

2 'I delivered thee when bound,
and, when wounded, healed thy wound;
sought thee wandering, set thee right,
turned thy darkness into light.

3 'Can a woman's tender care
cease towards the child she bare?
Yes, she may forgetful be,
yet will I remember thee.

4 'Mine is an unchanging love,
higher than the heights above,
deeper than the depths beneath,
free and faithful, strong as death.

5 'Thou shalt see my glory soon,
when the work of grace is done;
partner of my throne shalt be:
say, poor sinner, lov'st thou me?'

6 Lord, it is my chief complaint
that my love is weak and faint;
yet I love thee, and adore;
O for grace to love thee more!

WILLIAM COWPER 1731–1800

458

HAVE faith in God, my heart,
trust and be unafraid;
God will fulfil in every part
each promise he has made.

2 Have faith in God, my mind,
though oft thy light burns low;
God's mercy holds a wiser plan
than thou canst fully know.

3 Have faith in God, my soul,
his cross for ever stands;
and neither life nor death can pluck
his children from his hands.

4 Lord Jesus, make me whole;
grant me no resting place,
until I rest, heart, mind, and soul,
the captive of thy grace.

BRYN REES 1911–1983

459

HE wants not friends that hath thy love,
and may converse and walk with thee,
and with thy saints here and above,
with whom for ever I must be.

2 In the blest fellowship of saints
is wisdom, safety, and delight;
and when my heart declines and faints,
it's raisèd by their heat and light.

3 As for my friends, they are not lost;
the several vessels of thy fleet,
though parted now, by tempests tossed,
shall safely in the haven meet.

4 Still we are centred all in thee,
members, though distant, of one Head;
in the same family we be,
by the same faith and spirit led.

5 Before thy throne we daily meet
as joint-petitioners to thee;
in spirit we each other greet,
and shall again each other see.

6 The heavenly hosts, world without end,
shall be my company above;
and thou, my best and surest Friend,
who shall divide me from thy love?

RICHARD BAXTER 1615–1691

460

HELP us, O Lord, to learn
the truths thy word imparts:
to study that thy laws may be
inscribed upon our hearts.

2 Help us, O Lord, to live
the faith which we proclaim,
that all our thoughts and words and deeds
may glorify thy name.

3 Help us, O Lord, to teach
the beauty of thy ways,
that yearning souls may find the Christ,
and sing aloud his praise.

WILLIAM WATKINS REID *b.* 1923

461

HELP us to help each other, Lord,
each other's cross to bear;
let each his friendly aid afford,
and feel another's care.

2 Up into thee, our living head,
let us in all things grow,
and by thy sacrifice be led
the fruits of love to show.

3 Touched by the lodestone of thy love
let all our hearts agree;
and ever towards each other move,
and ever move towards thee.

4 This is the bond of perfectness,
thy spotless charity.
O let us still, we pray, possess
the mind that was in thee.

CHARLES WESLEY * 1707–1788

462

HERE from all nations, all tongues, and all peoples,
countless the crowd but their voices are one;
vast is the sight and majestic their singing:
'God has the victory; he reigns from the throne!'

2 These have come out of the hardest oppression,
now they may stand in the presence of God,
serving their Lord day and night in his temple,
ransomed and cleansed by the Lamb's precious blood.

3 Gone is their thirst and no more shall they hunger,
God is their shelter, his power at their side:
sun shall not pain them, no burning will torture;
Jesus the Lamb is their shepherd and guide.

4 He will go with them to clear living water
flowing from springs which his mercy supplies;
gone is their grief and their trials are over,
God wipes away every tear from their eyes.

5 Blessing and glory and wisdom and power
be to the Saviour again and again;
might and thanksgiving and honour for ever
be to our God: Alleluia! Amen.

CHRISTOPHER M. IDLE *b.* 1938
from Revelation 7

463

HOLY Trinity of Love,
perfect peace that has no end;
you are our eternal hope:
maker, guide and human friend.

2 Through earth's devastating storms,
thunder-clouds that hide your face,
still, creator-God, you hold
chaos in the grip of grace.

3 Through earth's troubles and alarms,
more than ocean's countless waves,
Christ, command our fears, 'Be still';
give the peace our spirit craves.

4 Holy Spirit, when life's storms
overwhelm us, and we drown;
lifted by your peace and power,
we still tread the chaos down.

5 Holy, holy, holy God,
pain and death, the throes of hell,
cannot conquer! Even now,
we believe, all shall be well.

ALAN GAUNT *b.* 1935

464

HOW good is the God we adore,
our faithful, unchangeable friend;
whose love is as great as his power,
and neither knows measure nor end.

2 'Tis Jesus, the first and the last,
whose Spirit shall guide us safe home:
we'll praise him for all that is past,
and trust him for all that's to come.

JOSEPH HART * 1712–1768

465

HOW lovely is your dwelling-place,
O Lord of hosts, to me;
my thirsting soul longs eagerly
within your courts to be.

2 Beside your altars, Lord of all,
the swallows find a nest;
happy are those who dwell with you
and praise you without rest;

3 And happy those whose hearts are set
upon the pilgrim ways:
you are the water when they thirst,
their guide towards your face.

4 How blest are they that in your house
for ever give you praise:
one day with you is better spent
than thousands in dark ways.

5 The Lord will hold back no good thing
from those who justly live;
to all who trust, the Lord of hosts
will all his blessings give.

based on Psalm 84 in *Scottish Psalter* 1650

466

HOW shall I sing that majesty
which angels do admire?
Let dust in dust and silence lie;
sing, sing, ye heavenly choir.
Thousands of thousands stand around
thy throne, O God most high;
ten thousand times ten thousand sound
thy praise; but who am I?

2 Thy brightness unto them appears,
while I thy footsteps trace;
a sound of God comes to my ears,
but they behold thy face:
I shall, I fear, be dark and cold,
with all my fire and light;
yet when thou dost accept their gold,
Lord, treasure up my mite.

3 Enlighten with faith's light my heart,
inflame it with love's fire,
then shall I sing and take my part
with that celestial choir.
They sing, because thou art their sun;
Lord, send a beam on me;
for where heaven is but once begun,
there alleluias be.

4 How great a being, Lord, is thine,
which doth all beings keep!
Thy knowledge is the only line
to sound so vast a deep:
thou art a sea without a shore,
a sun without a sphere;
thy time is now and evermore,
thy place is everywhere.

JOHN MASON * 1646–1694

467

HOW sweet the name of Jesus sounds
in a believer's ear!
It soothes his sorrows, heals his wounds,
and drives away his fear.

2 It makes the wounded spirit whole,
and calms the troubled breast;
'tis manna to the hungry soul,
and to the weary rest.

3 Dear name! the rock on which I build,
my shield and hiding-place,
my never-failing treasury filled
with boundless stores of grace.

4 Jesus! my Shepherd, Brother, Friend,
my Prophet, Priest, and King,
my Lord, my Life, my Way, my End,
accept the praise I bring.

5 Weak is the effort of my heart,
   and cold my warmest thought;
but when I see thee as thou art,
   I'll praise thee as I ought.

6 Till then I would thy love proclaim
   with every fleeting breath;
and may the music of thy name
   refresh my soul in death.

JOHN NEWTON * 1725–1807

468

I DANCED in the morning, when the world was begun,
and I danced in the moon and the stars and the sun,
and I came down from heaven and I danced on the earth;
at Bethlehem I had my birth.
Dance, then, wherever you may be;
I am the Lord of the Dance, said he,
and I'll lead you all, wherever you may be,
and I'll lead you all in the Dance, said he.

2 I danced for the scribe and the pharisee,
but they would not dance and they wouldn't follow me.
I danced for the fishermen, for James and John;
they came with me and the Dance went on:
Dance, then, wherever you may be ...

3 I danced on the Sabbath and I cured the lame;
the holy people said it was a shame.
They whipped and they stripped and they hung me on high,
and they left me there on a cross to die:
Dance, then, wherever you may be ...

4 I danced on a Friday when the sky turned black;
it's hard to dance with the devil on your back.
They buried my body and they thought I'd gone;
but I am the Dance and I still go on:
Dance, then, wherever you may be ...

5 They cut me down and I leapt up high;
I am the life that'll never, never die;
I'll live in you if you'll live in me:
I am the Lord of the Dance, said he:
Dance, then, wherever you may be ...

SYDNEY CARTER *b.* 1915

469

I HEARD the voice of Jesus say,
'Come unto me and rest;
lay down, thou weary one, lay down
thy head upon my breast':
I came to Jesus as I was,
weary and worn and sad;
I found in him a resting-place,
and he has made me glad.

2 I heard the voice of Jesus say,
'Behold, I freely give
the living water, thirsty one;
stoop down and drink and live':
I came to Jesus, and I drank
of that life-giving stream;
my thirst was quenched, my soul revived,
and now I live in him.

3 I heard the voice of Jesus say,
'I am this dark world's light;
look unto me, thy morn shall rise,
and all thy day be bright':
I looked to Jesus, and I found
in him my star, my sun;
and in that light of life I'll walk
till travelling days are done.

HORATIUS BONAR 1808–1889

470

I, THE Lord of sea and sky,
I have heard my people cry.
All who dwell in dark and sin,
  my hand will save.
I who made the stars of night,
I will make their darkness bright.
Who will bear my light to them?
  Whom shall I send?
Here I am, Lord, is it I, Lord?
I have heard you calling in the night.
I will go, Lord, if you lead me.
I will hold your people in my heart.

2 I, the Lord of snow and rain,
I have borne my people's pain,
I have wept for love of them,
  they turn away.
I will break their hearts of stone,
give them hearts for love alone,
I will speak my word to them.
  Whom shall I send?
Here I am, Lord ...

3 I, the Lord of wind and flame,
I will tend the poor and lame,
I will set a feast for them,
  my hand will save.
Finest bread I will provide
till their hearts be satisfied,
I will give my life to them.
  Whom shall I send?
Here I am, Lord ...

DAN SCHUTTE *b.* 1947

471

I TO the hills will lift mine eyes;
from whence doth come mine aid?
My safety cometh from the Lord,
who heaven and earth hath made.

2 Thy foot he'll not let slide, nor will
he slumber that thee keeps;
behold, he that keeps Israel,
he slumbers not, nor sleeps.

3 The Lord thee keeps; the Lord thy shade
on thy right hand doth stay;
the moon by night thee shall not smite,
nor yet the sun by day.

4 The Lord shall keep thy soul; he shall
preserve thee from all ill;
henceforth thy going out and in
God keep for ever will.

Psalm 121
Scottish Psalter 1650 *

472

I WAITED for the Lord my God,
and patiently did bear;
at length to me he did incline
my voice and cry to hear.

2 He took me from a fearful pit,
and from the miry clay,
and on a rock he set my feet,
establishing my way.

3 He put a new song in my mouth,
our God to magnify:
many shall see it, and shall fear,
and on the Lord rely.

4 To do thy will I take delight,
O thou my God that art;
yea, that most holy law of thine
I have within my heart.

5 In thee let all be glad, and joy,
who seeking thee abide;
who thy salvation love, say still,
the Lord be magnified.

Psalm 40
Scottish Psalter 1650

473

I'LL praise my Maker while I've breath;
and when my voice is lost in death
praise shall employ my nobler powers:
my days of praise shall ne'er be past
while life and thought and being last,
or immortality endures.

2 Happy are they whose hopes rely
on Israel's God! He made the sky,
and earth and sea, with all their train:
his truth for ever stands secure;
he saves the oppressed, he feeds the poor,
and none shall find his promise vain.

3 The Lord pours eyesight on the blind;
the Lord supports the fainting mind;
he sends the labouring conscience peace;
he helps the stranger in distress,
the widow and the fatherless,
and grants the prisoner sweet release.

4 I'll praise him while he lends me breath;
and when my voice is lost in death
praise shall employ my nobler powers:
my days of praise shall ne'er be past
while life and thought and being last,
or immortality endures.

ISAAC WATTS * 1674–1748
based on Psalm 146

474

IMMORTAL, invisible, God only wise,
in light inaccessible hid from our eyes,
most blessèd, most glorious, the Ancient of Days,
almighty, victorious, thy great name we praise.

2 Unresting, unhasting, and silent as light,
nor wanting, nor wasting, thou rulest in might;
thy justice like mountains high soaring above
thy clouds which are fountains of goodness and love.

3 To all life thou givest, to both great and small;
in all life thou livest, the true life of all;
we blossom and flourish as leaves on the tree,
and wither and perish; but naught changeth thee.

4 Great Father of glory, pure Father of light,
thine angels adore thee, all veiling their sight;
all laud we would render: O help us to see
'tis only the splendour of light hideth thee.

W. Chalmers Smith 1824–1908
1 Timothy 1. 17

475

IMMORTAL Love for ever full,
for ever flowing free,
for ever shared, for ever whole,
a never-ebbing sea.

2 Our outward lips confess the name
all other names above;
love only knoweth whence it came
and comprehendeth love.

3 We may not climb the heavenly steeps
to bring the Lord Christ down;
in vain we search the lowest deeps,
for him no depths can drown:

4 But warm, sweet, tender, even yet
a present help is he;
and faith has still its Olivet,
and love its Galilee.

*5 The healing of his seamless dress
is by our beds of pain;
we touch him in life's throng and press,
and we are whole again.

*6 Through him the first fond prayers are said
our lips of childhood frame;
the last low whispers of our dead
are burdened with his name.

7 Alone, O Love ineffable,
thy saving name is given;
to turn aside from thee is hell,
to walk with thee is heaven.

John Greenleaf Whittier 1807–1892

476

IN a world where people walk in darkness,
let us turn our faces to the light,
to the light of God revealed in Jesus,
to the Daystar scattering our night.
For the light is stronger than the darkness
and the day will overcome the night,
though the shadows linger all around us,
let us turn our faces to the light.

2 In a world where suffering of the helpless
casts a shadow all along the way,
let us bear the cross of Christ with gladness
and proclaim the dawning of the day.
For the light ...

3 let us light a candle in the darkness,
in the face of death a sign of life;
as a sign of hope where all seemed hopeless,
as a sign of peace in place of strife.
For the light is stronger than the darkness
and the day will overcome the night,
though the shadows linger all around us,
let us turn our faces to the light.

Robert Willis *b.* 1947

477

IN Christ there is no east or west,
in him no south or north,
but one great fellowship of love
throughout the whole wide earth.

2 In him shall true hearts everywhere
their high communion find;
his service is the golden cord,
close binding humankind.

3 Join hands, then, children of the faith,
whate'er your race may be;
who serves my Father as his child
is surely kin to me.

4 In Christ now meet both east and west,
in him meet south and north;
all Christlike souls are one in him,
throughout the whole wide earth.

JOHN OXENHAM * 1852–1941

478

IN heavenly love abiding,
no change my heart shall fear;
and safe is such confiding,
for nothing changes here:
the storm may roar without me,
my heart may low be laid;
but God is round about me,
and can I be dismayed?

2 Wherever he may guide me,
no want shall turn me back;
my Shepherd is beside me,
and nothing can I lack:
his wisdom ever waketh,
his sight is never dim,
he knows the way he taketh,
and I will walk with him.

3 Green pastures are before me,
which yet I have not seen;
bright skies will soon be o'er me,
where darkest clouds have been;
my hope I cannot measure,
my path to life is free;
my Saviour has my treasure,
and he will walk with me.

ANNA LAETITIA WARING * 1820–1910

479

IN praise of God meet duty and delight,
angels and creatures, flesh and spirits blest:
in praise is earth transfigured by the sound
and sight of heaven's everlasting feast.

2 The desert is refreshed by songs of praise,
relaxed the frown of pride, the stress of grief;
in praise forgotten all our human spite;
in praise the burdened heart finds sure relief.

3 In praise our art and craft together meet,
inspired, obedient, patient, practical;
in praise join instrument and voice and sound
to make one music for the Lord of all.

4 No skill of ours, no music made on earth,
no mortal song could scale the height of heaven;
yet stands that cross, through grace ineffable
the instrument of praise to sinners given.

5 So, confident and festive, let us sing
of wisdom, power and mercy there made known;
the song of Moses and the Lamb be ours,
through Christ raised up to life in God alone.

ERIK ROUTLEY * 1917–1982

480

IN the cross of Christ I glory,
towering o'er the wrecks of time:
all the light of sacred story
gathers round its head sublime.

2 When the woes of life o'ertake me,
hopes deceive, and fears annoy,
never shall the cross forsake me;
lo! it glows with peace and joy.

3 When the sun of bliss is beaming
light and love upon my way,
from the cross the radiance streaming
adds more lustre to the day.

4 Bane and blessing, pain and pleasure,
by the cross are sanctified;
peace is there that knows no measure,
joys that through all time abide.

5 In the cross of Christ I glory,
towering o'er the wrecks of time:
all the light of sacred story
gathers round its head sublime.

JOHN BOWRING 1792–1872

481

JERUSALEM, my happy home,
name ever dear to me,
when shall my labours have an end,
thy joys when shall I see?

2 When shall these eyes thy heaven-built walls
and pearly gates behold,
thy bulwarks with salvation strong,
and streets of shining gold?

3 Apostles, martyrs, prophets, there
around my Saviour stand;
and all I love in Christ below
will join the glorious band.

4 Jerusalem, my happy home,
when shall I come to thee?
When shall my labours have an end,
thy joys when shall I see?

5 O Christ, do thou my soul prepare
for that bright home of love;
that I may see thee and adore,
with all thy saints above.

based on 'F.B.P.' *c.* 1600

482

JERUSALEM the golden,
with milk and honey blest,
beneath thy contemplation
sink heart and voice opprest.
I know not, O I know not
what joys await us there,
what radiancy of glory,
what bliss beyond compare.

2 They stand, those halls of Sion,
conjubilant with song,
and bright with many an angel,
and all the martyr throng;
the Prince is ever with them,
the daylight is serene,
the pastures of the blessèd
are decked in glorious sheen.

3 There is the throne of David;
and there, from care released,
the shout of them that triumph,
the song of them that feast;
and they, who with their leader
have conquered in the fight,
for ever and for ever
are clad in robes of white.

4 O sweet and blessèd country,
the home of God's elect!
O sweet and blessèd country
that eager hearts expect!
Jesu, in mercy bring us
to that dear land of rest;
who art, with God the Father
and Spirit, ever blest.

BERNARD OF CLUNY 12th century
tr. J. M. NEALE * 1818–1866

483

JESU, my Lord, my God, my all,
hear me, blest Saviour, when I call;
hear me, and from thy dwelling-place
pour down the riches of thy grace:
Jesu, my Lord, I thee adore,
O make me love thee more and more.

2 Jesu, too late I thee have sought,
how can I love thee as I ought?
And how extol thy matchless fame,
the glorious beauty of thy name?
Jesu, my Lord ...

3 Jesu, what didst thou find in me,
that thou hast dealt so lovingly?
How great the joy that thou hast brought,
so far exceeding hope or thought!
Jesu, my Lord ...

4 Jesu, of thee shall be my song,
to thee my heart and soul belong;
all that I am or have is thine,
and thou, sweet Saviour, thou art mine.
Jesu, my Lord, I thee adore,
O make me love thee more and more.

HENRY COLLINS 1827–1919

484

JESU, priceless treasure,
source of purest pleasure,
truest friend to me;
ah! how long in anguish
shall my spirit languish
yearning, Lord, for thee?
Thine I am,
O spotless Lamb,
I will suffer
naught to hide thee,
naught I ask beside thee.

2 In thine arms I rest me,
foes who would molest me
  cannot reach me here.
Though the earth be shaking,
every heart be quaking,
  Jesus calms my fear;
    lightnings flash
    and thunders crash;
    yet, though sin
    and hell assail me,
Jesus will not fail me.

*3 Satan, I defy thee;
death, I now decry thee;
  fear, I bid thee cease.
World, thou shalt not harm me
nor thy threats alarm me
  while I sing of peace.
    God's great power
    guards every hour;
    earth and all
    its depths adore him,
silent bow before him.

4 Hence with earthly treasure!
Thou art all my pleasure,
  Jesus, all my choice.
Hence, thou empty glory!
naught to me thy story,
  told with tempting voice.
    Pain or loss,
    or shame or cross,
    shall not from
    my Saviour move me,
since he deigns to love me.

5 Hence, all fear and sadness!
For the Lord of gladness,
Jesus, enters in;
they who love the Father,
though the storms may gather,
still have peace within;
yea, whate'er
I here must bear,
thou art still
my purest pleasure,
Jesu, priceless treasure!

JOHANN FRANCK 1618–1677
tr. CATHERINE WINKWORTH * 1827–1878

485

JESU, the very thought of thee
with sweetness fills the breast;
but sweeter far thy face to see,
and in thy presence rest.

2 No voice can sing, nor heart can frame,
nor can the memory find
a sweeter sound than Jesu's name,
the Saviour of mankind.

3 O hope of every contrite heart,
O joy of all the meek,
to those who ask how kind thou art,
how good to those who seek!

4 But what to those who find? Ah, this
nor tongue nor pen can show;
the love of Jesus, what it is
none but his loved ones know.

5 Jesu, our only joy be thou,
as thou our prize wilt be;
in thee be all our glory now,
and through eternity.

Jesu, dulcis memoria
Latin, c. 12th century
tr. EDWARD CASWALL 1814–1878

ALTERNATIVE VERSION

O JESU, King most wonderful,
thou Conqueror renowned,
thou sweetness most ineffable,
in whom all joys are found!

2 When once thou visitest the heart,
then truth begins to shine,
then earthly vanities depart,
then kindles love divine.

3 Thee, Jesu, may our voices bless,
thee may we love alone,
and ever in our lives express
the image of thine own.

4 Abide with us, and let thy light
shine, Lord, on every heart;
dispel the darkness of our night,
and joy to all impart.

5 Jesu, our love and joy, to thee,
the Virgin's holy Son,
all might and praise and glory be
while endless ages run.

Jesu, Rex admirabilis
Latin, c. 12th century
tr. EDWARD CASWALL 1814–1878

486

JESU, thou joy of loving hearts,
  thou fount of life, thou light of men;
from the best bliss that earth imparts
  we turn unfilled to thee again.

2 Thy truth unchanged hath ever stood;
  thou savest those that on thee call;
to them that seek thee thou art good,
  to them that find thee, all in all.

3 We taste thee, O thou living bread,
  and long to feast upon thee still;
we drink of thee, the fountain-head,
  and thirst our souls from thee to fill.

4 Our restless spirits yearn for thee,
  where'er our changeful lot is cast,
glad when thy gracious smile we see,
  blest when our faith can hold thee fast.

5 O Jesu, ever with us stay;
  make all our moments calm and bright;
chase the dark night of sin away;
  shed o'er the world thy holy light.

Jesu, dulcedo cordium
Latin, 12th century
tr. RAY PALMER 1808–1887

487

JESUS, good above all other,
gentle child of gentle mother,
in a stable born our brother,
  give us grace to persevere.

2 Jesus, cradled in a manger,
for us facing every danger,
living as a homeless stranger,
  make we thee our King most dear.

3 Jesus, for thy people dying,
risen Master, death defying,
Lord in heaven, thy grace supplying,
keep us to thy presence near.

4 Jesus, who our sorrows bearest,
all our thoughts and hopes thou sharest,
thou to us the truth declarest;
help us all thy truth to hear.

5 Lord, in all our doings guide us;
pride and hate shall ne'er divide us;
we'll go on with thee beside us,
and with joy we'll persevere.

Percy Dearmer 1867–1936
partly based on J. M. Neale 1818–1866

488

JESUS, humble was your birth
when you came from heaven to earth;
every day in all we do,
make us humble, Lord, like you.

2 Jesus, strong to help and heal,
showing that your love is real;
every day in all we do,
make us strong and kind like you.

3 Jesus, when you were betrayed,
still you trusted God and prayed;
every day in all we do,
help us trust and pray like you.

4 Jesus, risen from the dead,
with us always, as you said;
every day in all we do,
help us live and love like you.

Patrick Appleford * *b.* 1924

489

JESUS, Lord, we look to thee,
let us in thy name agree:
show thyself the Prince of peace;
bid all strife for ever cease.

2 Make us of one heart and mind,
courteous, pitiful, and kind,
lowly, meek in thought and word,
altogether like our Lord.

3 Let us for each other care,
each the other's burden bear;
to thy church the pattern give,
show how true believers live.

4 Free from anger and from pride,
let us thus in God abide;
all the depths of love express,
all the heights of holiness.

CHARLES WESLEY * 1707–1788

490

JESUS shall reign where'er the sun
does his successive journeys run;
his kingdom stretch from shore to shore,
till moons shall wax and wane no more.

2 People and realms of every tongue
dwell on his love with sweetest song,
and infant voices shall proclaim
their early blessings on his name.

3 Blessings abound where'er he reigns:
the prisoner leaps to lose his chains;
the weary find eternal rest,
and all the sons of want are blest.

4 To him shall endless prayer be made,
and praises throng to crown his head;
his name like incense shall arise
with every morning sacrifice.

5 Let every creature rise and bring
peculiar honours to our King;
angels descend with songs again,
and earth repeat the loud Amen.

Isaac Watts * 1674–1748
Psalm 72

491

JESUS, these eyes have never seen
that radiant form of thine;
the veil of sense hangs dark between
thy blessèd face and mine.

2 I see thee not, I hear thee not,
yet art thou oft with me;
and earth hath ne'er so dear a spot
as where I meet with thee.

3 Yet, though I have not seen, and still
must rest in faith alone,
I love thee, dearest Lord, and will,
unseen, but not unknown.

4 When death these mortal eyes shall seal,
and still this throbbing heart,
the rending veil shall thee reveal
all glorious as thou art.

Ray Palmer 1808–1887

492

JESUS, where'er thy people meet,
there they behold thy mercy-seat;
where'er they seek thee thou art found,
and every place is hallowed ground.

2 For thou, within no walls confined,
inhabitest the humble mind;
such ever bring thee when they come,
and, going, take thee to their home.

3 Dear Shepherd of thy chosen few,
thy former mercies here renew;
here to our waiting hearts proclaim
the sweetness of thy saving name.

4 Here may we prove the power of prayer
to strengthen faith and sweeten care,
to teach our faint desires to rise,
and bring all heaven before our eyes.

5 Lord, we are few, but thou art near;
nor short thine arm, nor deaf thine ear:
O rend the heavens, come quickly down,
and make a thousand hearts thine own!

William Cowper 1731–1800

493

JOIN all the glorious names
of wisdom, love, and power,
that ever mortals knew,
that angels ever bore:
all are too mean to speak his worth,
too mean to set my *Saviour* forth.

2 But O what gentle terms,
what condescending ways
doth our *Redeemer* use
to teach his heavenly grace!
Mine eyes with joy and wonder see
what forms of love he bears for me.

*3 Great *Prophet* of my God,
my tongue would bless thy name;
by thee the joyful news
of our salvation came:
the joyful news of sins forgiven,
of hell subdued and peace with heaven.

*4 Jesus my great *High-Priest*
offered his blood and died;
my guilty conscience seeks
no sacrifice beside:
his powerful blood did once atone,
and now it pleads before the throne.

5 My dear almighty *Lord,*
my *Conqueror* and my *King,*
thy sceptre and thy sword,
thy reign of grace, I sing;
thine is the power: behold I sit
in willing bonds before thy feet.

6 Now let my soul arise,
and tread the tempter down;
my *Captain* leads me forth
to conquest and a crown.
A feeble saint shall win the day,
though death and hell obstruct the way.

7 Should all the hosts of death,
and powers of hell unknown,
put their most dreadful forms
of rage and mischief on,
I shall be safe, for *Christ* displays
superior power, and guardian grace.

Isaac Watts 1674–1748

494

KING of glory, King of peace,
I will love thee;
and, that love may never cease,
I will move thee.
Thou hast granted my request,
thou hast heard me;
thou didst note my working breast,
thou hast spared me.

2 Wherefore with my utmost art
I will sing thee,
and the cream of all my heart
I will bring thee.
Though my sins against me cried,
thou didst clear me,
and alone, when they replied,
thou didst hear me.

3 Seven whole days, not one in seven,
I will praise thee;
in my heart, though not in heaven,
I can raise thee.
Small it is, in this poor sort
to enrol thee:
e'en eternity's too short
to extol thee.

GEORGE HERBERT 1593–1633

495

LEAD, kindly light, amid the encircling gloom,
lead thou me on;
the night is dark, and I am far from home;
lead thou me on.
Keep thou my feet; I do not ask to see
the distant scene; one step enough for me.

2 I was not ever thus, nor prayed that thou
shouldst lead me on;
I loved to choose and see my path; but now
lead thou me on.
I loved the garish day, and, spite of fears,
pride ruled my will: remember not past years.

3 So long thy power hath blest me, sure it still
will lead me on,
o'er moor and fen, o'er crag and torrent, till
the night is gone,
and with the morn those angel faces smile,
which I have loved long since, and lost awhile.

JOHN HENRY NEWMAN 1801–1890

496

LEAD us, heavenly Father, lead us
o'er the world's tempestuous sea;
guard us, guide us, keep us, feed us,
for we have no help but thee;
yet possessing every blessing,
if our God our Father be.

2 Saviour, breathe forgiveness o'er us:
all our weakness thou dost know;
thou didst tread this earth before us,
thou didst feel its keenest woe;
lone and dreary, faint and weary,
through the desert thou didst go.

3 Spirit of our God, descending,
fill our hearts with heavenly joy,
love with every passion blending,
pleasure that can never cloy:
thus provided, pardoned, guided,
nothing can our peace destroy.

JAMES EDMESTON 1791–1867

497

LET all the world in every corner sing,
my God and King.
The heavens are not too high,
his praise may thither fly:
the earth is not too low,
his praises there may grow.
Let all the world in every corner sing,
my God and King.

2 Let all the world in every corner sing,
my God and King.
The church with psalms must shout,
no door can keep them out;
but above all the heart
must bear the longest part.
Let all the world in every corner sing,
my God and King.

George Herbert 1593–1633

498

LET us, with a gladsome mind,
praise the Lord, for he is kind:
For his mercies ay endure,
ever faithful, ever sure.

2 Let us blaze his name abroad,
for of gods he is the God:

3 He with all-commanding might
filled the new-made world with light:

4 He the golden-tressèd sun
caused all day his course to run:

5 And the hornèd moon at night
'mid her spangled sisters bright:

6 All things living he doth feed,
his full hand supplies their need:

7 Let us, with a gladsome mind,
praise the Lord, for he is kind:
For his mercies ay endure,
ever faithful, ever sure.

JOHN MILTON * 1608–1674
Psalm 136

499

LIFT high the cross, the love of Christ proclaim
till all the world adore his sacred name.

2 Come, let us follow where our Captain trod,
our King victorious, Christ the Son of God:

*3 Led on their way by this triumphant sign,
the hosts of God in conquering ranks combine:

*4 Each new-born soldier of the Crucified
bears on his brow the seal of him who died:

*5 This is the sign which Satan's legions fear
and angels veil their faces to revere:

*6 Saved by the cross whereon their Lord was slain,
earth's fallen children their lost home regain:

*7 From north and south, from east and west they raise
in growing unison their song of praise:

8 O Lord, once lifted on the glorious tree,
as thou hast promised, draw us unto thee:

9 Let every race and every language tell
of him who saves our souls from death and hell:

10 From farthest regions let them homage bring,
and on his cross adore their Saviour King:

11 Set up thy throne, that earth's despair may cease
beneath the shadow of its healing peace:

12 For thy blest cross which doth for all atone
creation's praises rise before thy throne:

Lift high the cross, the love of Christ proclaim
till all the world adore his sacred name.

G. W. Kitchin * 1827–1912
and M. R. Newbolt * 1874–1956

500

'LIFT up your hearts!' We lift them, Lord, to thee;
here at thy feet none other may we see:
'lift up your hearts!' E'en so, with one accord,
we lift them up, we lift them to the Lord.

2 Above the level of the former years,
the mire of sin, the slough of guilty fears,
the mist of doubt, the blight of love's decay,
O Lord of light, lift all our hearts to-day.

3 Above the swamps of subterfuge and shame,
the deeds, the thoughts, that honour may not name,
the halting tongue that dares not tell the whole,
O Lord of truth, lift every Christian soul.

4 Lift every gift that thou thyself hast given:
low lies the best till lifted up to heaven;
low lie the bounding heart, the teeming brain,
till, sent from God, they mount to God again.

5 Then, as the trumpet-call in after years,
'lift up your hearts!' rings pealing in our ears,
still shall those hearts respond with full accord,
'we lift them up, we lift them to the Lord!'

H. Montagu Butler 1833–1918

501

LIGHT of the minds that know him,
  may Christ be light to mine!
my sun in risen splendour,
  my light of truth divine;
my guide in doubt and darkness,
  my true and living way,
my clear light ever shining,
  my dawn of heaven's day.

2 Life of the souls that love him,
  may Christ be ours indeed!
the living bread from heaven
  on whom our spirits feed;
who died for love of sinners
  to bear our guilty load,
and make of life's brief journey
  a new Emmaus road.

3 Strength of the wills that serve him,
  may Christ be strength to me,
who stilled the storm and tempest,
  who calmed the tossing sea;
his Spirit's power to move me,
  his will to master mine,
his cross to carry daily
  and conquer in his sign.

4 May it be ours to know him
  that we may truly love,
and loving, fully serve him
  as serve the saints above;
till in that home of glory
  with fadeless splendour bright,
we serve in perfect freedom
  our strength, our life, our light.

TIMOTHY DUDLEY-SMITH *b.* 1926
based on a prayer of
ST AUGUSTINE OF HIPPO 354–430

502

LIGHT'S abode, celestial Salem,
vision whence true peace doth spring,
brighter than the heart can fancy,
mansion of the highest King;
O how glorious are the praises
which of thee the prophets sing!

2 There for ever and for ever
alleluia is outpoured;
for unending, for unbroken,
is the feast-day of the Lord;
all is pure and all is holy
that within thy walls is stored.

3 There no cloud or passing vapour
dims the brightness of the air;
endless noon-day, glorious noon-day,
from the Sun of suns is there;
there no night brings rest from labour,
for unknown are toil and care.

*4 O how glorious and resplendent,
fragile body, shalt thou be,
when endued with so much beauty,
full of health and strong and free,
full of vigour, full of pleasure
that shall last eternally.

*5 Now with gladness, now with courage,
bear the burden on thee laid,
that hereafter these thy labours
may with endless gifts be paid;
and in everlasting glory
thou with brightness be arrayed.

6 Laud and honour to the Father,
laud and honour to the Son,
laud and honour to the Spirit,
ever Three and ever One,
consubstantial, co-eternal,
while unending ages run.

Ascribed to THOMAS À KEMPIS *c.* 1380–1471
tr. J. M. NEALE * 1818–1866

503

LORD, dismiss us with thy blessing,
fill our hearts with joy and peace;
let us each, thy love possessing,
triumph in redeeming grace;
O refresh us,
travelling through this wilderness.

2 Thanks we give, and adoration,
for thy gospel's joyful sound;
may the fruits of thy salvation
in our hearts and lives abound;
may thy presence
with us evermore be found.

JOHN FAWCETT 1740–1817

504

LORD, I have made thy word my choice,
my lasting heritage:
there shall my noblest powers rejoice,
my warmest thoughts engage.

2 I'll read the histories of thy love,
and keep thy laws in sight,
while through the promises I rove
with ever-fresh delight.

3 'Tis a broad land of wealth unknown,
where springs of life arise,
seeds of immortal bliss are sown,
and hidden glory lies.

Isaac Watts 1674–1748
from Psalm 119

505

LORD Jesus Christ,
you have come to us,
you are one with us,
Mary's Son;
cleansing our souls from all their sin,
pouring your love and goodness in;
Jesus, our love for you we sing,
living Lord.

*2 Lord Jesus Christ,
now and every day,
teach us how to pray,
Son of God.
You have commanded us to do
this in remembrance, Lord, of you:
into our lives your power breaks through,
living Lord.

3 Lord Jesus Christ,
you have come to us,
born as one of us,
Mary's Son.
Led out to die on Calvary,
risen from death to set us free,
living Lord Jesus, help us see,
you are Lord.

4 Lord Jesus Christ,
I would come to you,
live my life for you,
Son of God.
All your commands I know are true,
your many gifts will make me new,
into my life your power breaks through,
living Lord.

PATRICK APPLEFORD *b.* 1924

506

LORD of all being, throned afar,
thy glory flames from sun and star;
centre and soul of every sphere,
yet to each loving heart how near!

2 Sun of our life, thy quickening ray
sheds on our path the glow of day;
star of our hope, thy softened light
cheers the long watches of the night.

3 Our midnight is thy smile withdrawn,
our noontide is thy gracious dawn,
our rainbow arch thy mercy's sign;
all, save the clouds of sin, are thine.

4 Lord of all life, below, above,
whose light is truth, whose warmth is love,
before thy ever-blazing throne
we ask no lustre of our own.

5 Grant us thy truth to make us free,
and kindling hearts that burn for thee,
till all thy living altars claim
one holy light, one heavenly flame.

OLIVER WENDELL HOLMES 1809–1894

507

LORD of all hopefulness, Lord of all joy,
whose trust, ever childlike, no cares could destroy,
be there at our waking, and give us, we pray,
your bliss in our hearts, Lord, at the break of the day.

2 Lord of all eagerness, Lord of all faith,
whose strong hands were skilled at the plane and the lathe,
be there at our labours, and give us, we pray,
your strength in our hearts, Lord, at the noon of the day.

3 Lord of all kindliness, Lord of all grace,
your hands swift to welcome, your arms to embrace,
be there at our homing, and give us, we pray,
your love in our hearts, Lord, at the eve of the day.

4 Lord of all gentleness, Lord of all calm,
whose voice is contentment, whose presence is balm,
be there at our sleeping, and give us, we pray,
your peace in our hearts, Lord, at the end of the day.

JAN STRUTHER (JOYCE PLACZEK) 1901–1953

508

LORD of all power, I give you my will,
in joyful obedience your tasks to fulfil.
Your bondage is freedom, your service is song,
and, held in your keeping, my weakness is strong.

2 Lord of all wisdom, I give you my mind,
rich truth that surpasses man's knowledge to find.
What eye has not seen and what ear has not heard
is taught by your Spirit and shines from your word.

3 Lord of all bounty, I give you my heart;
I praise and adore you for all you impart:
your love to inspire me, your counsel to guide,
your presence to cheer me, whatever betide.

4 Lord of all being, I give you my all;
if e'er I disown you I stumble and fall;
but, sworn in glad service your word to obey,
I walk in your freedom to the end of the way.

JACK C. WINSLOW * 1882–1974

509

LORD of all, to whom alone
all our heart's desires are known,
when we stand before thy throne,
Jesu, hear and save.

2 Son of Man, before whose eyes
every secret open lies,
at thy great and last assize,
Jesu, hear and save.

3 Son of God, whose angel host
(thou hast said) rejoiceth most
o'er the sinner who was lost,
Jesu, hear and save.

4 Saviour, who didst not condemn
those who touched thy garment's hem,
mercy show to us and them:
Jesu, hear and save.

5 Lord, the Way to sinners shown,
Lord, the Truth by sinners known,
Love incarnate on the throne,
Jesu, hear and save.

C. A. ALINGTON 1872–1955

510

LORD of the home, your only Son
received a mother's tender love,
and from an earthly father won
his vision of your home above.

2 Help us, O Lord, our homes to make
your Holy Spirit's dwelling place;
our hands' and hearts' devotion take
to be the servants of your grace.

3 Teach us to keep our homes so fair
that, were our Lord a child once more,
he might be glad our hearth to share,
and find a welcome at our door.

4 Lord, may your Spirit sanctify
each household duty we fulfil;
may we our Master glorify
in glad obedience to your will.

ALBERT F. BAYLY 1901–1984

511

LORD of the worlds above
how pleasant and how fair
the dwellings of thy love,
thy earthly temples, are!
To thine abode
my heart aspires,
with warm desires
to see my God.

2 O happy souls that pray
where God appoints to hear!
O happy ones that pay
their constant service there!
They praise thee still;
and happy they
that love the way
to Sion's hill.

3 They go from strength to strength
through this dark vale of tears,
till each arrives at length,
till each in heaven appears:
O glorious seat!
when God our King
shall thither bring
our willing feet.

ISAAC WATTS 1674–1748
Psalm 84

512

LORD, speak to me, that I may speak
in living echoes of thy tone;
as thou hast sought, so let me seek
thy erring children lost and lone.

2 O lead me, Lord, that I may lead
the wandering and the wavering feet;
O feed me, Lord, that I may feed
thy hungering ones with manna sweet.

3 O strengthen me, that, while I stand
firm on the rock, and strong in thee,
I may stretch out a loving hand
to wrestlers with the troubled sea.

4 O teach me, Lord, that I may teach
the precious things thou dost impart;
and wing my words, that they may reach
the hidden depths of many a heart.

5 O give thine own sweet rest to me,
that I may speak with soothing power
a word in season, as from thee,
to weary ones in needful hour.

6 O use me, Lord, use even me,
just as thou wilt, and when, and where,
until thy blessèd face I see,
thy rest, thy joy, thy glory share.

FRANCES RIDLEY HAVERGAL 1836–1879

513

LORD, the light of your love is shining,
in the midst of the darkness, shining;
Jesus, light of the world, shine upon us,
set us free by the truth you now bring us,
shine on me:
Shine, Jesus, shine,
fill this land with the Father's glory;
blaze, Spirit, blaze,
set our hearts on fire.
Flow, river, flow,
flood the nations with love and mercy;
send forth your word,
Lord, and let there be light!

2 Lord, I come to your awesome presence,
from the shadows into your radiance;
by the blood I may enter your brightness,
search me, try me, consume all my darkness:
shine on me:
Shine, Jesus, shine, ...

3 As we gaze on your kingly brightness,
so our faces display your likeness,
ever changing from glory to glory,
mirrored here, may our lives tell your story:
shine on me:
Shine, Jesus, shine,
fill this land with the Father's glory;
blaze, Spirit, blaze,
set our hearts on fire.
Flow, river, flow,
flood the nations with love and mercy;
send forth your word,
Lord, and let there be light!

GRAHAM KENDRICK *b.* 1950

514

LORD, thy church on earth is seeking
thy renewal from above;
teach us all the art of speaking
with the accent of thy love.
We would heed thy great commission:
'Go now into every place –
preach, baptize, fulfil my mission,
serve with love and share my grace'.

2 Freedom give to those in bondage,
lift the burdens caused by sin.
Give new hope, new strength and courage,
grant release from fears within.
Light for darkness; joy for sorrow;
love for hatred; peace for strife:
these and countless blessings follow
as the Spirit gives new life.

3 In the streets of every city
where the bruised and lonely dwell,
let us show the Saviour's pity,
let us of his mercy tell;
to all lands and peoples bringing
all the richness of thy word,
till the world, thy praises singing,
hails thee Christ, Redeemer, Lord.

HUGH SHERLOCK * 1905–1998

515

LORD, thy word abideth,
and our footsteps guideth;
who its truth believeth
light and joy receiveth.

2 When our foes are near us,
then thy word doth cheer us,
word of consolation,
message of salvation.

3 When the storms are o'er us,
and dark clouds before us,
then its light directeth,
and our way protecteth.

4 Who can tell the pleasure,
who recount the treasure
by thy word imparted
to the simple-hearted?

5 Word of mercy, giving
succour to the living;
word of life, supplying
comfort to the dying.

6 O that we discerning
its most holy learning,
Lord, may love and fear thee,
evermore be near thee!

H. W. BAKER 1821–1877

516

LOVE divine, all loves excelling,
joy of heaven, to earth come down,
fix in us thy humble dwelling,
all thy faithful mercies crown.
Jesu, thou art all compassion,
pure unbounded love thou art;
visit us with thy salvation,
enter every trembling heart.

2 Come, almighty to deliver,
  let us all thy grace receive;
suddenly return, and never,
  never more thy temples leave.
Thee we would be always blessing,
  serve thee as thy hosts above;
pray, and praise thee, without ceasing,
  glory in thy perfect love.

3 Finish then thy new creation:
  pure and spotless let us be;
let us see thy great salvation
  perfectly restored in thee;
changed from glory into glory
  till in heaven we take our place,
till we cast our crowns before thee,
  lost in wonder, love, and praise.

CHARLES WESLEY * 1707–1788

517

LOVING Shepherd of thy sheep,
keep thy lamb, in safety keep;
nothing can thy power withstand,
none can pluck me from thy hand.

2 Loving Saviour, thou didst give
thine own life that we might live,
and the hands outstretched to bless
bear the cruel nails' impress.

3 I would praise thee every day,
gladly all thy will obey,
like thy blessèd ones above
happy in thy precious love.

4 Loving Shepherd, ever near,
teach thy lamb thy voice to hear;
suffer not my steps to stray
from the straight and narrow way.

5 Where thou leadest I would go,
walking in thy steps below,
till before my Father's throne
I shall know as I am known.

Jane E. Leeson 1809–1881

518

MAKE me a captive, Lord,
and then I shall be free;
force me to render up my sword
and I shall conqueror be.
I sink in life's alarms
when by myself I stand;
imprison me within thine arms,
and strong shall be my hand.

2 My heart is weak and poor
until it master find;
it has no spring of action sure,
it varies with the wind.
It cannot freely move,
till thou hast wrought its chain;
enslave it with thy matchless love,
and deathless it shall reign.

3 My will is not my own
till thou hast made it thine;
if it would reach a monarch's throne
it must its crown resign;
it only stands unbent,
amid the clashing strife,
when on thy bosom it has leant
and found in thee its life.

George Matheson 1842–1906

519

MAKE me a channel of your peace.
Where there is hatred, let me bring your love;
where there is injury, your pardon, Lord;
and where there's doubt, true faith in you.
O Master, grant that I may never seek
so much to be consoled as to console,
to be understood as to understand,
to be loved, as to love with all my soul.

2 Make me a channel of your peace.
Where there's despair in life, let me bring hope;
where there is darkness, only light;
and where there's sadness, ever joy.
O Master, grant that I may never seek
so much to be consoled as to console,
to be understood as to understand,
to be loved, as to love with all my soul.

3 Make me a channel of your peace.
It is in pardoning that we are pardoned,
in giving to all men that we receive,
and in dying that we're born to eternal life.

SEBASTIAN TEMPLE 1928–1997
from a prayer of ST FRANCIS OF ASSISI c. 1182–1226

520

MAY the grace of Christ our Saviour,
and the Father's boundless love,
with the Holy Spirit's favour,
rest upon us from above.

2 Thus may we abide in union
with each other and the Lord,
and possess, in sweet communion,
joys which earth cannot afford.

JOHN NEWTON 1725–1807
2 Corinthians 13. 14

521

MAY the mind of Christ my Saviour
live in me from day to day,
by his love and power controlling
all I do or say.

2 May the word of God dwell richly
in my heart from hour to hour,
so that all may see I triumph
only through his power.

3 May the peace of God my Father
rule my life in everything,
that I may be calm to comfort
sick and sorrowing.

4 May the love of Jesus fill me,
as the waters fill the sea;
him exalting, self abasing –
this is victory.

5 May I run the race before me,
strong and brave to face the foe,
looking only unto Jesus
as I onward go.

KATE BARCLAY WILKINSON 1859–1928

522

MY faith looks up to thee,
thou Lamb of Calvary,
Saviour divine!
Now hear me while I pray,
take all my guilt away,
O let me from this day
be wholly thine.

2 May thy rich grace impart
strength to my fainting heart,
my zeal inspire;
as thou hast died for me,
O may my love to thee
pure, warm, and changeless be,
a living fire.

3 While life's dark maze I tread,
and griefs around me spread,
be thou my guide;
bid darkness turn to day,
wipe sorrow's tears away,
nor let me ever stray
from thee aside.

4 When ends life's transient dream,
when death's cold sullen stream
shall o'er me roll,
blest Saviour, then in love
fear and distrust remove;
O bear me safe above,
a ransomed soul.

RAY PALMER * 1808–1887

523

MY God, how wonderful thou art,
thy majesty how bright,
how beautiful thy mercy-seat
in depths of burning light!

2 How dread are thine eternal years,
O everlasting Lord,
by prostrate spirits day and night
incessantly adored!

3 How wonderful, how beautiful,
the sight of thee must be,
thine endless wisdom, boundless power,
and aweful purity!

4 O how I fear thee, living God,
with deepest, tenderest fears,
and worship thee with trembling hope
and penitential tears!

5 Yet I may love thee too, O Lord,
almighty as thou art,
for thou hast stooped to ask of me
the love of my poor heart.

6 No earthly father loves like thee,
no mother, e'er so mild,
bears and forbears as thou hast done
with me, thy sinful child.

7 Father of Jesus, love's reward,
what rapture will it be,
prostrate before thy throne to lie
and gaze and gaze on thee!

F. W. FABER 1814–1863

524

MY God, I love thee; not because
I hope for heaven thereby,
nor yet because who love thee not
are lost eternally.

2 Thou, O my Jesus, thou didst me
upon the cross embrace;
for me didst bear the nails and spear,
and manifold disgrace;

3 And griefs and torments numberless,
and sweat of agony;
yea, death itself — and all for me
who was thine enemy.

4 Then why, O blessèd Jesu Christ,
should I not love thee well?
Not for the sake of winning heaven,
nor of escaping hell;

5 Not from the hope of gaining aught,
not seeking a reward;
but as thyself hast lovèd me,
O ever-loving Lord.

6 So would I love thee, dearest Lord,
and in thy praise will sing;
solely because thou art my God,
and my most loving King.

O Deus ego amo te
Latin, 17th century
tr. EDWARD CASWALL * 1814–1878

525

NAME of all majesty,
fathomless mystery,
King of the ages
by angels adored;
power and authority,
splendour and dignity,
bow to his mastery,
Jesus is Lord!

2 Child of our destiny,
God from eternity,
love of the Father
on sinners outpoured;
see now what God has done
sending his only Son,
Christ the belovèd One,
Jesus is Lord!

3 Saviour of Calvary,
costliest victory,
darkness defeated
and Eden restored;
born as a man to die,
nailed to a cross on high,
cold in the grave to lie,
Jesus is Lord!

4 Source of all sovereignty,
light, immortality,
life everlasting
and heaven assured;
so with the ransomed, we
praise him eternally,
Christ in his majesty,
Jesus is Lord!

TIMOTHY DUDLEY-SMITH *b.* 1926

526

NEARER, my God, to thee,
nearer to thee!
E'en though it be a cross
that raiseth me,
still all my song shall be:
'Nearer, my God, to thee,
nearer to thee!'

2 Though, like the wanderer,
the sun gone down,
darkness be over me,
my rest a stone;
yet in my dreams I'd be
nearer, my God, to thee,
nearer to thee!

3 There let the way appear
steps unto heaven –
all that thou sendest me
in mercy given –
angels to beckon me
nearer, my God, to thee,
nearer to thee!

4 Then, with my waking thoughts
bright with thy praise,
out of my stony griefs
Bethel I'll raise;
so by my woes to be
nearer, my God, to thee,
nearer to thee!

Sarah Flower Adams 1805–1848
Genesis 28. 10–22

527

NEW songs of celebration render
to him who has great wonders done.
Love sits enthroned in ageless splendour:
come and adore the Mighty One.
He has made known his great salvation
which all his friends with joy confess:
he has revealed to every nation
his everlasting righteousness.

2 Joyfully, heartily resounding,
let every instrument and voice
peal out the praise of grace abounding,
calling the whole world to rejoice.
Trumpets and organs, set in motion
such sounds as make the heavens ring;
all things that live in earth and ocean,
make music for your mighty King.

3 Rivers and seas and torrents roaring,
honour the Lord with wild acclaim;
mountains and stones look up adoring
and find a voice to praise his name.
Righteous, commanding, ever glorious,
praises be his that never cease:
just is our God, whose truth victorious
establishes the world in peace.

Erik Routley 1917–1982
Psalm 98

528

NOT far beyond the sea, nor high
above the heavens, but very nigh
thy voice, O God, is heard.
For each new step of faith we take
thou hast more truth and light to break
forth from thy holy word.

2 Rooted and grounded in thy love,
with saints on earth and saints above
we join in full accord,
to grasp the breadth, length, depth, and height,
the crucified and risen might
of Christ, the Incarnate Word.

3 Help us to press toward that mark,
and, though our vision now is dark,
to live by what we see.
So, when we see thee face to face,
thy truth and light our dwelling-place
for evermore shall be.

George B. Caird 1917–1984

529

NOTHING distress you,
nothing affright you,
everything passes,
  God will abide.
Patient endeavour
accomplishes all things;
who God possesses
  needs naught beside.

2 Lift your mind upward,
fair are his mansions,
nothing distress you,
  cast fear away.
Follow Christ freely,
his love will light you,
nothing affright you,
  in the dark way.

3 See the world's glory!
Fading its splendour,
everything passes,
  all is denied.
Look ever homeward
to the eternal;
faithful in promise
  God will abide.

4 Love in due measure
measureless goodness;
patient endeavour,
  run to love's call!
Faith burning brightly
be your soul's shelter;
who hopes, believing,
  accomplishes all.

5 Hell may assail you,
it cannot move you;
sorrows may grieve you,
faith may be tried.
Though you have nothing,
he is your treasure:
who God possesses
needs naught beside.

from *Nada te turbe*
by St Teresa of Avila 1515–1582
tr. Colin P. Thompson *b.* 1945

530

NOW thank we all our God
with heart and hands and voices,
who wondrous things hath done,
in whom his world rejoices;
who from our mother's arms
hath blessed us on our way
with countless gifts of love,
and still is ours to-day.

2 O may this bounteous God
through all our life be near us,
with ever joyful hearts
and blessèd peace to cheer us;
and keep us in his grace,
and guide us when perplexed,
and free us from all ills
in this world and the next.

3 All praise and thanks to God
the Father now be given,
the Son, and him who reigns
with them in highest heaven,
the one eternal God,
whom earth and heaven adore;
for thus it was, is now,
and shall be evermore.

MARTIN RINKART 1586–1649
tr. CATHERINE WINKWORTH 1827–1878

531

O CHRIST the Word incarnate,
O wisdom from on high,
O truth unchanged, unchanging,
O light of our dark sky,
we praise thee for the radiance
that from the hallowed page,
a lantern to our footsteps
shines on from age to age.

2 The Church from her dear Master
received the gift divine,
and still that light she lifteth
o'er all the earth to shine;
it is the precious treasury
where gems of truth are stored;
it is the heaven-drawn picture
of Christ, the living Word.

3 O make thy Church, dear Saviour,
a lamp of burnished gold,
to bear before the nations
thy true light, as of old;
O teach thy wandering pilgrims
by this their path to trace,
till, clouds and darkness ended,
they see thee face to face.

W. WALSHAM HOW * 1823–1897

532

O FOR a closer walk with God,
  a calm and heavenly frame;
a light to shine upon the road
  that leads me to the Lamb!

2 What peaceful hours I once enjoyed,
  how sweet their memory still!
But they have left an aching void
  the world can never fill.

3 Return, O holy Dove, return,
  sweet messenger of rest:
I hate the sins that made thee mourn
  and drove thee from my breast.

4 The dearest idol I have known,
  whate'er that idol be,
help me to tear it from thy throne
  and worship only thee.

5 So shall my walk be close with God,
  calm and serene my frame;
so purer light shall mark the road
  that leads me to the Lamb.

WILLIAM COWPER 1731–1800

533

O FOR a heart to praise my God,
  a heart from sin set free;
a heart that's sprinkled with the blood
  so freely shed for me:

2 A heart resigned, submissive, meek,
  my great Redeemer's throne;
where only Christ is heard to speak,
  where Jesus reigns alone:

3 A humble, lowly, contrite heart,
believing, true, and clean,
which neither life nor death can part
from him that dwells within:

4 A heart in every thought renewed,
and full of love divine;
perfect and right and pure and good —
a copy, Lord, of thine.

5 Thy nature, gracious Lord, impart,
come quickly from above;
write thy new name upon my heart,
thy new best name of Love.

CHARLES WESLEY * 1707–1788
Psalm 51. 10

534

O FOR a thousand tongues to sing
my dear Redeemer's praise,
the glories of my God and King,
the triumphs of his grace!

2 Jesus! the name that charms our fears,
that bids our sorrows cease;
'tis music in the sinner's ears,
'tis life and health and peace.

3 He breaks the power of cancelled sin,
he sets the prisoner free:
his blood can make the foulest clean;
his blood availed for me.

4 He speaks; and, listening to his voice,
new life the dead receive,
the mournful broken hearts rejoice,
the humble poor believe.

5 Hear him, ye deaf; his praise, ye dumb,
your loosened tongues employ;
ye blind, behold your Saviour come;
and leap, ye lame, for joy!

6 My gracious Master and my God,
assist me to proclaim
and spread through all the earth abroad
the honours of thy name.

CHARLES WESLEY 1707–1788

535

O GOD in heaven, whose loving plan
ordained for us our parents' care,
and, from the time our life began,
the shelter of a home to share;
our Father, on the homes we love
send down thy blessing from above.

2 May young and old together find
in Christ, the Lord of every day,
that fellowship our homes may bind
in joy and sorrow, work and play.
Our Father, on the homes we love
send down thy blessing from above.

3 The sins that mar our homes forgive;
from all self-seeking set us free;
parents and children, may we live
in glad obedience to thee.
Our Father, on the homes we love
send down thy blessing from above.

4 O Father, in our homes preside,
their duties shared as in thy sight;
in kindly ways be thou our guide,
on mirth and trouble shed thy light.
Our Father, on the homes we love
send down thy blessing from above.

HUGH MARTIN * 1890–1964

536

O GOD of Bethel, by whose hand
thy people still are fed,
who through this weary pilgrimage
hast all our fathers led;

2 Our vows, our prayers, we now present
before thy throne of grace;
God of our fathers, be the God
of their succeeding race.

3 Through each perplexing path of life
our wandering footsteps guide;
give us each day our daily bread,
and raiment fit provide.

4 O spread thy covering wings around
till all our wanderings cease,
and at our Father's loved abode
our souls arrive in peace.

PHILIP DODDRIDGE 1702–1751
Genesis 28. 20–22

537

O GOD, our help in ages past,
our hope for years to come,
our shelter from the stormy blast,
and our eternal home;

2 Under the shadow of thy throne
thy saints have dwelt secure;
sufficient is thine arm alone,
and our defence is sure.

3 Before the hills in order stood,
or earth received her frame,
from everlasting thou art God,
to endless years the same.

4 A thousand ages in thy sight
are like an evening gone,
short as the watch that ends the night
before the rising sun.

5 Time, like an ever-rolling stream,
bears all its sons away;
they fly forgotten, as a dream
dies at the opening day.

6 O God, our help in ages past,
our hope for years to come,
be thou our guard while troubles last,
and our eternal home.

ISAAC WATTS 1674–1748
Psalm 90

538

O JESUS, I have promised
to serve thee to the end;
be thou for ever near me,
my Master and my Friend:
I shall not fear the battle
if thou art by my side,
nor wander from the pathway
if thou wilt be my guide.

*2 O let me feel thee near me:
the world is ever near;
I see the sights that dazzle,
the tempting sounds I hear;
my foes are ever near me,
around me and within;
but, Jesus, draw thou nearer,
and shield my soul from sin.

3 O let me hear thee speaking
in accents clear and still
above the storms of passion,
the murmurs of self-will;
O speak to reassure me,
to hasten or control;
O speak, and make me listen,
thou guardian of my soul.

4 O Jesus, thou hast promised
to all who follow thee,
that where thou art in glory
there shall thy servant be;
and, Jesus, I have promised
to serve thee to the end:
O give me grace to follow,
my Master and my Friend.

5 O let me see thy foot-marks,
and in them plant mine own;
my hope to follow duly
is in thy strength alone:
O guide me, call me, draw me,
uphold me to the end;
and then in heaven receive me,
my Saviour and my Friend.

J. E. BODE 1816–1874

539

O JESUS, King most wonderful;
thou conqueror renowned,
thou sweetness most ineffable,
in whom all joys are found!

2 When once thou visitest the heart,
then truth begins to shine,
then earthly vanities depart,
then kindles love divine.

3 O Jesus, light of all below!
Thou fount of living fire,
surpassing all the joys we know,
and all we can desire:

4 Jesus, may all confess thy name,
thy wondrous love adore;
and, seeking thee, themselves inflame
to seek thee more and more.

*5 Thee may our tongues for ever bless,
thee may we love alone,
and ever in our lives express
the image of thine own.

*6 Abide with us, and let thy light
shine, Lord, on every heart;
dispel the darkness of our night,
and joy to all impart.

7 Jesus, our love and joy, to thee,
the Father's only Son,
all might, and praise, and glory be,
while endless ages run.

Jesu, Rex admirabilis
Latin, *c.* 12th century
tr. EDWARD CASWALL 1814–1878

540

O LORD of heaven and earth and sea,
to thee all praise and glory be.
How shall we show our love to thee
who givest all?

*2 The golden sunshine, vernal air,
sweet flowers and fruit, thy love declare;
when harvests ripen, thou art there,
who givest all.

3 For peaceful homes, and healthful days,
for all the blessings earth displays,
we owe thee thankfulness and praise,
who givest all.

4 Thou didst not spare thine only Son,
but gav'st him for a world undone,
and freely with that blessèd One
thou givest all.

5 Thou giv'st the Holy Spirit's dower,
Spirit of life and love and power,
and dost his sevenfold graces shower
upon us all.

6 For souls redeemed, for sins forgiven,
for means of grace and hopes of heaven,
Father, what can to thee be given,
who givest all?

*7 We lose what on ourselves we spend,
we have as treasure without end
whatever, Lord, to thee we lend,
who givest all.

8 To thee, from whom we all derive
our life, our gifts, our power to give:
O may we ever with thee live,
who givest all.

CHRISTOPHER WORDSWORTH 1807–1885

541

O LOVE divine, how sweet thou art!
When shall I find my longing heart
all taken up by thee?
I thirst, I faint, I die to prove
the greatness of redeeming love,
the love of Christ to me.

2 Stronger his love than death or hell;
its riches are unsearchable:
the first-born sons of light
desire in vain its depth to see;
they cannot reach the mystery,
the length and breadth and height.

*3 God only knows the love of God;
O that it now were shed abroad
in this poor stony heart!
For love I sigh, for love I pine;
this only portion, Lord, be mine,
be mine this better part.

4 For ever would I take my seat
with Mary at the Master's feet:
be this my happy choice;
my only care, delight, and bliss,
my joy, my heaven on earth, be this,
to hear the Bridegroom's voice!

5 Thy only love do I require,
nothing on earth beneath desire,
nothing in heaven above:
let earth and heaven, and all things go,
give me thine only love to know,
give me thine only love.

CHARLES WESLEY * 1707–1788

542

O LOVE that wilt not let me go,
I rest my weary soul in thee;
I give thee back the life I owe,
that in thine ocean depths its flow
may richer, fuller be.

2 O light that followest all my way,
I yield my flickering torch to thee;
my heart restores its borrowed ray,
that in thy sunshine's blaze its day
may brighter, fairer be.

3 O joy that seekest me through pain,
I cannot close my heart to thee;
I trace the rainbow through the rain,
and feel the promise is not vain,
that morn shall tearless be.

4 O cross that liftest up my head,
I dare not ask to fly from thee;
I lay in dust life's glory dead,
and from the ground there blossoms red
life that shall endless be.

GEORGE MATHESON 1842–1906

543

O PRAISE ye the Lord! Praise him in the height;
rejoice in his word, ye angels of light;
ye heavens adore him by whom ye were made,
and worship before him, in brightness arrayed.

2 O praise ye the Lord! Praise him upon earth,
in tuneful accord, ye sons of new birth;
praise him who hath brought you his grace from above,
praise him who hath taught you to sing of his love.

3 O praise ye the Lord, all things that give sound;
each jubilant chord re-echo around;
loud organs, his glory forth tell in deep tone,
and, sweet harp, the story of what he hath done.

4 O praise ye the Lord! Thanksgiving and song
to him be outpoured all ages along:
for love in creation, for heaven restored,
for grace of salvation, O praise ye the Lord!

H. W. BAKER 1821–1877
based on Psalm 150

544

O RAISE your eyes on high and see,
there stands our sovereign Lord;
his glory is this day revealed,
his word a two-edged sword.

2 We glimpse the splendour and the power
of him who conquered death,
the Christ in whom the universe
knows God's creating breath.

3 Of every creed and nation King
in him all strife is stilled;
the promise made to Abraham
in him has been fulfilled.

4 The prophets stand and with great joy
give witness as they gaze;
the Father with a sign has sealed
our trust, our hope, our praise.

RALPH WRIGHT *b.* 1938

545

O SING a song of Bethlehem,
of shepherds watching there,
and of the news that came to them
from angels in the air:
the light that shone on Bethlehem
fills all the world today;
of Jesus' birth and peace on earth
the angels sing alway.

2 O sing a song of Nazareth,
of sunny days of joy,
O sing of fragrant flowers' breath
and of the sinless Boy:
for now the flowers of Nazareth
in every heart may grow;
now spreads the fame of his dear name
on all the winds that blow.

3 O sing a song of Galilee,
of lake and woods and hill,
of him who walked upon the sea
and bade its waves be still:
for though, like waves on Galilee,
dark seas of trouble roll,
when faith has heard the Master's word
falls peace upon the soul.

4 O sing a song of Calvary,
its glory and dismay;
of him who hung upon the tree
and took our sins away:
for he who died on Calvary
is risen from the grave,
and Christ our Lord, by heaven adored,
is mighty now to save.

LOUIS F. BENSON 1855–1930

546

O WORSHIP the King, all glorious above;
O gratefully sing his power and his love;
our shield and defender, the Ancient of Days,
pavilioned in splendour and girded with praise.

2 O tell of his might, O sing of his grace,
whose robe is the light, whose canopy space;
his chariots of wrath the deep thunder clouds form,
and dark is his path on the wings of the storm.

*3 The earth with its store of wonders untold,
Almighty, thy power hath founded of old;
hath stablished it fast by a changeless decree,
and round it hath cast, like a mantle, the sea.

4 Thy bountiful care what tongue can recite?
It breathes in the air, it shines in the light;
it streams from the hills, it descends to the plain,
and sweetly distils in the dew and the rain.

5 Frail children of dust, and feeble as frail,
in thee do we trust, nor find thee to fail;
thy mercies how tender, how firm to the end,
Our Maker, Defender, Redeemer, and Friend.

6 O measureless might, ineffable love,
while angels delight to hymn thee above,
thy humbler creation, though feeble their lays,
with true adoration shall sing to thy praise.

ROBERT GRANT 1779–1838
Psalm 104

547

OFT in danger, oft in woe,
onward, Christians, onward go;
bear the toil, maintain the strife,
strengthened with the bread of life.

2 Onward, Christians, onward go,
join the war, and face the foe;
will ye flee in danger's hour?
Know ye not your Captain's power?

3 Let not sorrow dim your eye;
soon shall every tear be dry:
let not fears your course impede;
great your strength, if great your need.

4 Let your drooping hearts be glad;
march in heavenly armour clad;
fight, nor think the battle long:
soon shall victory wake your song.

5 Onward then in battle move;
more than conquerors ye shall prove:
though opposed by many a foe,
Christian soldiers, onward go.

HENRY KIRKE WHITE 1785–1806
and others

548

ONE more step along the world I go,
one more step along the world I go;
from the old things to the new,
keep me travelling along with you:
And it's from the old I travel to the new;
keep me travelling along with you.

2 Round the corners of the world I turn,
more and more about the world I learn;
all the new things that I see
you'll be looking at along with me.
And it's from the old ...

3 As I travel through the bad and good,
keep me travelling the way I should;
where I see no way to go
you'll be telling me the way, I know:
And it's from the old ...

4 Give me courage when the world is rough,
keep me loving though the world is tough;
leap and sing in all I do,
keep me travelling along with you:
And it's from the old ...

5 You are older than the world can be,
you are younger than the life in me;
ever old and ever new,
keep me travelling along with you.
And it's from the old I travel to the new;
keep me travelling along with you.

SYDNEY CARTER *b.* 1915

549

ONWARD, Christian soldiers,
marching as to war,
with the cross of Jesus
going on before:
Christ the royal Master
leads against the foe;
forward into battle,
see, his banners go!
Onward, Christian soldiers,
marching as to war,
with the cross of Jesus
going on before!

*2 At the sign of triumph
Satan's host doth flee;
on then, Christian soldiers,
on to victory!
Hell's foundations quiver
at the shout of praise;
brothers, lift your voices,
loud your anthems raise:

*3 Like a mighty army
moves the church of God;
brothers, we are treading
where the saints have trod:
we are not divided,
all one body we,
one in hope and doctrine,
one in charity:

4 Crowns and thrones may perish,
kingdoms rise and wane,
but the church of Jesus
constant will remain:
gates of hell can never
'gainst that church prevail;
we have Christ's own promise,
and that cannot fail:

5 Onward, then, ye people,
join our happy throng,
blend with ours your voices
in the triumph song:
glory, laud, and honour
unto Christ the King,
this through countless ages
men and angels sing:

SABINE BARING-GOULD * 1834–1924

550

OUR Father, by whose servants
our house was built of old,
whose hand hath crowned her children
with blessings manifold,
for thine unfailing mercies
far-strewn along our way,
with all who passed before us,
we praise thy name today.

2 The changeful years unresting
their silent course have sped,
new comrades ever bringing
in comrades' steps to tread:
and some are long forgotten,
long spent their hopes and fears;
safe rest they in thy keeping,
who changest not with years.

3 They reap not where they laboured,
we reap what they have sown;
our harvest may be garnered
by ages yet unknown.
The days of old have dowered us
with gifts beyond all praise:
our Father, make us faithful
to serve the coming days.

G. W. BRIGGS 1875–1959

551

OUR hunger cries from plenty, Lord:
   for bread which does not turn to stone;
for peace the world can never give;
   for truth unreached, for love unknown.

2 'Let all who hunger come to me!'
   Christ's bread is life, his word is true;
our lives are grounded in that love
   which is creating all things new.

3 Enlarge the boundaries of our love,
   O Life of God, so freely given,
till all whom hunger breaks are whole
   through Christ, the broken bread of heaven.

COLIN P. THOMPSON *b.* 1945

552

OUR Saviour's infant cries were heard,
   and met by human love,
before he preached one saving word
   or prayed to God above.
By trusting Christ to human care,
   God blessed for evermore
the care of children everywhere –
   the bruised, the lost, the poor.

2 Whoever calms a child by night
   or guides a youth by day,
serves him whose birth by lantern-light
   was on a bed of hay.
For Christ, who was a refugee
   from Herod and his sword,
is seeking now, through us, to be
   our children's friend and Lord.

THOMAS H. TROEGER *b.* 1945

553

PEACE, perfect peace, in this dark world of sin?
The blood of Jesus whispers peace within.

2 Peace, perfect peace, by thronging duties pressed?
To do the will of Jesus, this is rest.

3 Peace, perfect peace, death shadowing us and ours?
Jesus has vanquished death and all its powers.

4 Peace, perfect peace, our future all unknown?
Jesus we know, and he is on the throne.

5 It is enough: earth's struggles soon shall cease,
and Jesus call to heaven's perfect peace.

EDWARD H. BICKERSTETH 1825–1906

554

POUR out thy Spirit from on high,
and thine assembled servants bless;
graces and gifts to each supply,
and clothe thy priests with righteousness.

2 Within thy temple when they stand,
to teach the truth as taught by thee,
Saviour, like stars in thy right hand
let all thy church's pastors be.

3 Wisdom and zeal and faith impart,
firmness with meekness, from above,
to bear thy people in their heart,
and love the souls whom thou dost love;

4 To watch and pray and never faint,
by day and night their guard to keep,
to warn the sinner, cheer the saint,
to feed thy lambs and tend thy sheep.

5 So, when their work is finished here,
may they in hope their charge resign;
when the Chief Shepherd shall appear,
O God, may they and we be thine.

James Montgomery * 1771–1854

555

PRAISE, my soul, the King of heaven,
to his feet thy tribute bring;
ransomed, healed, restored, forgiven,
who like me his praise should sing?
Alleluia, alleluia,
praise the everlasting King.

2 Praise him for his grace and favour
to our fathers in distress;
praise him still the same for ever,
slow to chide, and swift to bless:
Alleluia, alleluia,
glorious in his faithfulness.

3 Father-like, he tends and spares us,
well our feeble frame he knows;
in his hands he gently bears us,
rescues us from all our foes:
Alleluia, alleluia,
widely as his mercy flows.

4 Angels, help us to adore him;
ye behold him face to face;
sun and moon, bow down before him,
dwellers all in time and space:
Alleluia, alleluia,
praise with us the God of grace.

Henry Francis Lyte 1793–1847
from Psalm 103

556

PRAISE the Lord! Ye heavens, adore him;
praise him, angels, in the height;
sun and moon, rejoice before him,
praise him, all ye stars and light.
Praise the Lord! for he hath spoken;
worlds his mighty voice obeyed:
laws, which never shall be broken,
for their guidance he hath made.

2 Praise the Lord! for he is glorious;
never shall his promise fail:
God hath made his saints victorious;
sin and death shall not prevail.
Praise the God of our salvation;
hosts on high, his power proclaim;
heaven and earth and all creation,
laud and magnify his name!

Foundling Hospital Collection c. 1796
Psalm 148

557

PRAISE to the Holiest in the height,
and in the depth be praise:
in all his words most wonderful,
most sure in all his ways.

2 O loving wisdom of our God!
When all was sin and shame,
a second Adam to the fight
and to the rescue came.

3 O wisest love! that flesh and blood,
which did in Adam fail,
should strive afresh against the foe,
should strive and should prevail;

4 And that a higher gift than grace
should flesh and blood refine,
God's presence and his very self,
and essence all-divine.

5 O generous love! that he, who smote
in Man for man the foe,
the double agony in Man
for man should undergo;

6 And in the garden secretly,
and on the cross on high,
should teach his brethren, and inspire
to suffer and to die.

7 Praise to the Holiest in the height,
and in the depth be praise:
in all his words most wonderful,
most sure in all his ways.

JOHN HENRY NEWMAN 1801–1890

558

PRAISE to the Lord, the Almighty, the King of creation;
O my soul, praise him, for he is thy health and salvation:
all ye who hear,
now to his temple draw near,
joining in glad adoration.

2 Praise to the Lord, who o'er all things so
wondrously reigneth,
shieldeth thee gently from harm, or when
fainting sustaineth:
hast thou not seen
how thy heart's wishes have been
granted in what he ordaineth?

3 Praise to the Lord, who doth prosper thy work
and defend thee;
surely his goodness and mercy shall daily attend thee:
ponder anew
what the Almighty can do,
if to the end he befriend thee.

4 Praise to the Lord! O let all that is in me adore him!
All that hath life and breath, come now with
praises before him!
Let the Amen
sound from his people again:
gladly for aye we adore him!

JOACHIM NEANDER 1650–1680
tr. CATHERINE WINKWORTH * 1827–1878

559

PRAY for the church afflicted and oppressed,
for all who suffer for the gospel's sake,
that Christ may show us how to serve them best
in that one kingdom Satan cannot shake.
But how much more than us they have to give,
who by their dying show us how to live!

2 Pray for Christ's dissidents, who daily wait,
as Jesus waited in the olive grove,
the unjust trial, the pre-determined fate,
the world's contempt for reconciling love.
Shall all they won for us, at such a cost,
be by our negligence or weakness lost?

3 Pray that if times of testing should lay bare
what sort we are, who call ourselves his own,
we may be counted worthy then to wear,
with quiet fortitude, Christ's only crown:
the crown that in his saints he wears again
the crown of thorns that signifies his reign.

F. PRATT GREEN 1903–2000

560

PRAY that Jerusalem may have
peace and felicity:
let them that love thee and thy peace
have still prosperity.

2 Therefore I wish that peace may still
within thy walls remain,
and ever may thy palaces
prosperity retain.

3 Now, for my friends' and brethren's sake,
peace be in thee, I'll say;
and for the house of God our Lord
I'll seek thy good alway.

Scottish Psalter 1650
Psalm 122

561

PRAYER is the soul's sincere desire,
uttered or unexpressed;
the motion of a hidden fire
that trembles in the breast.

2 Prayer is the simplest form of speech
that infant lips can try,
prayer the sublimest strains that reach
the Majesty on high.

3 Prayer is the Christian's vital breath,
the Christian's native air,
his watchword at the gates of death:
he enters heaven with prayer.

4 Prayer is the contrite sinner's voice,
returning from his ways;
while angels in their songs rejoice,
and cry, 'Behold, he prays!'

5 The saints in prayer appear as one,
in word and deed and mind;
while with the Father and the Son
sweet fellowship they find.

6 Nor prayer is made on earth alone:
the Holy Spirit pleads,
and Jesus on the eternal throne
for sinners intercedes.

7 O Thou by whom we come to God,
the Life, the Truth, the Way,
the path of prayer thyself hast trod:
Lord, teach us how to pray!

JAMES MONTGOMERY 1771–1854

562

PUT thou thy trust in God,
in duty's path go on;
walk in his strength with faith and hope,
so shall thy work be done.

2 Commit thy ways to him,
thy works into his hands,
and rest on his unchanging word,
who heaven and earth commands.

3 Though years on years roll on,
his covenant shall endure;
though clouds and darkness hide his path,
the promised grace is sure.

4 Give to the winds thy fears;
hope, and be undismayed:
God hears thy sighs and counts thy tears;
God shall lift up thy head.

5 Through waves and clouds and storms
his power will clear thy way:
wait thou his time; the darkest night
shall end in brightest day.

6 Leave to his sovereign sway
to choose and to command;
so shalt thou, wondering, own his way,
how wise, how strong his hand.

PAUL GERHARDT 1607–1676
tr. JOHN WESLEY 1703–1791 and others

563

REJOICE! The Lord is King,
your Lord and King adore;
mortals, give thanks and sing,
and triumph evermore:
Lift up your heart, lift up your voice;
rejoice, again I say, rejoice.

2 Jesus the Saviour reigns,
the God of truth and love;
when he had purged our stains,
he took his seat above:
Lift up your heart, ...

3 His kingdom cannot fail;
he rules o'er earth and heaven;
the keys of death and hell
are to our Jesus given:
Lift up your heart, ...

4 He sits at God's right hand
till all his foes submit,
and bow to his command,
and fall beneath his feet:
Lift up your heart, ...

5 Rejoice in glorious hope;
Jesus the judge shall come,
and take his servants up
to their eternal home:
We soon shall hear the archangel's voice;
the trump of God shall sound: rejoice!

CHARLES WESLEY 1707–1788

564

RESTORE in us, O God,
the splendour of your love;
renew your image in our hearts,
and all our sins remove.

2 O Spirit, wake in us
the wonder of your power;
from fruitless fear unfurl our lives
like springtime bud and flower.

3 Bring us, O Christ, to share
the fullness of your joy;
baptise us in the risen life
that death cannot destroy.

4 Three-personed God, fulfil
the promise of your grace,
that we, when all our searching ends,
may see you face to face.

CARL P. DAW JR *b.* 1944

565

ROCK of ages, cleft for me,
let me hide myself in thee;
let the water and the blood,
from thy riven side which flowed,
be of sin the double cure:
cleanse me from its guilt and power.

2 Not the labours of my hands
can fulfil thy law's demands;
could my zeal no respite know,
could my tears for ever flow,
all for sin could not atone:
thou must save, and thou alone.

3 Nothing in my hand I bring,
simply to thy cross I cling;
naked, come to thee for dress;
helpless, look to thee for grace;
foul, I to the fountain fly;
wash me, Saviour, or I die.

4 While I draw this fleeting breath,
when my eyelids close in death,
when I soar through tracts unknown,
see thee on thy judgement throne;
Rock of ages, cleft for me,
let me hide myself in thee.

A. M. TOPLADY * 1740–1778

566

SHEPHERD divine, our wants relieve
in this our evil day;
to all thy tempted followers give
the power to watch and pray.

2 Long as our fiery trials last,
long as the cross we bear,
O let our souls on thee be cast
in never-ceasing prayer.

3 The Spirit's interceding grace
give us in faith to claim;
to wrestle till we see thy face,
and know thy hidden name.

4 Till thou thy perfect love impart,
till thou thyself bestow,
be this the cry of every heart,
'I will not let thee go.'

5 I will not let thee go, unless
thou tell thy name to me;
with all thy great salvation bless,
and make me all like thee.

6 Then let me on the mountain-top
behold thy open face;
where faith in sight is swallowed up,
and prayer in endless praise.

CHARLES WESLEY * 1707–1788
Genesis 32. 24–30

567

SING, all creation, sing to God in gladness,
joyously serve him, singing hymns of homage,
chanting his praises, come before his presence:
praise the Almighty!

2 Know that our God is Lord of all the ages;
he is our maker: we are all his creatures,
people he fashioned, sheep he leads to pasture:
praise the Almighty!

3 Enter his temple, ringing out his praises;
sing in thanksgiving as you come before him;
blessing his bounty, glorify his greatness:
praise the Almighty!

4 Great in his goodness is the Lord we worship;
steadfast his kindness, love that knows no ending;
faithful his word is, changeless, everlasting:
praise the Almighty!

JAMES QUINN *b.* 1919
Psalm 100

568

SING alleluia forth ye saints on high,
and let the church on earth make glad reply:
To Christ the King, sing alleluia!

2 To him who is both Word of God and Son,
who, out of love, our nature did put on:

3 To him who, born of Mary, shared our life,
and in his manhood triumphed in the strife:

4 To him who did for all our sins atone,
in naked majesty on Calvary's throne:

5 To him who rose victorious from the dead
and reigns on high, his people's Lord and Head:

6 To him who sent the Holy Spirit's grace
to bear the Father's love to every race:

7 To him, the universal Saviour, now
let every knee in adoration bow:

8 Let men and angels praise our Lord and King,
and all creation, too, its tribute bring:
To Christ the King, sing alleluia!

G. B. Timms * 1910–1997

569

SING praise to God who reigns above,
the God of all creation,
the God of power, the God of love,
the God of our salvation;
with healing balm my soul he fills,
and every faithless murmur stills:
to God all praise and glory!

2 The Lord is never far away,
but, through all grief distressing,
an ever-present help and stay,
our peace and joy and blessing;
as with a mother's tender hand
he leads his own, his chosen band:
to God all praise and glory!

3 Thus all my gladsome way along
I sing aloud thy praises,
that all may hear the grateful song
my voice unwearied raises;
be joyful in the Lord, my heart;
both soul and body bear your part:
to God all praise and glory!

JOHANN JAKOB SCHÜTZ 1640–1690
tr. FRANCES ELIZABETH COX 1812–1897

570

SING to the Lord a joyful song,
lift up your hearts, your voices raise;
to us his gracious gifts belong,
to him our songs of love and praise.

2 For life and love, for rest and food,
for daily help and nightly care,
sing to the Lord, for he is good,
and praise his name, for it is fair.

3 For strength to those who on him wait,
his truth to prove, his will to do,
praise ye our God, for he is great;
trust in his name, for it is true.

4 For joys untold, that from above
cheer those who love his sweet employ,
sing to our God, for he is Love,
exalt his name, for it is Joy.

5 Sing to the Lord of heaven and earth,
whom angels serve and saints adore,
the Father, Son, and Holy Ghost,
to whom be praise for evermore.

J. S. B. MONSELL 1811–1875

571

SOLDIERS of Christ, arise,
and put your armour on,
strong in the strength which God supplies,
through his eternal Son;

2 Strong in the Lord of Hosts,
and in his mighty power:
who in the strength of Jesus trusts
is more than conqueror.

3 Stand then in his great might,
with all his strength endued;
and take, to arm you for the fight,
the panoply of God.

4 From strength to strength go on,
wrestle and fight and pray;
tread all the powers of darkness down,
and win the well-fought day;

5 that, having all things done,
and all your conflicts past,
ye may o'ercome, through Christ alone,
and stand entire at last.

CHARLES WESLEY 1707–1788
Ephesians 6. 10–18

572

SOMETIMES a light surprises
the Christian while he sings:
it is the Lord who rises
with healing in his wings;
when comforts are declining,
he grants the soul again
a season of clear shining
to cheer it after rain.

2 In holy contemplation
we sweetly then pursue
the theme of God's salvation,
and find it ever new:
set free from present sorrow,
we cheerfully can say,
'E'en let the unknown morrow
bring with it what it may':

3 It can bring with it nothing
but he will bear us through;
who gives the lilies clothing
will clothe his people too:
beneath the spreading heavens
no creature but is fed;
and he who feeds the ravens
will give his children bread.

4 Though vine nor fig-tree neither
their wonted fruit should bear,
though all the fields should wither,
nor flocks nor herds be there;
yet, God the same abiding,
his praise shall tune my voice;
for, while in him confiding,
I cannot but rejoice.

William Cowper 1731–1800

573

SON of God, eternal Saviour,
source of life and truth and grace,
Son of Man, whose birth incarnate
hallows all our human race,
thou, our Head, who, throned in glory,
for thine own dost ever plead,
fill us with thy love and pity;
heal our wrongs, and help our need.

*2 As thou, Lord, hast lived for others,
so may we for others live;
freely have thy gifts been granted,
freely may thy servants give:
thine the gold and thine the silver,
thine the wealth of land and sea,
we but stewards of thy bounty,
held in solemn trust for thee.

3 Come, O Christ, and reign among us,
King of love, and Prince of peace;
hush the storm of strife and passion,
bid its cruel discords cease;
by thy patient years of toiling,
by thy silent hours of pain,
quench our fevered thirst of pleasure,
shame our selfish greed of gain.

4 Son of God, eternal Saviour,
source of life and truth and grace,
Son of Man, whose birth incarnate
hallows all our human race,
thou who prayedst, thou who willest,
that thy people should be one,
grant, O grant our hope's fruition:
here on earth thy will be done.

S. C. Lowry 1855–1932

574

SONGS of praise the angels sang,
heaven with alleluias rang,
when creation was begun,
when God spake and it was done.

2 Songs of praise awoke the morn
when the Prince of peace was born;
songs of praise arose when he
captive led captivity.

3 Heaven and earth must pass away;
songs of praise shall crown that day:
God will make new heavens and earth;
songs of praise shall hail their birth.

4 And shall we alone be dumb
till that glorious kingdom come?
No, the church delights to raise
psalms and hymns and songs of praise.

5 Saints below, with heart and voice,
still in songs of praise rejoice;
learning here, by faith and love,
songs of praise to sing above.

6 Hymns of glory, songs of praise,
Father, unto thee we raise,
Jesu, glory unto thee,
with the Spirit, ever be.

JAMES MONTGOMERY * 1771–1854

575

SPIRIT of God, descend upon my heart;
wean it from earth; through all its pulses move;
stoop to my weakness, mighty as thou art,
and make me love thee as I ought to love.

2 I ask no dream, no prophet-ecstasies,
no sudden rending of the veil of clay,
no angel-visitant, no opening skies;
but take the dimness of my soul away.

3 Hast thou not bid me love thee, God and King –
all, all thine own, soul, heart, and strength, and mind?
I see thy cross – there teach my heart to cling:
O let me seek thee, and O let me find!

4 Teach me to feel that thou art always nigh;
teach me the struggles of the soul to bear,
to check the rising doubt, the rebel sigh;
teach me the patience of unanswered prayer.

5 Teach me to love thee as thine angels love,
one holy passion filling all my frame —
the baptism of the heaven-descended dove,
my heart an altar, and thy love the flame.

GEORGE CROLY 1780–1860

576

SPIRIT of holiness, wisdom and faithfulness,
Wind of the Lord, blowing strongly and free;
strength of our serving and joy of our worshipping,
Spirit of God, bring your fullness to me.

1 You came to interpret and teach us effectively
all that the Saviour has spoken and done;
to glorify Jesus is all your activity,
promise and gift of the Father and Son:
Spirit of holiness, ...

2 You came with your gifts to supply all our poverty,
pouring your love on the church in her need;
you came with your fruit for our growth to maturity,
richly refreshing the souls that you feed:
Spirit of holiness, ...

3 You came to the world in its pride and futility,
warning of dangers, directing us home;
now with us and in us, we welcome your company:
Spirit of Christ, in his name you have come:
Spirit of holiness, ...

CHRISTOPHER M. IDLE *b.* 1938

577

STAND up, and bless the Lord,
ye people of his choice;
stand up, and bless the Lord your God
with heart and soul and voice.

2 Though high above all praise,
above all blessing high,
who would not fear his holy name,
and laud and magnify?

3 O for the living flame
from his own altar brought,
to touch our lips, our mind inspire,
and wing to heaven our thought.

4 God is our strength and song,
and his salvation ours;
then be his love in Christ proclaimed
with all our ransomed powers.

5 Stand up, and bless the Lord,
the Lord your God adore;
stand up, and bless his glorious name
henceforth for evermore.

JAMES MONTGOMERY 1771–1854

578

STAND up, stand up for Jesus,
ye soldiers of the cross!
Lift high his royal banner,
it must not suffer loss.
From victory unto victory
his army he shall lead,
till every foe is vanquished,
and Christ is Lord indeed.

2 Stand up, stand up for Jesus,
the solemn watchword hear;
if while ye sleep he suffers,
away with shame and fear.
Where'er ye meet with evil,
within you or without,
charge for the God of battles,
and put the foe to rout.

3 Stand up, stand up for Jesus,
stand in his strength alone;
the arm of flesh will fail you,
ye dare not trust your own.
Put on the gospel armour,
each piece put on with prayer;
when duty calls or danger
be never wanting there.

4 Stand up, stand up for Jesus,
the strife will not be long;
this day the noise of battle,
the next the victor's song.
To him that overcometh
a crown of life shall be;
he with the King of glory
shall reign eternally.

George Duffield 1818–1888

579

STEAL away, steal away,
steal away to Jesus.
Steal away, steal away home,
I ain't got long to stay here.

2 My Lord he calls me;
he calls me by the thunder;
the trumpet sounds within-a my soul;
I ain't got long to stay here.

3 Green trees are bending,
poor sinner stands a-trembling;
the trumpet sounds within-a my soul;
I ain't got long to stay here.

Steal away, steal away,
steal away to Jesus.
Steal away, steal away home,
I ain't got long to stay here.

Afro-American spiritual

580

SWEET is the work, my God, my King,
to praise thy name, give thanks and sing,
to show thy love by morning light,
and talk of all thy truth at night.

2 Sweet is the day of sacred rest,
no mortal cares disturb my breast;
O may my heart in tune be found,
like David's harp of solemn sound!

3 My heart shall triumph in the Lord,
and bless his works, and bless his word;
thy works of grace, how bright they shine,
how deep thy counsels, how divine!

4 And I shall share a glorious part,
when grace has well refined my heart,
and fresh supplies of joy are shed,
like holy oil, to cheer my head.

5 Then shall I see and hear and know
all I desired or wished below;
and every power find sweet employ
in that eternal world of joy.

ISAAC WATTS * 1674–1748
based on Psalm 92

581

TAKE my life, and let it be
consecrated, Lord, to thee;
take my moments and my days,
let them flow in ceaseless praise.

2 Take my hands, and let them move
at the impulse of thy love;
take my feet, and let them be
swift and beautiful for thee.

3 Take my voice, and let me sing
always, only, for my King;
take my lips, and let them be
filled with messages from thee.

4 Take my silver and my gold;
not a mite would I withhold;
take my intellect, and use
every power as thou shalt choose.

5 Take my will, and make it thine:
it shall be no longer mine;
take my heart: it is thine own;
it shall be thy royal throne.

6 Take my love; my Lord, I pour
at thy feet its treasure-store;
take myself, and I will be
ever, only, all for thee.

FRANCES RIDLEY HAVERGAL 1836–1879

582

TAKE up thy cross, the Saviour said,
if thou wouldst my disciple be;
deny thyself, the world forsake,
and humbly follow after me.

2 Take up thy cross: let not its weight
fill thy weak spirit with alarm;
his strength shall bear thy spirit up,
and brace thy heart, and nerve thine arm.

3 Take up thy cross, nor heed the shame,
nor let thy foolish pride rebel:
thy Lord for thee the cross endured,
to save thy soul from death and hell.

4 Take up thy cross then in his strength,
and calmly every danger brave;
'twill guide thee to a better home,
and lead to victory o'er the grave.

5 Take up thy cross, and follow Christ,
nor think till death to lay it down;
for only they who bear the cross
may hope to wear the glorious crown.

6 To thee, great Lord, the One in Three,
all praise for evermore ascend:
O grant us in our home to see
the heavenly life that knows no end.

C. W. Everest 1814–1877

583

TEACH me, my God and King,
in all things thee to see;
and what I do in anything
to do it as for thee.

2 A man that looks on glass,
on it may stay his eye;
or, if he pleaseth, through it pass,
and then the heaven espy.

3 All may of thee partake;
nothing can be so mean
which, with this tincture, *For thy sake,*
will not grow bright and clean.

4 A servant with this clause
makes drudgery divine;
who sweeps a room, as for thy laws,
makes that and the action fine.

5 This is the famous stone
that turneth all to gold;
for that which God doth touch and own
cannot for less be told.

GEORGE HERBERT 1593–1633

584

THANKS to God whose word was spoken
in the deed that made the earth.
His the voice that called a nation,
his the fires that tried her worth.
God has spoken:
praise him for his open word.

2 Thanks to God whose Word Incarnate
glorified the flesh of man;
deeds and words and death and rising
tell the grace in heaven's plan.
God has spoken:
praise him for his open word.

3 Thanks to God whose word was written
in the Bible's sacred page,
record of the revelation
showing God to every age.
God has spoken:
praise him for his open word.

4 Thanks to God whose word is published
in the tongues of every race.
See its glory undiminished
by the change of time or place.
God has spoken:
praise him for his open word.

5 Thanks to God whose word is answered
by the Spirit's voice within.
Here we drink of joy unmeasured,
life redeemed from death and sin.
God is speaking:
praise him for his open word.

R. T. Brooks 1918–1985

585

THE church's one foundation
is Jesus Christ her Lord;
she is his new creation
by water and the word:
from heaven he came and sought her
to be his holy Bride;
with his own blood he bought her,
and for her life he died.

2 Elect from every nation,
yet one o'er all the earth,
her charter of salvation
one Lord, one faith, one birth;
one holy name she blesses,
partakes one holy food,
and to one hope she presses
with every grace endued.

*3 Though with a scornful wonder
men see her sore opprest,
by schisms rent asunder,
by heresies distrest;
yet saints their watch are keeping,
their cry goes up, 'How long?'
And soon the night of weeping
shall be the morn of song.

4 'Mid toil and tribulation,
and tumult of her war,
she waits the consummation
of peace for evermore;
till with the vision glorious
her longing eyes are blest,
and the great church victorious
shall be the church at rest.

5 Yet she on earth hath union
with God the Three in One,
and mystic sweet communion
with those whose rest is won:
O happy ones and holy!
Lord, give us grace that we,
like them, the meek and lowly,
on high may dwell with thee.

S. J. STONE 1839–1900

586

THE God of Abraham praise
who reigns enthroned above,
Ancient of everlasting days,
and God of love:
Jehovah, great I AM,
by earth and heaven confest;
we bow and bless the sacred name
for ever blest.

*2 The God of Abraham praise,
at whose supreme command
from earth we rise, and seek the joys
at his right hand:
we all on earth forsake
its wisdom, fame, and power;
and him our only portion make,
our shield and tower.

3 Though nature's strength decay,
and earth and hell withstand,
to Canaan's bounds we urge our way
at his command:
the watery deep we pass,
with Jesus in our view;
and through the howling wilderness
our way pursue.

4 The goodly land we see,
with peace and plenty blest:
a land of sacred liberty
and endless rest;
there milk and honey flow,
and oil and wine abound,
and trees of life for ever grow,
with mercy crowned.

5 There dwells the Lord our King,
the Lord our Righteousness,
triumphant o'er the world of sin,
the Prince of peace:
on Sion's sacred height
his kingdom he maintains,
and glorious with his saints in light
for ever reigns.

*6 He keeps his own secure,
he guards them by his side,
arrays in garment white and pure
his spotless Bride:
with streams of sacred bliss,
beneath serener skies,
with all the fruits of paradise,
he still supplies.

*7 Before the great Three-One
they all exulting stand,
and tell the wonders he hath done
through all their land:
the listening spheres attend,
and swell the growing fame,
and sing in songs which never end
the wondrous name.

*8 The God who reigns on high
the great archangels sing,
and 'Holy, Holy, Holy,' cry,
'almighty King,
who was, and is the same,
and evermore shall be.
Jehovah, Father, great I AM,
we worship thee.'

9 Before the Saviour's face
the ransomed nations bow,
o'erwhelmed at his almighty grace
for ever new;
he shows his prints of love
they kindle to a flame,
and sound through all the worlds above
the slaughtered Lamb.

10 The whole triumphant host
give thanks to God on high;
'hail, Father, Son, and Holy Ghost,'
they ever cry:
hail, Abraham's God, and mine,
(I join the heavenly lays)
all might and majesty are thine,
and endless praise.

THOMAS OLIVERS 1725–1799
based on the Hebrew *Yigdal*

587

THE God of love my shepherd is,
and he that doth me feed;
while he is mine and I am his,
what can I want or need?

2 He leads me to the tender grass,
where I both feed and rest;
then to the streams that gently pass:
in both I have the best.

3 Or if I stray, he doth convert,
and bring my mind in frame,
and all this not for my desert,
but for his holy name.

4 Yea, in death's shady black abode
well may I walk, not fear;
for thou art with me, and thy rod
to guide, thy staff to bear.

5 Surely thy sweet and wondrous love
shall measure all my days;
and, as it never shall remove,
so neither shall my praise.

GEORGE HERBERT 1593–1633
Psalm 23

588

THE great Creator of the worlds,
the sovereign God of heaven,
his holy and immortal truth
to all on earth has given.

2 He sent no angel of his host
to bear his mighty word,
but him through whom the worlds were made,
the everlasting Lord.

3 He sent him not in wrath and power,
but grace and peace to bring;
in kindness, as a king might send
his son, himself a king.

4 He sent him down as sending God;
in flesh to us he came;
as one with us he dwelt with us,
and bore a human name.

5 He came as Saviour to his own,
the way of love he trod;
he came to win us by good will,
for force is not of God.

6 Not to oppress, but summon all
their truest life to find,
in love God sent his Son to save,
not to condemn mankind.

from *Epistle to Diognetus* c. 150
tr. F. BLAND TUCKER * 1895–1984

589

THE King of love my shepherd is,
whose goodness faileth never;
I nothing lack if I am his
and he is mine for ever.

2 Where streams of living water flow
my ransomed soul he leadeth,
and where the verdant pastures grow
with food celestial feedeth.

3 Perverse and foolish oft I strayed,
but yet in love he sought me,
and on his shoulder gently laid,
and home rejoicing brought me.

4 In death's dark vale I fear no ill
with thee, dear Lord, beside me;
thy rod and staff my comfort still,
thy cross before to guide me.

5 Thou spread'st a table in my sight;
thy unction grace bestoweth;
and O what transport of delight
from thy pure chalice floweth!

6 And so through all the length of days
thy goodness faileth never:
good Shepherd, may I sing thy praise
within thy house for ever.

H. W. BAKER 1821–1877
Psalm 23

590

'THE kingdom is upon you!'
the voice of Jesus cries,
fulfilling with its message
the wisdom of the wise;
it lightens with fresh insight
the striving human mind,
creating new dimensions
of faith for all to find.

2 'God's kingdom is upon you!'
the message sounds today,
it summons every pilgrim
to take the questing way,
with eyes intent on Jesus,
our leader and our friend,
who trod faith's road before us,
and trod it to the end.

3 The kingdom is upon us!
Stirred by the Spirit's breath,
we glory in its freedom
from emptiness and death;
we celebrate its purpose,
its mission and its goal,
alive with the conviction
that Christ can make us whole.

ROBERT WILLIS *b.* 1947

591

THE kingdom of God is justice and joy,
for Jesus restores what sin would destroy;
God's power and glory in Jesus we know,
and here and hereafter the kingdom shall grow.

2 The kingdom of God is mercy and grace,
the captives are freed, the sinners find place,
the outcast are welcomed God's banquet to share,
and hope is awakened in place of despair.

3 The kingdom of God is challenge and choice,
believe the good news, repent and rejoice!
His love for us sinners brought Christ to his cross,
our crisis of judgement for gain or for loss.

4 God's kingdom is come, the gift and the goal,
in Jesus begun, in heaven made whole;
the heirs of the kingdom shall answer his call,
and all things cry 'Glory!' to God all in all.

BRYN REES * 1911–1983

592

THE Lord is King! lift up thy voice,
O earth, and all ye heavens, rejoice;
from world to world the joy shall ring,
'The Lord omnipotent is King!'

2 The Lord is King! who then shall dare
resist his will, distrust his care,
or murmur at his wise decrees,
or doubt his royal promises?

3 He reigns! ye saints, exalt your strains;
your God is King, your Father reigns;
and he is at the Father's side,
the Man of love, the Crucified.

4 Alike pervaded by his eye
all parts of his dominion lie:
this world of ours and worlds unseen,
and thin the boundary between!

5 One Lord one empire all secures;
he reigns, and life and death are yours;
through earth and heaven one song shall ring,
'The Lord omnipotent is King!'

JOSIAH CONDER 1789–1855

593

THE Lord my pasture shall prepare,
and feed me with a shepherd's care;
his presence shall my wants supply,
and guard me with a watchful eye;
my noonday walks he shall attend,
and all my midnight hours defend.

2 When in the sultry glebe I faint,
or on the thirsty mountain pant,
to fertile vales and dewy meads
my weary wandering steps he leads,
where peaceful rivers, soft and slow,
amid the verdant landscape flow.

3 Though in a bare and rugged way
through devious lonely wilds I stray,
thy bounty shall my pains beguile;
the barren wilderness shall smile
with sudden greens and herbage crowned,
and streams shall murmur all around.

4 Though in the paths of death I tread,
with gloomy horrors overspread,
my steadfast heart shall fear no ill,
for thou, O Lord, art with me still:
thy friendly staff shall give me aid,
and guide me through the dreadful shade.

JOSEPH ADDISON * 1672–1719
Psalm 23

594

THE Lord's my Shepherd, I'll not want;
he makes me down to lie
in pastures green; he leadeth me
the quiet waters by.

2 My soul he doth restore again,
and me to walk doth make
within the paths of righteousness,
e'en for his own name's sake.

3 Yea, though I walk through death's dark vale,
yet will I fear none ill;
for thou art with me, and thy rod
and staff me comfort still.

4 My table thou hast furnishèd
in presence of my foes;
my head thou dost with oil anoint,
and my cup overflows.

5 Goodness and mercy all my life
shall surely follow me;
and in God's house for evermore
my dwelling-place shall be.

Scottish Psalter 1650
Psalm 23

595

THE Son of God his glory hides
to dwell with parents poor;
and he who made the heavens abides
in dwelling-place obscure.

2 Those mighty hands that stay the sky
no earthly toil refuse;
and he who set the stars on high
an humble trade pursues.

3 He in whose sight the angels stand,
at whose behest they fly,
now yields himself to man's command,
and lays his glory by.

4 For this thy lowliness revealed,
Jesu, we thee adore,
and praise to God the Father yield
and Spirit evermore.

JEAN DE SANTEUL 1630–1697
tr. JOHN CHANDLER 1806–1876
and others

596

THERE in God's garden stands the tree of wisdom
whose leaves hold forth the healing of the nations:
tree of all knowledge, tree of all compassion,
tree of all beauty.

2 Its name is Jesus, name that says 'Our Saviour':
there on its branches see the scars of suffering:
see where the tendrils of our human selfhood
feed on its lifeblood.

3 Thorns not its own are tangled in its foliage;
our greed has starved it, our despite has choked it;
yet, look, it lives! Its grief has not destroyed it,
nor fire consumed it.

4 See how its branches reach to us in welcome;
hear what the voice says, 'Come to me, ye weary:
give me your sickness, give me all your sorrow:
I will give blessing'.

5 All heaven is singing, 'Thanks to Christ whose Passion
offers in mercy healing, strength and pardon:
peoples and nations, take it, take it freely'.
Amen, my Master.

ERIK ROUTLEY 1917–1982
based on the Hungarian of
KIRÀLY IMRE VON PÉCSELYI *c.* 1590–*c.* 1641

597

THERE is a land of pure delight,
where saints immortal reign;
infinite day excludes the night,
and pleasures banish pain.

2 There everlasting spring abides,
and never-withering flowers;
death, like a narrow sea, divides
that heavenly land from ours.

3 Sweet fields beyond the swelling flood
stand dressed in living green;
so to the Jews old Canaan stood,
while Jordan rolled between.

4 But timorous mortals start and shrink
to cross the narrow sea,
and linger shivering on the brink,
and fear to launch away.

5 O could we make our doubts remove,
those gloomy doubts that rise,
and see the Canaan that we love
with unbeclouded eyes;

6 Could we but climb where Moses stood,
and view the landscape o'er,
not Jordan's stream, nor death's cold flood,
should fright us from the shore!

ISAAC WATTS 1674–1748

598

THERE'S a wideness in God's mercy
like the wideness of the sea;
there's a kindness in his justice
which is more than liberty.

2 There is no place where earth's sorrows
are more felt than up in heaven;
there is no place where earth's failings
have such kindly judgement given.

3 For the love of God is broader
than the measures of man's mind;
and the heart of the Eternal
is most wonderfully kind.

4 But we make his love too narrow
by false limits of our own;
and we magnify his strictness
with a zeal he will not own.

5 There is plentiful redemption
in the blood that has been shed;
there is joy for all the members
in the sorrows of the Head.

6 There is grace enough for thousands
of new worlds as great as this;
there is room for fresh creations
in that upper home of bliss.

7 If our love were but more simple,
we should take him at his word;
and our lives would be all gladness
in the joy of Christ our Lord.

F. W. FABER * 1814–1863

599

THINE for ever! God of love,
hear us from thy throne above;
thine for ever may we be
here and in eternity.

2 Thine for ever! Lord of life,
shield us through our earthly strife;
thou the Life, the Truth, the Way,
guide us to the realms of day.

3 Thine for ever! O how blest
they who find in thee their rest!
Saviour, guardian, heavenly friend,
O defend us to the end.

*4 Thine for ever! Shepherd, keep
us thy frail and trembling sheep;
safe alone beneath thy care,
let us all thy goodness share.

5 Thine for ever! Thou our guide,
all our wants by thee supplied,
all our sins by thee forgiven,
lead us, Lord, from earth to heaven.

M. F. MAUDE 1819–1913

600

THOU art the Way: by thee alone
from sin and death we flee;
and they who would the Father seek
must seek him, Lord, by thee.

2 Thou art the Truth: thy word alone
true wisdom can impart;
thou only canst inform the mind
and purify the heart.

3 Thou art the Life: the rending tomb
proclaims thy conquering arm;
and those who put their trust in thee
nor death nor hell shall harm.

4 Thou art the Way, the Truth, the Life:
grant us that Way to know,
that Truth to keep, that Life to win,
whose joys eternal flow.

GEORGE WASHINGTON DOANE 1799–1859

601

THOU didst leave thy throne and thy kingly crown,
when thou camest to earth for me;
but in Bethlehem's home was there found no room
for thy holy nativity:
O come to my heart, Lord Jesus;
there is room in my heart for thee.

2 Heaven's arches rang when the angels sang,
proclaiming thy royal degree;
but in lowly birth didst thou come to earth,
and in great humility:
O come to my heart ...

3 The foxes found rest, and the bird had its nest
in the shade of the cedar tree;
but thy couch was the sod, O thou Son of God,
in the desert of Galilee:
O come to my heart ...

4 Thou camest, O Lord, with the living word
that should set thy people free;
but with mocking scorn and with crown of thorn
they bore thee to Calvary:
O come to my heart ...

5 When the heavens shall ring, and the angels sing,
at thy coming to victory,
let thy voice call me home, saying, 'Yet there is room,
there is room at my side for thee:'
O come to my heart, Lord Jesus;
there is room in my heart for thee.

EMILY ELLIOTT * 1836–1897

602

THOU hidden love of God, whose height,
   whose depth unfathomed, no-one knows,
I see from far thy beauteous light,
   inly I sigh for thy repose;
my heart is pained, nor can it be
at rest, till it finds rest in thee.

2 'Tis mercy all, that thou hast brought
   my mind to seek her peace in thee;
yet, while I seek but find thee not,
   no peace my wandering soul shall see;
O when shall all my wanderings end,
and all my steps to thee-ward tend?

3 Is there a thing beneath the sun
   that strives with thee my heart to share?
Ah, tear it thence, and reign alone,
   the Lord of every motion there!
Then shall my heart from earth be free,
when it hath found repose in thee.

4 O Love, thy sovereign aid impart
   to save me from low-thoughted care;
chase this self-will through all my heart,
   through all its latent mazes there;
make me thy duteous child, that I
ceaseless may 'Abba, Father!' cry.

5 Each moment draw from earth away
   my heart, that lowly waits thy call;
speak to my inmost soul, and say,
   'I am thy Love, thy God, thy All!'
To feel thy power, to hear thy voice,
to taste thy love, be all my choice.

GERHARD TERSTEEGEN 1697–1769
tr. JOHN WESLEY 1703–1791

603

THOU hidden source of calm repose,
thou all-sufficient love divine,
my help and refuge from my foes,
secure I am, if thou art mine:
and lo, from sin, and grief, and shame,
I hide me, Jesus, in thy name.

2 Thy mighty name salvation is,
and keeps my happy soul above;
comfort it brings, and power, and peace,
and joy, and everlasting love:
to me, with thy dear name, are given
pardon, and holiness, and heaven.

3 Jesus, my all in all thou art:
my rest in toil, my ease in pain,
the medicine of my broken heart,
in war my peace, in loss my gain,
my smile beneath the tyrant's frown,
in shame my glory and my crown;

4 In want my plentiful supply,
in weakness my almighty power,
in bonds my perfect liberty,
my light in Satan's darkest hour,
in grief my joy unspeakable,
my life in death, my heaven in hell.

CHARLES WESLEY 1707–1788

604

THROUGH all the changing scenes of life,
in trouble and in joy,
the praises of my God shall still
my heart and tongue employ.

2 O magnify the Lord with me,
with me exalt his name;
when in distress to him I called,
he to my rescue came.

3 The hosts of God encamp around
the dwellings of the just;
deliverance he affords to all
who on his succour trust.

4 O make but trial of his love,
experience will decide
how blest are they, and only they,
who in his truth confide!

5 Fear him, ye saints, and you will then
have nothing else to fear;
make you his service your delight,
your wants shall be his care.

6 To Father, Son, and Holy Ghost,
the God whom we adore,
be glory, as it was, is now,
and shall be evermore.

NAHUM TATE 1652–1715
and NICHOLAS BRADY 1659–1726
A New Version of the Psalms of David 1696 and 1698
Psalm 34

605

THROUGH the night of doubt and sorrow
onward goes the pilgrim band,
singing songs of expectation,
marching to the promised land.

2 Clear before us through the darkness
gleams and burns the guiding light;
pilgrim clasps the hand of pilgrim,
stepping fearless through the night.

3 One the light of God's own presence
o'er his ransomed people shed,
chasing far the gloom and terror,
brightening all the path we tread:

4 One the object of our journey,
one the faith which never tires,
one the earnest looking forward,
one the hope our God inspires:

5 One the strain that lips of thousands
lift as from the heart of one;
one the conflict, one the peril,
one the march in God begun:

6 One the gladness of rejoicing
on the far eternal shore,
where the one almighty Father
reigns in love for evermore.

*7 Onward, therefore, pilgrim brothers,
onward with the cross our aid;
bear its shame, and fight its battle,
till we rest beneath its shade.

*8 Soon shall come the great awaking,
soon the rending of the tomb;
then the scattering of all shadows,
and the end of toil and gloom.

BERNHARDT INGEMANN 1789–1862
tr. SABINE BARING-GOULD 1834–1924

606

THY hand, O God, has guided
thy flock, from age to age;
the wondrous tale is written,
full clear, on every page;
our fathers owned thy goodness,
and we their deeds record;
and both of this bear witness:
one church, one faith, one Lord.

2 Thy heralds brought glad tidings
to greatest, as to least;
they bade men rise, and hasten
to share the great King's feast;
and this was all their teaching,
in every deed and word,
to all alike proclaiming
one church, one faith, one Lord.

*3 When shadows thick were falling,
and all seemed sunk in night,
thou, Lord, didst send thy servants,
thy chosen sons of light.
On them and on thy people
thy plenteous grace was poured,
and this was still their message:
one church, one faith, one Lord.

4 Through many a day of darkness,
through many a scene of strife,
the faithful few fought bravely,
to guard the nation's life.
Their gospel of redemption,
sin pardoned, man restored,
was all in this enfolded:
one church, one faith, one Lord.

*5 And we, shall we be faithless?
Shall hearts fail, heads hand down?
Shall we evade the conflict,
and cast away our crown?
Not so: in God's deep counsels
some better thing is stored:
we will maintain, unflinching,
one church, one faith, one Lord.

6 Thy mercy will not fail us,
   nor leave thy work undone;
with thy right hand to help us,
   the victory shall be won;
and then, by men and angels,
   thy name shall be adored,
and this shall be their anthem:
   one church, one faith, one Lord.

E. H. Plumptre 1821–1891

607

THY kingdom come, O God,
   thy rule, O Christ, begin;
break with thine iron rod
   the tyrannies of sin.

2 Where is thy reign of peace
   and purity and love?
When shall all hatred cease,
   as in the realms above?

3 When comes the promised time
   that war shall be no more,
and lust, oppression, crime
   shall flee thy face before?

4 We pray thee, Lord, arise,
   and come in thy great might;
revive our longing eyes,
   which languish for thy sight.

5 Men scorn thy sacred name,
   and wolves devour thy fold;
by many deeds of shame
   we learn that love grows cold.

6 O'er lands both near and far
   thick darkness broodeth yet:
arise, O Morning Star,
   arise, and never set!

Lewis Hensley * 1824–1905

608

THY kingdom come! On bended knee
the passing ages pray;
and faithful souls have yearned to see
on earth that kingdom's day.

2 But the slow watches of the night
not less to God belong;
and for the everlasting right
the silent stars are strong.

3 And lo, already on the hills
the flags of dawn appear;
gird up your loins, ye prophet souls,
proclaim the day is near:

4 The day in whose clear-shining light
all wrong shall stand revealed,
when justice shall be throned in might,
and every hurt be healed;

5 When knowledge, hand in hand with peace,
shall walk the earth abroad:
the day of perfect righteousness,
the promised day of God.

F. L. HOSMER 1840–1929

609

TO God be the glory, great things he has done!
So loved he the world that he gave us his Son,
who yielded his life an atonement for sin
and opened the life-gate that all may go in.
Praise the Lord! Praise the Lord!
Let the earth hear his voice!
Praise the Lord! Praise the Lord!
Let the people rejoice!
O come to the Father, through Jesus the Son,
and give him the glory! Great things he has done!

2 O perfect redemption, the purchase of blood!
To every believer the promise of God!
The vilest offender who truly believes,
that moment from Jesus forgiveness receives.
Praise the Lord! ...

3 Great things he has taught us, great things he has done,
and great our rejoicing through Jesus the Son;
but purer and higher and greater will be
our wonder, our rapture, when Jesus we see.
Praise the Lord! Praise the Lord!
Let the earth hear his voice!
Praise the Lord! Praise the Lord!
Let the people rejoice!
O come to the Father, through Jesus the Son,
and give him the glory! Great things he has done!

FANNY CROSBY (FRANCES JANE VAN ALSTYNE) * 1820–1915

610

TO the name of our salvation
laud and honour let us pay,
which for many a generation
hid in God's foreknowledge lay,
but with holy exultation
we may sing aloud to-day.

2 Jesus is the name we treasure,
name beyond what words can tell;
name of gladness, name of pleasure,
ear and heart delighting well;
name of sweetness passing measure,
saving us from sin and hell.

3 'Tis the name that whoso preacheth
speaks like music to the ear;
who in prayer this name beseecheth
sweetest comfort findeth near;
who its perfect wisdom reacheth
heavenly joy possesseth here.

4 Jesus is the name exalted
over every other name;
in this name, whene'er assaulted,
we can put our foes to shame:
strength to them who else had halted,
eyes to blind, and feet to lame.

5 Therefore we in love adoring
this most blessèd name revere,
holy Jesu, thee imploring
so to write it in us here,
that hereafter heavenward soaring
we may sing with angels there.

Latin, *c.* 15th century
tr. J. M. NEALE * 1818–1866

611

WE bring you, Lord, our prayer and praise
that every child of earth
should live and grow in freedom's ways,
in dignity and worth.

2 We praise for such a task begun
to serve each other's need,
for every cause of justice won,
for every fetter freed.

3 Our prayers are for a world in pain
where force and fear prevail,
the plough becomes the sword again,
and hope and harvests fail.

4 Alike our prayer and praise express
the wants of humankind,
that those in bondage and distress
their larger freedoms find.

5 So may we still maintain the fight
till earth's oppressions cease
before the universal right
to liberty and peace.

6 In Christ we learn to love and care
and spread his truth abroad;
and in his Name we lift our prayer:
'Your kingdom come, O Lord.'

TIMOTHY DUDLEY-SMITH *b.* 1926

612

WE have a gospel to proclaim,
good news for all throughout the earth;
the gospel of a Saviour's name:
we sing his glory, tell his worth.

2 Tell of his birth at Bethlehem
not in a royal house or hall
but in a stable dark and dim,
the Word made flesh, a light for all.

3 Tell of his death at Calvary,
hated by those he came to save,
in lonely suffering on the cross;
for all he loved his life he gave.

4 Tell of that glorious Easter morn:
empty the tomb, for he was free.
He broke the power of death and hell
that we might share his victory.

5 Tell of his reign at God's right hand,
by all creation glorified.
He sends his Spirit on his church
to live for him, the Lamb who died.

6 Now we rejoice to name him King:
Jesus is Lord of all the earth.
This gospel-message we proclaim:
we sing his glory, tell his worth.

EDWARD J. BURNS *b.* 1938

613

WE pray for peace,
but not the easy peace
built on complacency
and not the truth of God.
We pray for real peace,
the peace God's love alone can seal.

2 We pray for peace,
but not the cruel peace,
leaving God's poor bereft
and dying in distress,
we pray for real peace,
enriching all the human race.

3 We pray for peace,
and not the evil peace,
defending unjust laws
and nursing prejudice,
but for the real peace
of justice, mercy, truth and love.

4 We pray for peace:
holy communion
with Christ our risen Lord
and every living thing;
God's will fulfilled on earth
and all his creatures reconciled.

*5 We pray for peace,
and for the sake of peace,
look to the risen Christ
who gives the grace we need,
to serve the cause of peace
and make our own self-sacrifice.

6 God, give us peace:
if you withdraw your love,
there is no peace for us
nor any hope of it.
With you to lead us on,
through death or tumult, peace will come.

ALAN GAUNT *b.* 1935

614

WE sing for all the unsung saints,
that countless, nameless throng,
who kept the faith and passed it on,
with hope steadfast and strong,
through all the daily griefs and joys
no chronicles record,
forgetful of their lack of fame,
but mindful of their Lord.

2 Though uninscribed with date or place,
with title, rank, or name,
as living stones their stories join
to form a hallowed frame
around the mystery in their midst:
the Lamb once sacrificed,
the Love that wrested life from death,
the wounded, risen Christ.

3 So we take heart from unknown saints
bereft of earthly fame,
those faithful ones who have received
a more enduring name:
for they reveal true blessing comes
when we our pride efface
and offer back our lives to be
the vessels of God's grace.

CARL P. DAW JR *b.* 1944

615

WHAT shall I do my God to love,
my loving God to praise?
The length, and breadth, and height to prove,
and depth of sovereign grace?

2 Thy sovereign grace to all extends,
immense and unconfined;
from age to age it never ends,
it reaches all mankind.

3 Throughout the world its breadth is known,
wide as infinity;
so wide it never passed by one,
or it had passed by me.

4 My trespass was grown up to heaven;
but, far above the skies,
in Christ abundantly forgiven,
I see thy mercies rise.

5 The depth of all-redeeming love
what angel tongue can tell?
O may I to the utmost prove
the gift unspeakable!

6 Come quickly, gracious Lord, and take
possession of thine own;
my longing heart vouchsafe to make
thine everlasting throne.

CHARLES WESLEY * 1707–1788

616

WHEN a knight won his spurs in the stories of old,
he was gentle and brave, he was gallant and bold;
with a shield on his arm and a lance in his hand,
for God and for valour he rode through the land.

2 No charger have I, and no sword by my side,
yet still to adventure and battle I ride,
though back into storyland giants have fled,
and the knights are no more and the dragons are dead.

3 Let faith be my shield and let joy be my steed
'gainst the dragons of anger, the ogres of greed;
and let me set free, with the sword of my youth,
from the castle of darkness the power of the truth.

JAN STRUTHER (JOYCE PLACZEK) 1901–1953

617

WHEN all thy mercies, O my God,
my rising soul surveys,
transported with the view, I'm lost
in wonder, love, and praise.

2 Unnumbered comforts to my soul
thy tender care bestowed,
before my infant heart conceived
from whom those comforts flowed.

3 When in the slippery paths of youth
with heedless steps I ran,
thine arm unseen conveyed me safe,
and led me up to man.

*4 Ten thousand thousand precious gifts
my daily thanks employ,
and not the least a cheerful heart
which tastes those gifts with joy.

5 Through every period of my life
thy goodness I'll pursue,
and after death in distant worlds
the glorious theme renew.

6 Through all eternity to thee,
a joyful song I'll raise;
for O, eternity's too short
to utter all thy praise.

JOSEPH ADDISON 1672–1719

618

WHEN, in our music, God is glorified,
and adoration leaves no room for pride,
it is as though the whole creation cried:
Alleluia!

2 How often, making music, we have found
a new dimension in the world of sound,
as worship moved us to a more profound
Alleluia!

3 So has the church, in liturgy and song,
in faith and love, through centuries of wrong,
borne witness to the truth in every tongue:
Alleluia!

4 And did not Jesus sing a psalm that night
when utmost evil strove against the Light?
Then let us sing, for whom he won the fight:
Alleluia!

5 Let every instrument be tuned for praise!
Let all rejoice who have a voice to raise!
And may God give us faith to sing always:
Alleluia!

F. PRATT GREEN 1903–2000

619

WHEN morning gilds the skies,
my heart awaking cries,
may Jesus Christ be praised:
alike at work and prayer
to Jesus I repair;
may Jesus Christ be praised.

*2 Whene'er the sweet church bell
peals over hill and dell,
may Jesus Christ be praised:
O hark to what it sings,
as joyously it rings,
may Jesus Christ be praised.

3 My tongue shall never tire
of chanting with the choir,
may Jesus Christ be praised:
this song of sacred joy,
it never seems to cloy,
may Jesus Christ be praised.

4 Does sadness fill my mind?
A solace here I find,
may Jesus Christ be praised:
or fades my earthly bliss?
My comfort still is this,
may Jesus Christ be praised.

5 The night becomes as day,
when from the heart we say,
may Jesus Christ be praised:
the powers of darkness fear,
when this sweet chant they hear,
may Jesus Christ be praised.

6 Be this, while life is mine,
my canticle divine,
may Jesus Christ be praised:
be this the eternal song
through ages all along,
may Jesus Christ be praised!

German, 19th century
tr. EDWARD CASWALL * 1814–1878

620

WHERE cross the crowded ways of life,
where sound the cries of race and clan,
above the noise of selfish strife,
we hear thy voice, O Son of Man.

2 In haunts of wretchedness and need,
on shadowed thresholds dark with fears,
from paths where hide the lures of greed,
we catch the vision of thy tears.

3 The cup of water given for thee
still holds the freshness of thy grace;
yet long these multitudes to see
the strong compassion of thy face.

4 O Master, from the mountain-side
make haste to heal these hearts of pain;
among these restless throngs abide,
O tread the city's streets again:

5 Till all shall come to learn thy love,
and follow where thy feet have trod;
till glorious from thy heaven above
shall come the city of our God.

FRANK MASON NORTH 1850–1935

621

WHO would true valour see,
let him come hither;
one here will constant be,
come wind, come weather;
there's no discouragement
shall make him once relent
his first avowed intent
to be a pilgrim.

2 Whoso beset him round
with dismal stories,
do but themselves confound,
his strength the more is.
No lion can him fright:
he'll with a giant fight,
but he will have the right
to be a pilgrim.

3 Hobgoblin nor foul fiend
can daunt his spirit;
he knows he at the end
shall life inherit.
Then, fancies, fly away;
he'll not fear what men say;
he'll labour night and day
to be a pilgrim.

JOHN BUNYAN 1628–1688

622

WILL you come and follow me,
if I but call your name?
Will you go where you don't know
and never be the same?
Will you let my love be shown,
will you let my love be known,
will you let my life be grown
in you and you in me?

2 Will you leave yourself behind
if I but call your name?
Will you care for cruel and kind
and never be the same?
Will you risk the hostile stare
should your life attract or scare?
Will you let me answer prayer
in you and you in me?

3 Will you let the blinded see
if I but call your name?
Will you set the prisoners free
and never be the same?
Will you kiss the leper clean,
and do such as this unseen,
and admit to what I mean
in you and you in me?

4 Will you love the 'you' you hide
if I but call your name?
Will you quell the fear inside
and never be the same?
Will you use the faith you've found
to reshape the world around,
through my sight and touch and sound
in you and you in me?

5 Lord, your summons echoes true
when you but call my name.
Let me turn and follow you
and never be the same.
In your company I'll go
where your love and footsteps show.
Thus I'll move and live and grow
in you and you in me.

JOHN BELL *b.* 1949
and GRAHAM MAULE *b.* 1958

623

WITH glorious clouds encompassed round,
whom angels dimly see,
will the Unsearchable be found,
or God appear to me?

2 Will he forsake his throne above,
himself to me impart?
Answer, thou Man of grief and love,
and speak it to my heart!

3 In manifested love explain
thy wonderful design;
what meant the suffering Son of Man,
the streaming blood divine?

4 Didst thou not in our flesh appear,
and live and die below,
that I may now perceive thee near,
and my Redeemer know?

5 Come then, and to my soul reveal
the heights and depths of grace,
the wounds which all my sorrows heal,
that dear disfigured face.

6 I view the Lamb in his own light,
whom angels dimly see,
and gaze, transported at the sight,
through all eternity.

CHARLES WESLEY * 1707–1788

624

WITH joy we meditate the grace
of our High Priest above;
his heart is made of tenderness,
and ever yearns with love.

2 Touched with a sympathy within,
he knows our feeble frame;
he knows what sore temptations mean
for he has felt the same.

3 He in the days of feeble flesh
poured out his cries and tears;
and, in his measure, feels afresh
what every member bears.

4 He'll never quench the smoking flax,
but raise it to a flame;
the bruisèd reed he never breaks,
nor scorns the meanest name.

5 Then let our humble faith address
his mercy and his power:
we shall obtain delivering grace
in every needful hour.

ISAAC WATTS * 1674–1748
Hebrews 4. 15–16 and 5. 7

625

WORD of God, come down on earth,
living rain from heaven descending;
touch our hearts and bring to birth
faith and hope and love unending.
Word almighty, we revere you;
Word made flesh, we long to hear you.

2 Word eternal, throned on high,
Word that brought to life creation,
Word that came from heaven to die,
crucified for our salvation,
saving Word, the world restoring,
speak to us, your love outpouring.

3 Word that speaks your Father's love,
one with him beyond all telling,
Word that sends us from above
God the Spirit, with us dwelling,
Word of truth, to all truth lead us,
Word of life, with one Bread feed us.

JAMES QUINN *b.* 1919

626

YE holy angels bright,
who wait at God's right hand,
or through the realms of light
fly at your Lord's command,
assist our song,
for else the theme
too high doth seem
for mortal tongue.

2 Ye blessèd souls at rest,
who ran this earthly race,
and now, from sin released,
behold the Saviour's face,
his praises sound,
as in his sight
with sweet delight
ye do abound.

3 Ye saints, who toil below,
adore your heavenly King,
and onward as ye go
some joyful anthem sing;
take what he gives
and praise him still,
through good and ill,
who ever lives.

4 My soul, bear thou thy part,
triumph in God above,
and with a well-tuned heart
sing thou the songs of love;
let all thy days
till life shall end,
whate'er he send,
be filled with praise.

RICHARD BAXTER 1615–1691
and J. H. GURNEY 1802–1862

627

YE servants of God, your Master proclaim,
and publish abroad his wonderful name;
the name all-victorious of Jesus extol:
his kingdom is glorious, and rules over all.

2 God ruleth on high, almighty to save;
and still he is nigh, his presence we have;
the great congregation his triumph shall sing,
ascribing salvation to Jesus our King.

3 Salvation to God who sits on the throne!
Let all cry aloud, and honour the Son.
The praises of Jesus the angels proclaim,
fall down on their faces, and worship the Lamb.

4 Then let us adore, and give him his right:
all glory and power, all wisdom and might,
and honour and blessing, with angels above,
and thanks never-ceasing, and infinite love.

CHARLES WESLEY * 1707–1788

628

YE that know the Lord is gracious,
ye for whom a corner-stone
stands, of God elect and precious,
laid that ye may build thereon,
see that on that sure foundation
ye a living temple raise,
towers that may tell forth salvation,
walls that may re-echo praise.

2 Living stones, by God appointed
each to his allotted place,
kings and priests, by God anointed,
shall ye not declare his grace?
Ye, a royal generation,
tell the tidings of your birth,
tidings of a new creation
to an old and weary earth.

3 Tell the praise of him who called you
out of darkness into light,
broke the fetters that enthralled you,
gave you freedom, peace and sight:
tell the tale of sins forgiven,
strength renewed and hope restored,
till the earth, in tune with heaven,
praise and magnify the Lord.

C. A. ALINGTON 1872–1955

INDEXES

INDEX OF AUTHORS, TRANSLATORS and SOURCES OF WORDS

*An asterisk * indicates an alteration to the original text*

INDEX OF FIRST LINES